Robert Traill

The Works of the Late Reverend Robert Traill, A.M.

Minister of the gospel in London. Vol. 2

Robert Traill

The Works of the Late Reverend Robert Traill, A.M.
Minister of the gospel in London. Vol. 2

ISBN/EAN: 9783337429300

Printed in Europe, USA, Canada, Australia, Japan

Cover: Foto ©Lupo / pixelio.de

More available books at **www.hansebooks.com**

THE
WORKS

OF

The late REVEREND

ROBERT TRAILL, A. M.

Minister of the Gospel in LONDON.

IN THREE VOLUMES.

VOL. II.

CONTAINING

Sixteen SERMONS on the LORD's PRAYER in John xvii. 24.———First printed in 1705.

Cui veritas comperta, sine Deo? Cui Deus cognitus, sine Christo? Cui Christus exploratus, sine Spiritu Sancto?
                                      TERTULLIAN.

GLASGOW:

Printed and Sold by JOHN BRYCE, at his Shop, opposite Gibson's-wynd, SALT-MARKET.
MDCCLXXV.

THE
PREFACE.

THREE things are simply necessary unto any man's having of true religion and godliness; sound principles of divine truth known, the savoury of that knowledge in the heart, and the power of that savoury in a man's worship and walk. There are no sound principles of saving truth, but in and from God's written word. There is no right savour of those principles, but in and by faith and love, which is in Christ Jesus, 2 Tim. i. 13. and iii. 15. It is by this savour of the knowledge of Christ, *as it is called*, 2 Cor. ii. 14. that the power of godliness is impressed on the heart, and expressed in the life of a believer. If the principles of truth be not from God's word, there can be no true religion; if the truth professed be consonant to God's word, and faith and love be wanting, it may be a man's notion and opinion, but it is not the man's religion; and if the power of known truth be not in his walk and conversation, neither should he himself, nor ought any other think, that such a man hath any religion at all.

They have done good service to the common-wealth of learning, who, leaving the unprofitable, speculative, and notional philosophy, have set upon the experimental. And any man may see, that theology hath been, especially by the school-men, as much corrupted; and that it is to be cured by reducing it unto practice and experience. For certainly religion consists not so much in the notions of truth in the mind, (in which the devils, the most irreligious of all creatures, exceed all men), as in the faith and love of truth in the heart, and in the fruits of that faith in the life.

There are two sorts of mysteries spoke of in the New Testament; the mystery of godliness, which centers in Jesus Christ, the Son of God, 1 Tim. iii. 16.; and the mystery of iniquity, which centers in Antichrist, the man of sin, and the son of per-

perdition, 2 Theff. ii. 3. 7. *These two mysteries are constant and direct contraries. Whoever is ignorant, or an unbeliever of the mystery of godliness, may easily be drawn, or driven, to be a believer of* the mystery of iniquity. *So it was foretold,* 2 Theff. ii. 10, 11, 12.; *and accordingly we daily see this awful judgment of God executed upon many. Neither is any thing more needful to make a man a real hater of Popery, than to be a sincere believer on Jesus Christ. It is true, that the excessive pride of the Pope, and his prelates, the cruelty of his domination, the frontless profaneness of his synagogue, and the visible worldly craft of his religion, is more than enough to make him and it hateful to Pagans, Jews, Turks, and Infidels. Yet to hate Popery spiritually, as it is a gross corruption of true Christianity (of which he falsly arrogates the name), is only found with the elect of God:* Rev. xiii. 8. And all that dwell upon the earth shall worship him, *(that is, the beast)*, whose names are not written in the book of life of the Lamb slain from the foundation of the world. *And to the same purpose is that in* Rev. xvii. 8.

It was not the clearness of light and knowledge, (in which this age doth much exceed the former), but the power of known truth on the hearts of Christ's witnesses against Antichrist, that carried them so honourably through the fiery trial.

It is unaccountable hypocrisy and folly in such as pretend to be followers of such martyrs for Christ, in their cause and testimony, and yet do mock that faith, and love, and communion with God, which were their support in their sufferings for it. If it be possible, it is very rare, and highly improbable, that a stranger to, much more a mocker at the power of godliness, should suffer extremity, and that chearfully, for the form of it.

We have also in these last and perilous times, some antichrists, that do deride both the mystery of godliness, and the mystery of iniquity. *They have no faith to take up the glory of* the mystery of godliness: *but they have sense and reason enough to take up the folly and knavery of* the mystery of iniquity: *A sort of men, to whom may be applied what* the evil spirit said to the vagabond Jews, exorcists, Acts xix. 15. Jesus I know, and Paul I know; but who are ye? *Which a witty minister took for his text, and raised this, more ingenious than grave, doctrine from it,* "That there are some men so
"bad

"bad, that the devil himself does not know what to make of them." These men I mean, do not halt betwixt God and Baal, betwixt Christ and Antichrist; but oppose both. If they escape Antichrist's rage in this world, they shall not escape the wrath of the Son of God in the next. They are such as have both heaven and hell against them, and fight against both. But whatever disturbance the church of Christ may meet with, and whatever danger and loss particular mens souls may sustain by other damnable heresies; yet the grand trial of the New Testament church, and the chief plague of the latter days, is from Antichrist. And no wise Christian can expect the fulfilment of the prophecies of the glory of the church of Christ, but in and by the ruin of Antichrist, and of his throne of iniquity.

And though Antichrist's interest in this nation seems to be pretty well excluded by Protestant laws and rulers, and yet more by the plain interest of the nation, as to all its valuable concerns; yet where the mystery of godliness is not duly esteemed, no man nor nation is secured from the malignant influence of the mystery of iniquity. And though Antichrist's throne seems to be fixed by long possession, and the blindness of most of the kings in Europe; yet there is that rottenness in its foundations, and that weight of wrath threatened in the word of God, as will sink it as a milstone in the sea, in due time.

It was with an eye to both these mysteries, that what you read, was preached some years since, and is now published.

It is neither from unacquaintedness with the genius of the present age, nor with my small talent, that I put forth these plain ordinary sermons; I well know, that they are not suited to the spirit of the day.

Nor should any importunity have prevailed (though I was not without some of the nearest and most pressing kind), if I had not some confidence towards God, that his truth is herein declared, (how weakly soever), and some hope that this work may be accepted with God through Jesus Christ, and may be of some use to his people; which I leave with the Lord, who alone giveth the increase.

It was praise-worthy charity in a great divine, now at rest with the Lord, to say, "He hoped that some were much obliged to the grace of God to whom the grace of God was little obliged."

THE PREFACE.

"liged." *To which I would add my desires, that some opposers and perverters of the grace of God, may yet fall under that power of his grace, as shall make them* know the grace of God in truth, Col. i. 6. *and* preach that faith they now seek to destroy, Gal. i. 23.

The edification and comfort of any believer, or the conviction of any unbeliever, will overpay the labour of this service. This is all I design and desire. I have neither sought patrons nor vouchers, besides the Spirit of God speaking in the scriptures of truth. At this bar all men and all doctrines must stand and be judged.

LONDON,
May 9. 1705.

ROBERT TRAILL.

SERMONS

SIXTEEN SERMONS
ON THE
LORD's PRAYER

In JOHN xvii. 24.——Firſt printed in 1705.

*Cui veritas comperta, ſine Deo? Cui Deus cognitus, ſine Chriſto?
Cui Chriſtas exploratus, ſine Spiritu Sancto?*
                                    TERTULLIAN.

By the late REVEREND
MR. ROBERT TRAILL, A. M.
Miniſter of the Goſpel in LONDON.

GLASGOW:

Printed by JOHN BRYCE, and Sold at his
Shop, oppoſite Gibſon's-wynd, SALT-MARKET.
M DCC LXXVI.

SERMONS
CONCERNING THE
LORD's PRAYER.
In John xvii. 24.

SERMON I.

John xvii. 24.

Father, I will that they also whom thou haſt given me, be with me where I am; that they may behold my glory which thou haſt given me: for thou lovedſt me before the foundation of the world.

YOU have heard many a good text taken out of the word of God; but though all be good, there is none better than this. Love the text, and love above all, the bleſſed firſt ſpeaker of it; and you will be the fitter to profit by what you hear ſpoken in his name from it.

The beſt of all ſermons, in chap. xiv, xv, xvi, is concluded with the beſt of all prayers in this chap. xvii. In this prayer, properly the Lord's prayer, (for that in Matth. vi. 9. is rather the pattern given for our praying, than the Lord's prayer), there are but few petitions, but they are all great ones. He prays,

1. For

1. For himself and his own glory, ver. 1, to 6. 2. Then for his people, to the end of this chapter. This ver. 24. contains his last petition for them. And passing the compellation *Father*, five times used in this prayer, thrice singly, as in ver. 1, 5, and 24. twice with an addition, *Holy Father*, ver. 11. *Righteous Father*, ver. 25. I take up two things in this petition.

1. The manner of our Lord's asking, *I will;* a singular way of praying.

2. The matter of Christ's prayer. And in it are four things.

1. The party he prays for; *they whom thou hast given me*. Only Jesus Christ could pray thus for the elect, as elect.

2. The blessing he prays for to them: *that they may be with me where I am*. Where was Christ when he said this? He was going to the garden, to his agony, to be taken that night, and to be crucified next morning, and laid in his grave the next evening. But here our Lord is praying as one in heaven. See ver. 11, 12. *And now I am no more in the world, but these are in the world, and I come to thee. While I was with them in the world, I kept them in thy name*. And he prays to have his people with him in heaven. He loved them so well, that he came to the world where they were; he loved them so well, that he endured what they deserved: and here he expresseth his love in desiring *that they may be with him where he is*. Christ and his people must be together.

3. In the matter of this prayer of Christ, we have the end why Christ prays for this blessing to them; *that they may behold my glory which thou hast given me*. Why would Christ have his people with him where he is? *That they may behold his glory*. Are they to receive no glory of their own? Yes, a great deal, surely; yea, they have got some already, verse 22. *The glory which thou gavest me* (to give), *I have given them;* and a great deal more they are to receive in heaven: but it stands in, and is advanced by their be-

beholding of Christ's glory. Had they not beheld Christ's glory before? John i. 14. *We beheld his glory, the glory as of the only begotten of the Father,* 2 Cor. iii. 18. *We all with open face behold as in a glass the glory of the Lord.* Isaiah, chap. vi. *saw his glory, and spake of him,* John xii. 41. Why then doth our Lord speak of the necessity of his people's being with him where he is, that they might behold his glory, since he can manifest his glory, and they by grace can behold it, even when they are where they are, and not yet where he is? The reason is this, Because believers now, though by faith they can see something of Christ's glory, yet it is but a very little they do, or can see. The light is small, and their eye but weak; but in that day that our Lord prays for, the discoveries of his glory will be greater, and the seeing eye of the glorified will be stronger, than now we can conceive.

4. In the matter of this prayer, we have the argument on which our Lord prays for this blessing to his people: *For thou lovedst me before the foundation of the world.* You know, that this phrase, *before the foundation of the world,* is an usual scripture-word for eternity: for the foundation of the world and time began together; creatures and time began together. Time is properly the measure of the duration of a creature; but God *inhabiteth eternity,* Isa. lvii. 15. Creatures dwell or sojourn in time. So that this argument of our Lord's is, *For thou lovedst me from eternity.* And it hath a mighty force in it. If our Lord had said, " I pray that they may be with me " where I am, *for thou lovedst them before the foundation of the world:*" he had spoke what he had oft told them, for they were given to Christ in love. But the argument is stronger, as Christ expresseth it. *For thou lovedst me.* " I love them, and would have them " where I am; they love me, and would be with me " where I am; thou lovest them, and wilt have them " where I am." But here is one argument more, *For thou lovedst me.* Jesus Christ the Son of God, as intrusted

trusted with the office of a Saviour, and charged with the chosen, was, and is the object of the Father's eternal delight and love; and on this love the salvation of all the elect stands more firm than the pillars of heaven or earth.

So much for the words of this verse. And from this little glance I have given you of them, you may plainly perceive, that here is a rich and deep mine, better than of gold that perisheth. The Lord help us to dig and find treasure, and to be enriched by it.

HEAD I. To begin with the first thing in the text, *the manner of Christ's praying* here, *I will:* a singular manner: About it I would premise three things.

1. This is a way and manner of praying, that we never read the like of it used by any saint in the word. Some of them have been very familiar with God, and the Lord hath encouraged them much by his condescendence to them; yet nothing of this *I will* is to be heard or read of in their prayers. *I will* is too high for a supplicant at God's footstool. Abraham was a great intimate with God, the first believer honoured with the noble name of *the friend of God:* yet this great friend, when pleading for Sodom, Gen. xviii. with what deep humility is his confidence mixed? Again, when pleading for Ishmael, Gen. xvii. 18. he saith, *O that Ishmael might live in thy sight!* Nothing like this *I will*. Abraham's grandson Jacob came a little nearer to this, Gen. xxxii. 26. *Let me go,* (saith the angel), *for the day breaketh;* Jacob answers, *I will not let thee go, except thou bless me;* "Give me thy blessing, and go when thou wilt." When he had got the blessing, he got an halting thigh, and a humbled heart whilst he lived, as he hints in Gen. xxxii. 30. *I have seen God face to face, and my life is preserved.* Not a word or thought of this, "I have seen God face to face, I have wrestled with him hand to hand, and have prevailed." No; he rather wonders that he

he got alive out of God's hands. Right Jacobs, true Israels, in and on their greatest prevailings with God, and blessings from him, are lowly, humble believers, yea, humbled by God's advancing of them. Moses, that great wrestler with God for Israel, though he expressed a holy resolvedness, yet nothing appears like this *I will*. Exod. xxxii. 10. *Let me alone,* (saith the Lord), *that my wrath may wax hot against them, and that I may consume them.* It is strange, that one man should as it were hold the Lord's hands, that one man's faith should stop the execution of a just sentence against a sinful people. Surely you may conclude, that the Lord is easy to be intreated. Again in Exodus xxxiii. 15. Moses said, *If thy presence go not with me* (or *us*), *carry us not up hence.* It is as good for us to die here, as to go any whither without thy presence. The wilderness, though waste and howling; and Canaan, though the glory of all lands, are alike to Moses without God's presence. Again, in Numb. xiv. 12. Moses hath a great offer from the Lord; *I will destroy this people, and make of thee a greater nation, and mightier than they.* Moses, in his zeal to God's glory, refuseth this proffer, and pleads still, and prevails; yet never *I will* is in all his importunity. No believer ever did, or ought to speak so to God; they should all ask according to his will, and forget and deny their own will. Yet Christ did say, *I will,* and might well say so.

2. This *I will* is not in a promise to us, but in a prayer to his Father. When the Lord promiseth to do, or give good to his people, it is very becoming to use this style, *I will do,* or *give,* or *be* so and so to my people. And it is this *I will* in a promise that faith fixeth on; as Jacob did, Gen. xxxii. 12. *Thou saidst, I will surely do thee good.* But our Lord is here praying; though I own that there is a great promise implied in it, as we shall hear.

3. There is nothing like this in all the account we have of Christ's prayers at other times, and other

occasions. We find, that our blessed Saviour was much given to prayer alone, Bless him for it, and love secret prayer the better, that he used it himself, and thereby hallowed it to our use. How our Lord spent those nights in the mountain in prayer, and what he prayed for, and how, we cannot tell, except by that in Heb. v. 7. There are *prayers and supplications offered up, with strong crying and tears.* Believers, you, sometimes when your hearts are full, want to be far from all company, that you may pour out your complaint to the Lord. Blessed Jesus did so in the days of his flesh, and filled the silent night with his crying; and watered the cold earth with his tears, more precious than *the dew of Hermon,* or any moisture (next to his blood) that ever fell on God's earth since the creation. Never were such sinless and precious tears in God's bottle, Psalm lvi. 8. Let yours drop, believers, and mix in the same bottle with his; and on this account sow them in hope, and you shall *reap in joy,* Psalm cxxvi. 5. But for Christ's prayers recorded in the gospel, we find our Lord prayed very humbly, though confidently. When he prays in his agony, not a word of *I will;* but, *Abba, let this cup pass from me, if thou wilt; nevertheless, not my will, but thine be done.* Christians, behold the amazing difference betwixt Christ's way of praying against his own hell, (so I may call it), and his praying for our heaven. When praying for himself, it is, *Father, if it be thy will, let this cup pass from me.* And no wonder; for every drop in that cup, was wrath, and curse, and death. One drop of it is everlasting poison to all that taste it, but to Jesus the Prince of life. This cup he drank chearfully: John xviii. 11. *The cup which my Father hath given me, shall I not drink it?* But when Christ is praying for his people's heaven, it is, *Father, I will that they may be with me where I am.* Again, when our Lord is dying on the cross, he prays, *Father, forgive them, for they know*
not

not what they do. And again, juſt at dying, *Father, into thy hands I commend my ſpirit,* Luke xxii. 34. and 46. All humble ſupplications; none of them ſo high and lofty (but yet it well became him) as this *I will.* I own, that Chriſt, in one inſtance on the croſs, put forth his divine power, and acted like a King and God, Luke xxiii. 42, 43. One of the malefactors that was crucified with him, (the happieſt death ever man had, next to dying for Chriſt, was to die with the Saviour, and to die receiving Chriſt's grace, and Chriſt's paſs to heaven), whatever Thomas meant in his words, John xi. 16. *Let us go, that we may die with him;* this happy malefactor had the beſt of it fulfilled on him: he died with Chriſt, and got eternal life on the ſame day. Surely that word was eminently fulfilled in this man, Eccl. vii. 1. *Better is the day of death, than the day of one's birth.* This man prays marvellouſly, *Lord, remember me when thou comeſt into thy kingdom.* Our Lord anſwers more marvellouſly, *Verily I ſay unto thee, To day ſhalt thou be with me in paradiſe.* As if Chriſt had ſaid, " Can thy faith " take me up as a king, and the diſpoſer of heaven, " notwithſtanding this thick and dark vail that is now " upon me? I will act as a God and Saviour to thee:" *To-day ſhalt thou be with me in paradiſe.* Theſe words have no ſmall aſpect to this text, *I will that they be with me where I am.*

Now let us ſee what may be in this ſingular word in Chriſt's prayer, *I will.* No ſaint ever prayed ſo; Chriſt himſelf in this prayer only here uſeth this word. There muſt be ſome ſingular things that made our Lord uſe this word in prayer, *I will;* and them I would look into.

1. We may lawfully conceive, that herein there is a breaking out of his divine glory as the Son of God equal with the Father, as in Phil. ii. 6,----10.; where the apoſtle marketh three things about Chriſt, none of which muſt be forgotten by Chriſtians. 1. The
divine

divine dignity of his person, ver. 6. 2. The depth of his low and humbled state, ver. 7, 8. 3. The height of his exalted state, ver. 9, 10, 11. So doth the apostle to the Hebrews, chap. i. 3. Now, tho' Christ's humbled and exalted state had, and have their several and distinct appearances; yet as his divine dignity was still the same in both states, in his lowest and at his highest, so there were now and then some beamings of his glory, even in his lowest state, John ii. 11. and in his triumphant entry to Jerusalem, even when he was going to be crucified. So we may think, that this singular word, *I will*, is used by Christ to display his divine glory; for it is a word that no mere man may use.

2. Our Lord had promised it to his disciples in John xiv. 2, 3.; and therefore prays thus for it. And we must think, that the doctrine delivered by Christ in his last sermon of consolation, and this last prayer of his, though in the first place designed for his apostles, yet are the common portion of all believers on Jesus Christ. Now Christ had promised, John xiv. 2, 3. that *where he was, there his people should be also*. If a poor believer have at any time a firm hold on a promise of God, how will he cleave to it, plead upon it, and urge it? as 2 Sam. vii. 27, 28, 29. But who can conceive what confidence of faith Jesus Christ the Son of God had, and did use, in pleading with his Father for the fulfilling of all his own promises to his people? Besides, all Christ's promises to his people, were made by him in his Father's name. No wonder then that our Lord says, *I will*.

3. Christ here gives us a copy and pattern of his intercession in heaven, that so much is spoke of. Christ here speaks as within the vail, ver. 4, 11, 12. as if he had done all his work, and were no more in the world. He had done so much, had but a little more to do, which also was speedily to be dispatched. Christ's intercession in heaven, is a kind and powerful remembrance of his people, and of all their concerns, managed,

naged with state and majesty; not as a supplicant at the footstool, but as a crowned prince on the throne, at the right hand of the Father. So it is expressed, Rom. viii. 34. Heb. i. 3. viii. 2. x. 12, 13. and xii. 2. This may be one reason of this great *I will*.

4. Here our Lord is making his will; and therefore *I will* is fitly put in. Christ is making his last will and testament, and praying it over to his Father, which he sealed next day with his blood; and here he tells what he wills to his people, even *that they may be with him where he is*. And nothing greater or better can be willed for them. Blessed for evermore are they that have this willed and bequeathed to them. And you have a word like this in Luke xxii. 29. *I appoint unto you a kingdom*: "I bequeath, "dispose it, make it over to you;" as the word may be rendered.

5. Our Lord had the price of this glory in his hand, ready now to lay down; and therefore he demands the purchase: for Christ was taken this night, and died next day. The price of the redeemed and of their salvation, a price agreed upon in the everlasting covenant, a price of infinite value in itself, a price the Father's wisdom and justice demanded, a price the Son promised to lay down in the fulness of time, a price on the payment whereof so great things were promised to Christ and his seed; this price is now in Christ's hand ready, presently to be told down. No wonder then, if Christ demand the purchase in this high word, *I will*. Believers, it passeth all your thoughts, it passeth the highest flights of your faith, to conceive that high assurance and confidence that our Lord Jesus had of the acceptance and success of that sacrifice of himself that he was now upon offering to his Father. Hence cometh this great *I will*.

6. This *I will* is but an echo to the known will of his Father. It doth not become us to say in our prayers, *I will*, because we do not perfectly know God's will; and when our desires clash with his will,

we

we do but dash against a rock. But Christ knew perfectly, that the thing he prays for, was the will of his Father, John vi. 38, 39, 40. When a believer hath a sure knowledge of God's will, his faith may plead boldly on it. We read of one bold word of blessed Luther. He hearing of the dangerous sickness of an eminent minister of the gospel, prayed for him, prevailed with the Lord for his life; and wrote to him, that he was assured, that the Lord would restore him, and preserve him to outlive Luther; which came to pass. In the close of this letter, he writes *Fiat voluntas mea ; mea, Domine, quia tua.* " Let my will " be done; mine, Lord, because thine."

7. *Lastly,* This *I will* in Christ's prayer for his people, shews how much his heart was set upon the eternal happiness of his people. He prays for it with all his heart. On this sweet theme I would offer a few things.

1st, Let us consider how Christ's love and will was on the necessary price of their salvation. How dear soever it was to him, whatever it cost him, his love was on laying it down; Luke xii. 50. *I have a baptism to be baptized with, and how am I straitened* (or *pained*) *till it be accomplished?* and it was a baptism in his own blood; and Luke xxii. 15. *With desire I have desired to eat this passover with you before I suffer :* and it was his last meal. Love to his Father, and love to his sheep, made our Lord long greatly to pay the price of redemption.

There are several thoughts in mens hearts about Christ's dying. 1. Some think of Christ's death as brought about by the wicked hands of sinners. This is a poor thought, if there be no more. This thought is natural to any that read the history of his death. Carnal men may hate Judas that betrayed him, Pilate that condemned him, the priests that cried *Crucify him,* and the people that did it. If this be all, I may say, the devils have a higher thought of Christ's death,

and

and that that comes nearer to the truth, than this sorry one. 2. Some go further, and think of Christ's death as it was a fulfilling of the purpose and word of God concerning him. This Christ teacheth us in Luke xxiv. 26. 44. 46.; and the apostles frequently in their preaching of Christ. 3. There is a higher thought of Christ's death; and that is, That Christ died, by the stroke of God's law and justice, for his people. Justice roused itself against our Lord: Zech. xiii. 7. *Awake, O sword, against my shepherd, and against the man that is my fellow, saith the Lord of hosts: smite the shepherd.* This sword was drawn and furbished, and did enter into his soul: Isa. liii. 5. *He was wounded for our transgressions, he was bruised for our iniquities.* Better were it that a man had never heard of Christ and of his death, than to hear, and not to know that his death was for his sins. This is Paul's first doctrine he taught; and he is an ignorant and proud preacher that follows not this pattern: 1 Cor. xv. 3. *For I delivered unto you first of all, that which I also received, that Christ died for our sins, according to the scriptures.* 4. The best thought of Christ's death is, That he died out of love to his people. Love made him come in the way of justice. Justice and the law saith as it were, " Thou, or they " must die. They have sinned, the law must be ful-" filled, justice must be satisfied." Blessed Jesus answers, " I love them too well to let them die; I will " rather die for them, that they may live." Christ's death is still laid on his love, John x. Gal. ii. 20. Eph. v. 25, 26. *He loved us, and washed us from our sins in his own blood,* Rev. i. 5.; that is, He loved us so that he shed his own blood for our sins; and then in the same love he washed us from our sins, in and by that blood which he shed in love. O such love! such blood! such washing! Here is salvation, and here only. It is a damning dream to expect it any where else.

2dly, Consider, as Christ's love was much set on the paying the price of redemption, so was his love and will as much set on the persons of the redeemed. He laid down the price, in love to the purchase. How can it enter into a man's thoughts, that the Son of God should lay down so great a price, and not know what he was to take up for it? that he should die, and not know for whom, nor who should be the better for it? His dying was in love; and did he not know whom he loved? His love is still spoke of as distinguishing and particular; for his *body*, his *people*, his *sheep*, whom he *knew*, John x.

3dly, the ways and means of bringing his redeemed to glory, were also much in Christ's love and will: John. xvii. 6. 26. *I have declared unto them thy name, and will declare it; that the love wherewith thou hast loved me, may be in them, and I in them;* and John x. 16. *And other sheep I have, which are not of this fold,* (are not of the Jews, but of the elect Gentiles) *: them also I must bring, and they shall hear my voice; and there shall be one fold, and one shepherd.* Every mean of grace, every blessing of the means, every drop of grace you receive, as Christ is the giver, so his love and will is in the bestowing it on you. All things that accompany salvation, are given with the love and will of Christ.

4thly, Lastly, Christ's will is upon the end itself, eternal glory. It is first in his design, though it be last in our enjoyment, as in this text. He will have his people *with him where he is.*

APPLICATION. There is one thing I would exhort you to from this doctrine, That Christ's love and will is fixed on the eternal glory of his people; and it is this. Let believers learn to own their eternal salvation as springing from the will of Christ, as well as from the blood of Christ. There was a saving will in Christ in shedding his saving blood: Heb. x. 10. *By the which will we are sanctified, (*i. e. justified and

and saved, in the style of that epistle, specially) *thro' the offering of the body of Jesus Christ once for all.* What this *will* is, is declared in the foregoing verses; to be the Father's will commanding the true sacrifice, and the Son's will in offering this commanded sacrifice. By this *will* we are saved; this *will*, thus fixed, thus accomplished in Christ's death.

There are three great advantages, which we shall reap by this looking on heaven, the prize of our calling, as willed by Jesus Christ.

1. It will stir you up to praise and glorify him. He that took on him the burden of our souls, and the care of our salvation, should surely bear the burden of all our songs for salvation, and for the hope of it. So the apostle sings, Rev. i. 5. Hearty praise to Jesus Christ for salvation can never be given, unless men know that all their salvation is owing to him alone; to his will, and to his blood. If a man ascribe any bit of his salvation to any thing or person besides Christ, that thing or person will bear away, or rob somewhat of the glory of salvation. But since all salvation is from Christ, all the glory of it should be given to him.

2. This will make your faith in Christ strong. What is strong faith? Christians usually think, that strong faith hath in it peace, joy, and comfort. But these are but the effects of it; and separable also, as in Psal. xxii. 1. Never was faith near so strong in any saint, as it was in the man Christ on the cross: and yet no joy or comfort was tasted by him then. But as to faith in believers, strong faith is when a believer gets far in, into the love and will of Jesus Christ. Now, this doctrine opens up Christ's love and will about our salvation; let us then enter into it. Faith makes several approaches to Christ for and about salvation.

1*st*, It seeketh, and findeth, and seeth atoning, reconciling blood, flowing from Christ's love: Rom. iii. 25. *God hath set him forth to be a propitiation* *through faith in his blood.* Eph. i. 7. *In whom we have redemption through his blood.*

2*dly*, Faith seeth life springing and growing out of Christ's grave. Alas! many are busy about Moses's grave, and have no business with Christ's grave. A believer seeth eternal life springing from Christ's death and grave.

3*dly*, Faith goes further; and through this blood of atonement, and this life giving death, it enters into Christ's love and will that was in his redeeming. As there was life to us in his death, so there was love to us in his dying for us, Gal. ii. 20. Rev. i. 5. But can faith go any further? Yes. Only one step more; and that is to the highest fountain of all this; even God's *eternal purpose which he purposed in Jesus Christ our Lord,* Eph. iii. 11. So that faith begins at Christ's death, riseth with him in his resurrection, seeth the virtue and power of all in Christ's love, and then riseth to the love of the Father that sent him, to that purpose of grace from which the Saviour and all salvation doth proceed. Can faith go any further? No. Here faith is at a stand. The believer is saved, and yet sinks and is overwhelmed in this depth; and, like one swallowed up, cries out, *O the depth of the riches both of the wisdom and knowledge of God! how unsearchable are his judgments, and his ways past finding out!* Rom. xi. 33. When faith gets a view of the unsearchable riches of God's grace in, by, and through Jesus Christ, then the believer longs to be in heaven, to behold the fountain-head of all grace and glory. Faith longs to cease to be faith. This is a strange and strong act of faith, a strange desire in a believer, " O when shall I cease to be a believer, and " become a seer! when shall the glass be done away, " and the full-eyed vision of glory succeed! 1 Cor. " xiii. 10, 11, 12. When shall both faith and hope " cease, and love fill their room?"

3. This seeing of Christ's heart and will about your salvation, will enable you to pray and labour
rightly

rightly for glory. What is it to do it rightly? It is to labour with courage, and to labour with humility. And Christians work prospereth, when those are united, as they always should be. How boldly may a believer say, I would be in heaven since Christ wills it? And how humbly should he say, I would be there; since his own will about it signifies nothing, and Christ's will is all?

Obj. How shall I know that I am in Christ's will for salvation? If I did know it, then I would give thanks, I would believe firmly, and would labour hard to obtain the possession of this glory.

Answ. To this I offer three things. 1. Consider how they behaved themselves, that with their own ears heard those very words from Christ's own mouth. It is a vain thought that readily riseth in all our hearts, that if we had been present, and had heard Christ praying thus for us in a special, particular way, that we might be with him where he is, that then we would believe our salvation if we were in the saddest distress. But now consider what great encouragement to faith Christ gave them. He told them, chap. xiv. 2, 3. *I go to prepare a place for you. I will come again, and receive you unto myself, that where I am, there ye may be also.* What more could they desire, than to have Christ telling them to their faces, "You and I must "indeed part for a little while; but you and I shall "quickly meet again, never to part more?" They did also with their ears hear Christ praying over his promise to them, to his Father, *I will that they be with me where I am.* Could such believers under all those advantages, so great, so singular, ever stagger again? Yes. Almost as soon as this encouraging sermon and prayer is ended, their faith was almost at an end too: John xvi. 31, 32. *Jesus answered them, Do ye now believe? Behold, the hour cometh, yea, is now come, that ye shall be scattered, every man to his own, and shall leave me alone.* I speak this, to check the vanity of that thought in Christians, that if they had but sufficient ground of the assurance of Christ's love, and of eternal glory, they would believe in every difficulty and trial. Yet you see how they behaved that had such grounds of faith from Christ's own lips, whilst bodily present with them, which you cannot expect or desire. And I hope none of you will imagine, that if he had been in those good mens places, and had had their helps, you would have behaved better than they did. Grounds of faith, if never so great, yet if not attended with the influence of the Spirit of faith, will never keep faith in life and vigour.

Answ. 2. What reason have you to doubt your interest in this prayer of Christ? You may say, I am so vile and unworthy, that I cannot believe that Christ willed me to be with him. If this be all, it is nothing, yea worse than nothing. 1. Hath not Christ willed eternal glory to many as bad as ever you were? Did he ever will heaven for worthiness in the persons that are to receive it? Is it not always willed to the praise of his own grace and love as the giver, and never as a recompence to the worth and loveliness of the receiver? 2. Christ will mend you ere he bring you to heaven. And a great work it is to *make you meet for it*, Col. i. 12.; a work that must be done, and that he only can do, and he can easily do it. 3. Right preparation for glory, flows from the faith of Christ's good-will to give it. It is a weak and ignorant, but common thought of Christians, that they ought not to look for heaven, nor trust Christ for eternal glory, till they be well advanced in holiness, and meetness for it. But as the first sanctification of our natures flows from our faith and trust in Christ for acceptance, so our farther sanctification and meetness for glory flows from the renewed and repeated exercise of faith on him. The hope of glory is purifying, 1 John iii. 3.

Answ. 3. Every believer hath the witness in himself, that he hath an interest in Christ's heart and will in this prayer: 1 John v. 10. *He that believeth on in the Son of God, hath the witness in himself.* The apostle is speaking of the many witnesses that are given to Jesus Christ as the Saviour. Three in heaven, ver. 7. three on earth, ver. 8. All are divine witnesses, and sufficient grounds of faith in Jesus Christ, ver. 9. Now, saith the apostle, ver. 10. *He that believeth on the Son of God,* (that trusts his soul, and its salvation, to this so well attested Saviour), *he hath the witness* (or *testimony*) *in himself.* 1. There are witnesses in heaven. 2. Witnesses on earth. 3. A testimony in the heart of a believer in Christ. Whoever believeth on Christ, that faith is an evidence sufficient (if he will require it to speak), and will regard its testimony: and both of them require actings of faith, to persuade him that he hath an interest in Christ's prayer here. On this I would glance at four things, and conclude.

1. Believers in Christ, what do you do when you believe? O that all believers did but know what they do when they believe! Do ye not, in every distinct act of faith, betrust your guilty perishing soul to the saving arm of Jesus Christ, upon the warrant of all that grace, mercy, and power, that belongs to Christ in his office of a Saviour? And is not this his willing of eternal glory, a great and glorious beam of that grace of our Lord Jesus Christ, by which ye believe to be saved? Acts xv. 11.

2. How came you by this your faith? Is it not his gift? He is the *author* of it, Heb. xii. 2. It is *given on Christ's behalf*, Phil. i. 29. Whenever you have an evidence in your heart, (and it is your own fault if you have it not daily), that you have true faith in Jesus Christ; if it be but weak, and cannot mount so high as it ought, raise it by this consideration, Whence came this spark of faith to be kindled in my heart? Did it naturally grow in my heart? No. Time was when I was without it, Eph. ii. 12. and loved to be without it. Did Satan plant it? No. I find him to be the great enemy of it; and I never felt his enmity,

mity, till I began to trust Jesus Christ; and it is that in me he mainly assaults. Did ministers, and the means of grace, plant faith in me? No. I enjoyed them when no faith was wrought in me; and when it is wrought, all their power, without Christ's grace and Spirit in concurring, cannot raise this faith to act and exercise. Therefore, surely, this faith came from Jesus Christ himself. Was it not from the work, and will, and love of Christ? How easy and native is the inference? If faith in Christ be the work of his love, how warrantably may I look, by that faith, for all the good that this love purposeth, promiseth, and prayeth for to me?

3. Can you call him to witness with a good conscience, that your great desire and will is to be with Christ in heaven? If the Lord should try you with this question, "Name that one thing that you would "have above all;" every believer hath his answer ready; it is, "Lord, that I may be ever with thee, "where thou art;" as David said, Psalm xxvii. 4. of God's house on earth. This I infer, If thy love be set on being with Christ where he is, be assured that Christ's love is set on the same blessing for thee; yea, thy desire after it, flows from his desire of it for thee.

4. Are you willing, yea pleased and delighted, to hold your title to eternal glory, by the will and testament of Jesus Christ? Are you willing to have and hold the crown by this tenure only, that it was bought by his blood, and willed to you by his testament? Every believer would be in heaven, because Christ is there; and is pleased to get and keep his place there, as willed to him by Jesus Christ. Heaven is a lovely name, and a more lovely thing; but not at all known by many, and but little by the best; but yet believers look for it, and expect it, as *the gift of God thro' Jesus Christ our Lord*, Rom. vi. 23. They plead for it as such; at last they receive it as grace, and eternally wear the crown as a crown of grace, as well as
a crown

a crown of glory. The glorified saint, as soon as he receives this crown, casts it at Christ's feet, Rev. iv. 10. or sets it on Christ's head, as if ashamed to wear a crown, where Christ the only Worthy is. Upon Christ's *head are many crowns,* Rev. xix. 12. His Father puts a crown on him, Heb. ii. 9. *crowned him with glory and honour;* his mother, the church, crowns him, Cant. iii. 11. with a crown of salvation; and every saved person puts on Christ's head the crown of the glory of their particular salvation. To conclude: They that are not willing to give the glory of all salvation to Jesus Christ, shall never receive any salvation from him. But for you that are willing to receive all from him, and are delighted to render the glory of all to him, his heart is towards you; his best wishes are for your good; and he will give you what he hath prepared for you, which is exceedingly above all that can be told you.

SERMON II.

JOHN xvii. 24.

Father, I will that they also whom thou hast given me, be with me where I am; that they may behold my glory which thou hast given me: for thou lovedst me before the foundation of the world.

THOSE great and saving words of our Lord Jesus Christ, have been taken up into two heads.
1. The manner of Christ's praying: *I will.* Of this last day.

HEAD II. *The matter of Christ's prayer.* And therein I took up four things. 1. The person he prays for; *they whom thou hast given me.* 2. The blessing he prays for to them; *that they may be with me where I am.* 3. The end our Lord prays for this blessing to them for; *that they may behold my glory which thou hast given me.* 4. The argument our Lord presseth this suit by; *for thou lovedst me before the foundation of the world.*

The *first* of these I would now speak to: *The designation and name of the persons Christ here prays for: They whom thou hast given me.* No man but Jesus Christ, who is more than a man, dare say in prayer, *I will;* nor pray for persons under this name as Christ did. All our prayers are to be out of one book; and we pray without book in a bad sense, when we go beyond it. The only book I mean, is God's written will in the holy scriptures. By this we are taught what to pray for, and how we should pray: and beyond this we cannot lawfully ask any thing; neither need we more for direction, but only the same Spirit that writ them, to assist us in the using of them, Rom. viii. 26.; that we may *pray in the Holy Ghost,* Jude, ver. 20. and *in the Spirit,* Eph. vi. 18. But our Lord Jesus Christ could not only pray out of God's revealed will in the scriptures, (for he testified of the scriptures, as they do of him, John v. 39.); but he could, and did pray out of the book of God's secret will. He prayed out of the book of life, and was acquainted with the original of the covenant. And thus he prays here for *them that were given him.*

From this I would raise three doctrines, and speak to one of them at this time.

OBS. 1. *There is a select company of the children of men given by the Father to the Son.*

OBS. 2. *This company given by the Father to the Son was, and is fully and exactly known by Jesus Christ.*

OBS.

Obs. 3. *That Jesus Christ is nearly concerned about their eternal salvation;* as his praying for it here witnesseth.

Obs. 1. *There was a select company of mankind given by the Father to his Son Jesus Christ, to be saved by him.*

This truth is several ways declared to us in the word; and yet more by Jesus Christ himself, than by any other; and yet more in this prayer, than any where else by him. And, if we may so conceive, this great depth of God was specially fit to be mentioned, when the receiver of them is speaking his heart about them to the giver of them. This is named six times in this short chapter. In ver. 2. *As thou hast given him power over all flesh, that he should give eternal life to as many as thou hast given him.* In ver. 6. we have it twice: *I have manifested thy name unto the men which thou gavest me out of the world: thine they were, and thou gavest them me; and they have kept thy word.* In ver. 9. *I pray not for the world, but for them which thou hast given me, for they are thine.* Ver. 11. *Holy Father, keep through thine own name, those whom thou hast given me.* And here again in ver. 24. *They whom thou hast given me.* There is a twofold giving of men to the Son by the Father. One is eternal, in the purpose of his grace; and this is mainly meant here. The other is in time; when the Father by his Spirit draws men to Christ, John vi. 44, 45. All the elect are given from eternity to the Son, to be redeemed by his blood; all the redeemed are in due time drawn by the Father to the Son, to be kept to eternal life.

On this giving of men to Christ, I would speak a little. 1. To the nature of it. And, 2. To the ends of it.

I. As to *the nature of it*. This giving of men to the Son to be redeemed and saved, is the same thing with election and predestination, Eph. i. 4. *He hath chosen us in Christ before the foundation of the world.* Ver. 5. *Having predestinated us unto the adoption of children by Jesus Christ to himself.* And ver. 11. *In whom also we have obtained an inheritance, being predestinated according to the purpose of him who worketh all things after the counsel of his own will.* The difference betwixt these two words is very small. *Election* points at the distinction of the persons on whom this grace fell from eternity. *Predestination* fixeth the end they were appointed to, 1 Thess. v. 9. Giving them to Christ, points forth the grand trustee with this great charge. The meaning of this word, *giving of men to Christ,* so oft used by our Lord, and hallowed by his using of it, hath these five things in it.

1. That there were divine transactions between the Father and Son about the saving of men. There was *a counsel of peace between them both,* Zech. vi. 13.; oft and plainly revealed in the word, yet a mystery unsearchable to all men, but firmly to be believed, reverently to be adored, and cautiously to be improved by us.

2. That there was but a select company of mankind that this counsel was about. Our Lord, who knew them best, still speaks thus of them, especially in this prayer: as hath been declared. He still speaks of them by way of distinction from the world. Whatever men may say of universal redemption, surely universal election is a contradiction in words. Election must be of a fixed determinate number. There is no election, if there be no passing by. If all be taken, there are none chosen. If there be an *election,* there is a *rest,* a *remnant,* (and this rest is a multitude), Rom. xi. 7. How great this number of the elect is, Christ and his Father knew; and the last day will declare, when they shall be brought altogether, and obtain *the kingdom prepared for them from the foundation of the world,*

world, and be adjudged to it by Chrift, as they are the *bleffed of his Father*, Matth. xxv. 34.

3. That this counfel about their falvation was from eternity. Time-election is as great a blunder as univerfal election. How oft is the eternity of it afferted in the word? Eph. i. 4. 2 Theff. ii. 13. 2 Tim. i. 9. Election is an immanent act of God about creatures; not on them, nor with them. It is in a tranfaction betwixt the Father and the Son, about men that were not, but were only to be; and to reap the benefit of it in time and to eternity.

4. It follows, that this grace of election muft be unchangeable, immutable, and unalterable. It never changeth, it never fails of its defigned effect. All God's counfels are fo: Ifa. xxv. 1. *Thy counfels of old are faithfulnefs and truth.* His *counfel ftands for ever, the thoughts of his heart to all generations*, Pfal. xxxiii. 11. *He is in one mind, and who can turn him? and what his foul defireth, even that he doth.* For he *performeth the thing which is appointed for me*, Job xxiii. 13, 14. Now, of this number of the elect given by the Father to the Son, there is no paring from it, no adding to it. The book of life admits of no corrections, blotting out; no additions, no new editions.

5. It is alfo implied, that in this giving of men to the Son, the Son of God, our Lord Jefus Chrift, hath a fpecial intereft. Thereby they are made his charge; and he *the Captain of their falvation, to bring thefe fons* of election-grace *to eternal glory*, Heb. ii. 10.

II. Of *the ends of this giving of men thus to Chrift by the Father*. It is a glorious act of God, and it is on glorious defigns and ends. Of fome of thefe, from the word, I would fpeak in thefe four particulars.

1. Herein is a moft clear difplaying of abfolute fovereignty in Jehovah. The glorious God is moft zealous for the glory of this name of his fovereignty, as what moft nearly concerns the glory of his Godhead;

and proud vain men are most averse to the owning of it. The apostle Paul is on this same doctrine in Rom. ix. and builds it on this same foundation, ver. 11.----19. He starts two strong objections against it; as carnal minds are fertile in vain arguings against divine counsels. And O that all advocates for them had been satisfied with Paul's answers, which are the only and strongest bulwarks of the Holy Ghost about this doctrine! *Object.* 1. is in ver. 14. *Is there unrighteousness with God?* Did God love Jacob, and hate Esau, before they had either done good or evil? ver. 11, 12, 13. Where is the righteousness of this? Jacob had done no good to deserve love; Esau had done no evil to deserve hatred. How does the apostle answer it? 1. By an abhorrence of the charge: *God forbid.* If we cannot see into the depth of God's counsels, let us still justify God,-as Jer. xii. 1.; and admire and adore the depth we cannot fathom, Rom. xi. 33. 2. He answers with a reason taken from God's old saying to Moses, ver. 15. Now, if Paul had been of some mens minds, he would have answered, That God foresaw, that though Jacob had done no good when he was in the womb, yet that in time he would be a holy man, a wrestler with God, and a great believer; and therefore God loved him, and therefore there was no unrighteousness with God. And so as to Esau, he would have said, God foresaw that he would prove a profane man, would sell his birth-right for a mess of pottage, grieve the hearts of his godly father and mother by his marriage, and hate to the death his godly brother Jacob; and therefore God hated Esau, and therefore there was no unrighteousness with God. But Paul instead of hinting any thing like this, gives an answer inconsistent with, and subversive of this notion. In ver. 15. *For he saith to Moses, I will have mercy on whom I will have mercy, and I will have compassion on whom I will have compassion.* See the apostle's inference from, and application of this word of God, ver. 16. *So then, it is not of him that willeth, nor of him that runneth, but of God that sheweth mercy.* And on the case of reprobate Pharaoh, ver. 27. he again infers, ver. 18. *Therefore hath he mercy on whom he will have mercy; and whom he will, he hardeneth.* He plainly layeth the sovereign will and pleasure of God, as the fixed foundation of the counsels of God about mens eternal state. Object. 2. In ver. 19. *Thou wilt say then unto me, Why doth he yet find fault? for who hath resisted his will?* A plausible strong like objection, in every natural man's heart. How doth he answer it? ver. 20. *Nay, but, O man, who art thou that repliest against God?* He calls it, ver. 19. *a saying to Paul*; here in ver. 20. he calls it *a replying against God.* But is challenging the objector, an answer to the objection? Yes, in part it is; as if Paul had said, "Dost thou know neither God nor thyself, that thou " cavillest against his will and counsels?" Thus Elihu answered Job, chap. xxxiii. 12, 13. *Behold, in this thou art not just: I will answer thee, that God is greater than man. Why dost thou strive against him? for he giveth not account* (or *he answereth not*) *of any of his matters.* And after Paul had checked the arrogance of the objector, he again lays the same ground of God's absolute sovereignty, ver. 20.----33. with many scriptures brought to the same purpose.

2. The second end of God's giving men to Jesus Christ, is, to glorify his free, infinite, and everlasting love to them that he gives. So in Eph. i. 4, 5, 6. The love of the Father shines in giving us to Christ to be redeemed; the love of the Son shines in his receiving of us; and these two loves (if I may call them so) do not eclipse, but enlighten one another, and make a glorious light to the eyes of a believer. Election is always in love, and from it, or with it. And this love hath no cause, but in the heart of the lover: *He loves because he loves*, Deut. vii. 7, 8. It had no beginning, it hath no intermission, and it shall have no ending. It is *from everlasting to everlasting*, Psal. ciii.

ciii. 17. It is *an everlasting love,* Jer xxxi. 3.; *therefore he draws with loving kindness,* (or *extended loving kindness unto thee*). And he never leaves off to draw thus, till he hath drawn them to heaven, and till he *hath crowned them with loving kindness and tender mercies,* Psal. ciii. 4. Here doth this blessed love shine, in giving men to Christ; and here believers should behold it.

3. Another end of God the Father's giving of men to his Son, is, that there may be a glorious and sure salvation brought about for them that are thus given in sovereign pleasure and love. If Adam had stood in that state wherein he was created, (I know not if it be allowable to wish that it had been so), it would have been but a poor low happiness that he would have conveyed to his posterity, in regard of what comes by the second Adam to his offspring. That it was uncertain, is evident by the issue. The first Adam was intrusted with his own and all his natural posterity's happiness, as with this charge, "So shall " it fare with thee, and all thine, as thy behaviour " is." In this behaviour commanded, he failed, fell himself, and dragged us all with him into the same pit of sin and misery. But now it hath pleased the Father to lodge the happiness of his elect in his Son's hand, where it is both more sure and more glorious than the former.

4. This giving of men to the Son, is in order to the raising up a great name of glory and honour to Jesus Christ. Great is his glory in being the repairer of this greatest breach which sin made betwixt God and man. This the apostle remarks in Rom. viii. 29. *For whom he did foreknow, he also did predestinate to be conformed to the image of his Son, that he might be the first-born among many brethren.* Of this further when we come to speak of Christ's glory, in this text; and shall now only mention a little of Christ's concern in them that are given to him.

All the redeemed, and all their concerns for their

salva-

salvation, are lodged in Christ's hand, and in his only. Their persons, and every thing that pertains to them, are given to him.

2. All the impediments of their salvation are laid on Christ, that by him they may be removed. These are many and great, as you know. There is sin, and the law with its curse for sin, and the holy justice and wrath of God, and the power of hell and death. When a sinner's eyes are opened to see those impediments of salvation, it is no wonder he say with the disciples, *Who then can be saved?* All these impediments Christ did remove. But how? By taking them on himself, and removing them out of our way. For all the impediments of our salvation were impediments laid in Christ's way to his glory. He must not enter into his own glory, till he had removed the impediments of the elect's salvation. There could be no impediments in Christ's way to his glory, without his relation to his people. As he was the Son of God, eternal glory was his natural right and possession; but when he comes to be Surety and Mediator, he *must first suffer, ere he enter into his glory,* Luke xxiv. 26. 46. He must *purge our sins by himself,* Heb. i. 3. He must *put away sin by the sacrifice of himself,* Heb. ix. 26. He must *through death destroy him that had the power of death, that is, the devil,* Heb. ii. 14. He must be *made under the law, that he may redeem them that were under the law,* Gal. iv. 4, 5. He *redeemed us from the curse of the law, being made a curse for us,* Gal. iii. 13. He must *make an entrance to the holiest of all for us, by his blood;* he must *consecrate the way for us by his flesh,* Heb. x. 19, 20. He must *enter into the holy place by his own blood, having obtained eternal redemption for us,* Heb. ix. 12. Thus, by our Lord Jesus Christ, all the gates of hell are shut on the elect, and none can open them; and all the gates of heaven are opened, and none can shut them on them that are given him.

3. All the parts and pieces of salvation are in Christ's hand, and do come to us by him. The *acceptance of our persons*, is in and through this beloved, Eph. i. 6. The *forgiveness of our sins* is through his blood, Eph. i. 7. Our *quickening, when dead in sins, our rising, and sitting in heavenly places*, is with Christ and in him, Eph. ii. 4, 5, 6. Our title and right to heaven is singly owing to him. What right hath a sinner to heaven? No more, and no other, than he hath to Jesus Christ. If he be united to Christ by faith in him, he is an heir of God, and an heir of glory; a joint heir with Christ, Rom. viii. 17. Nay, our sanctification, which is begun glory, 2 Cor. iii. 18. is but a beam of this Sun of Righteousness darted in upon our souls. Unless Christ had been made sanctification to us, there had never been a sanctified man or woman in the world.

4. The actual possession of the kingdom is owing to Jesus Christ. We have a right to it in him; our charter of it is sealed by his blood; we have the earnest of it by his Spirit; we are kept to it, and it kept for us, by his power; and at last we receive it out of his own hand, John x. 28. *I give unto them eternal life*. It is too great, and too good a gift, to be given by any but blessed Jesus.

I would conclude with a few words of application.
1. Learn to see with wonder and adoration the high spring of the well of life and salvation for poor men. It is in the Father's giving of men to the Son. Nothing is before it, and all the blessings of grace and glory flow from it. From hence is the creating of the world, that these men might be born in it; from hence came the permitting and ordering of Adam's fall, that the Redeemer might be needful; from this Christ comes into the world, to redeem them; from this comes the gospel, as a light to seek those lost ones; from this cometh the Spirit, to make the gospel effectual,

fectual, that *they who are ordained to eternal life, may believe,* Acts xiii. 48.

2. Labour to see your own concern in this giving to the Son. It is but a deep and dangerous speculation without this care. Many poor questions are in people's heads, and many poor ways of answering them are in mens hearts. Some would fain know if they have any grace and true holiness; others go farther, and they would fain know if they have faith, the spring of holiness; some would fain know their title and right to heaven. There is an allowed room and place for these inquiries, and the like. But how few, even of true Christians, ask this question, *Was I given by the Father to the Son?* It is a question that may be made, and may be answered to satisfaction. Christ tells his disciples it, Luke x. 20. Paul knew it, 1 Thess. v. 9. Peter bids us *give diligence to make our calling and election sure,* 2 Pet. i. 10. But because there is some difficulty and danger in managing this inquiry, I would offer a few things about it.

Advice 1. Lay it down as a fixed persuasion in your heart, that satisfaction in this matter would be of great advantage to your souls. 1. This would bring you to the top of the mount. As Moses on the top of Pisgah saw the earthly Canaan; so you, from the sight of your election-grace, may find it both an easy and a comfortable thing, to view all the streams of grace and mercy towards you. You would then see whence they spring, and whither they run. 2. This sight would keep you low and humble. The most humbling thought is this, " I was of mere sovereign " grace given by the Father to the Son." A false pretender to this blessing may be proud; but the true believer of it is always humbled by it. Whence is it that there is so much pride amongst Christians? why are they puffed up so soon and so much? Is it not always on the account of what they do, are, or receive? Here is a blessing, where none of those puffing-up things are; a blessing that hath no sort of respect to what we are, have, or do. 3. The knowledge of this bleſſing of electing love, is of great uſe in extreme trials. We are called to lay our account with them; the Lord brings them on us; and we need all the armour of God againſt them, Eph. vi. 10.; and *the hope of ſalvation is a helmet* in the evil day, 1 Theſſ. v. 8, 9. And this knowledge that we are *appointed to ſalvation,* is the ground of this hope. Chriſt comforts the hearts of his people with this, Luke xii. 32. *Fear not, little flock; for it is your Father's good pleaſure to give you the kingdom.* Chriſt tells Ananias, that Paul was *a choſen veſſel,* who was to do and ſuffer much for his name, Acts ix. 15, 16.; Ananias tells it Paul; and Paul repeats it, in the midſt of his ſufferings, in a great aſſembly, Acts xxii. 14, 15.

Advice 2. For as great advantages as this knowledge hath in it, think not, attempt not the attaining of it by a ſudden leap; but you muſt aſcend to it by degrees. It was a good ſaying, I think, of the bleſſed martyr Mr. Bradford, "No man ſhould go to the "univerſity of predeſtination, till he be well trained "up in the grammar-ſchool of faith and repentance." If this, or the like method, be neglected, no good can, but much hurt will enſue. God's decrees are ſome way like the mount that muſt not be touched; but you muſt firſt worſhip at a diſtance, and then make a reverend and awful approach. This is not only holy ground, but it is unſearchable by us. Now know, that though electing love hath no cauſe nor ground for it without God himſelf, yet it hath great and noble fruits, and in the decree of the end, ſalvation, there is a wiſe deſign of fit means and ways to compaſs this end: 2 Theſſ. ii. 13. *But we are bound to give thanks always to God for you, brethren, beloved of the Lord, becauſe God hath from the beginning choſen you to ſalvation, through ſanctification of the Spirit, and belief of the truth;* and 1 Pet. i. 2. *Elect according to the foreknowledge of God the Father, through ſanctification of the Spirit unto obedience, and ſprinkling of the blood of Jesus Christ.* There is a *work of faith, and labour of love, and patience of hope,* whereby *the election of God* may be *known,* 1 Thess. i. 3, 4. You must not leap immediately up to the purpose of God, but climb up thereto by the steps he hath prescribed in his revealed will.

Advice 3. You must be at great pains about this. This knowledge of your own concern in this giving to the Son, is not easily acquired; wherefore the apostle saith, 2 Peter i. 10. *Give diligence* (and verse 5. *Give all diligence*) *to make your calling and election sure.* God's part in your calling and election is sure enough; and needs none of your labour to make it surer. But to make it sure to yourselves, and to make the knowledge thereof sure and clear to you, diligence is needful, and diligence will do it. Alas! who bestow any diligence about this greatest concern? Search out the fruits and marks of election: and when you find any of them, then, and not before, climb up this high tree of the Father's giving you to Jesus Christ.

Advice 4. Be not discouraged if it doth not yet appear to you, that you were given by the Father to the Son. It may be, though you do not see it. Many of the given do not for a long time know it; yea, I see no great danger in saying, that not a few of the given to the Son may be in darkness, and doubts, and fears about it, till the last and brightest day declare it, and till the last sentence proclaims it, *Come, ye blessed of my Father,* (blessed by this giving), *inherit the kingdom prepared for you from the foundation of the world,* Math. xxv. 34. It is wisely ordered by the Lord, that all that are given to the Son, do not (tho' they should endeavour it) know that they were given; and that they that are not given, cannot know it; that the book of life is not always legible to all believers, and that the book of death cannot be read by any unbeliever. It would be a miserable world, if the reprobate could be as sure of their being past by, as the elect may be of their being chosen to salvation.

If

If therefore any of you be in the dark about your own election, be not discouraged; it may be, though you do not know it. And to such discouraged souls I would speak a few words.

Object. It may be some of you may say, that this is strange doctrine.

Answ. I am sorry that this doctrine is so rarely taught; and I am sure, that it is not only the doctrine of Christ, and of his apostles; but that the work of the gospel in conversion of sinners, and in the edification, growth, and holiness of saints, did prosper more, when such doctrine was more commonly taught than now. Discouraged souls about this doctrine, answer these.

1. Can you hear of this giving of some by the Father to the Son, and bless the giver, the Father; and the receiver, the Son; and count all the given a happy remnant? A heart grumbling and replying against this sovereign grace of God, I dare not say is a sure token of one not given, but it is surely a very bad thing. But, on the contrary, it is a hopeful sign of an interest in this great blessing, when a poor creature, in his deepest distress and fears about his own salvation, hath a high value for electing love, and reckons them blessed indeed that are sharers thereof. He admires and adores this design, even when doubtful of his own interest therein.

2. Can you be sure that you were not given to the Son? No, surely. God hath not, will not reveal it. Thy heart is blind and deceitful; do not trust it. Satan knows it not, and is a lyar, especially when he pretends to teach thee God's secret purposes. The devil was never on God's counsel; why should you regard his whispers? He is a reprobate, condemned spirit, raging against God, and strives to infuse his own spirit and temper into sinners. Say then, "If I " know not that I was given to the Son, I cannot " know, I should not conclude, none can prove, that " I was not given to him."

3. Is

3. Is Christ as God's gift precious to you? 1 Pet. ii. 6, 7, 8. Then it is sure you were given to Christ? It is a deep secret, who are given by the Father to the Son; but it is an open plain truth, that *the Father hath sent the Son to be the Saviour of the world*, 1 John iv. 14. How do you like him; how do you esteem and love him? Say then, " Although I am " not sure that I was given to Christ, I am sure that " Christ is come as a Saviour, just such a one as I " need."

4. Can you give yourselves to Jesus Christ to be saved by him? Then were you given to him, to be redeemed by him. Your faith on him, speaks your election in him. True faith is *the faith of God's elect*, Titus i. 1. Why so called, but because all, and only God's elect, get it, and have it; and because election may be known by it; because faith flows from electing love, and should lead the believer up to this love as its original and spring? Answer then, thou that knows not that thou wast given to Christ by the Father, dost thou give thyself to Christ? Seest thou no hand in heaven nor earth, to intrust thy soul in, but Christ's? Hast thou so seen him in his skill and good-will to save lost sinners, that thou hast, daily dost, and resolvest still to bring, and lay, and leave thy perishing soul on Jesus Christ, as on him that *speaketh in righteousness, mighty to save?* Isa. lxiii. 1. Then thou wast given to Jesus Christ. Go on in trusting him, and in living by faith on him; and he will make you know, that *he loved you, and gave himself for you*, Gal. ii. 20. And if thou knowest that he gave himself for thee in time, conclude, that thou wast given to him by the Father from eternity, and that thou shalt to eternity be with him where he is.

SERMON

SERMON III.

JOHN xvii. 24.

Father, I will that they also whom thou hast given me, be with me where I am; that they may behold my glory which thou hast given me: for thou lovedst me before the foundation of the world.

PETER gives a good testimony to Jesus Christ, in John vi. 68. *Thou hast the words of eternal life.* And here these words are eminently. Christ himself is *eternal life*, 1 John i. 2. And in this text we have him that was and is essential, eternal life, praying for and willing of communicated eternal life to all his people.

The first thing I took up in the matter of Christ's prayer in this verse, was the name and description of them he prays for; *they whom thou hast given me.* From this part of the verse I named three doctrines.

1. That there was a *select company of mankind given by the Father to the Son, to be redeemed and saved.* On this I spoke last day.

OBSERV. 2. *This company given to Christ are well known to him.* Christ knows them all, particularly, fully, exactly. Christ doth not here pray, as we ought, for the elect, on the general truth revealed in the word, that there is a body of the elect, though we know not who they be; but Christ hath them all now as in his eye and heart particularly. Paul was in his eye, and all that were to believe on him through grace. Why are we commanded to pray for all men, though Christ did not, John xvii. 9, 10.? Because we
know

know not particularly who are the elect, but Christ did.

On this truth I would offer a few things in proof of it, and then apply it. For this doctrine looks like a deep and barren point; yet it is profitable.

1. For proof of this, *that the elect are known to Jesus Christ*. Let us see what he himself speaks of it, John x. Once in that parable, ver. 3. *He calleth his own sheep by name, and leadeth them out.* You will never believe, till Christ call you by name. Again, in the doctrine taught by him on the parable, ver. 14. *I am the good Shepherd,* (O how well doth it become Christ to commend himself! You will never love him, till Christ himself commend himself to you), *and know my sheep.* And ver. 27. *My sheep hear my voice, and I know them, and they follow me.* Ver. 28. *And I give unto them eternal life.* Well doth Christ know to whom he gives eternal life. Woe to them to whom he will say, *I never knew you,* Matth. vii. 24. Little better is that word in John x. 26. *But ye believe not; because ye are not of my sheep, as I said unto you.* Christ knew who were his sheep, and who not; who were gathered into his fold, and who were yet straying as lost sheep on the mountains: verse 16. *And other sheep I have, which are not of this fold; them also I must bring, and they shall hear my voice.* The grounds of this truth are.

1*st*, Christ, as God, knoweth all things, and therefore knows who are given to him. It is a pity, that when the godhead of the Son shines so very brightly in the new testament, any should doubt and deny it. And it is pity also, that the deniers of this rock of the church of Christ should not renounce the name of Christians; or that any true Christian should afford this honourable name to such apostates. Peter, when asked by his Master about his love to him, John xxi. 17. answers by a humble appeal to his all-knowing.

He that knows all things, must know who were given him by the Father.

2dly, The Son of God was a party concerned in this transaction. As the Father was the giver of the elect, the Son was the receiver of them. Will any say, that the Father knew not whom he gave, when his foreknowledge is so expresly told in Rom. viii. 29.? It is equally absurd to say, that the Son knew not whom he received. And as the Father's giving was of particular, distinct, and distinguished persons; so was the Son's receiving of such persons. Hence our Lord says of them in his prayer, ver 9, 10. *I pray for them; I pray not for the world, but for them which thou hast given me, for they are thine. And all mine are thine, and thine are mine, and I am glorified in them.* This transaction betwixt the Father and Son, was a business, as of high sovereignty about mankind, and of infinite love to the given, so was it passed in infinite wisdom. *The manifold wisdom of God is in this eternal purpose which he purposed in Christ Jesus our Lord*, Eph. iii. 9, 10, 11. It is a high reflection on all the glory of God in this transaction, to say, that the Father knew not particularly whom he gave to the Son, or that the Son knew not who were given to him.

3dly, Christ's knowing who were given to him, is the ground of his undertaking and dispatching the work of redemption. This work he undertook in love; this love is still acted on persons, Gal. ii. 20. Rev. i. 5. These persons must be known to Christ, if so beloved by him.

4thly, It is this knowledge in Christ that is the ground of Christ's patience and pains on the elect. If any will say, that Christ, in dying, designed no more for Peter than for Judas, (God forgive them, and open their eyes); I hope they will not say, but Christ did more for Peter than for Judas. The visible difference that is betwixt Christ's way of dealing with men, flows from his knowing of them that are given to him. There are some that Christ deals with in and by the gospel; and, upon their first refusal, he leaves them, and Christ and they never meet till the last day: others he waits long upon, and yet he leaves them at last. But there are some that Christ deals with; and though they refuse him again and again, yet he will never leave them, till he hath gained their hearts, and saved them. Paul thought he was the rarest instance of this: 1 Tim. i. 16. *Howbeit, for this cause I obtained mercy, that in me first (in me the chief* sinner) *Jesus Christ might show forth all long-suffering, for a pattern to them which should hereafter believe on him to life everlasting.* Yet we may say, that there are some in heaven, and some on earth, that have been as great patterns as Paul; tho' they were not so filled with the Holy Ghost as he; nor Christ's grace in calling them set so on a candlestick for all ages, as it was in his case. It may be Paul never heard Christ preach, nor saw his face, though he was brought up at Jerusalem in Christ's time, Acts xxii. 3. and xxvi. 4. It is like he heard no more of him, but by the common report, and by the slanders of the Pharisees, Christ's constant enemies. It was but blind zeal of the law that locked him up in unbelief, and made him hate Christ's name and people. But how many have been since Paul, that have lived long under the light of the gospel, whom the Lord have striven long with, and they have as long striven against him, whom yet he hath subdued at last? Blessed be his name; and may such instances be multiplied to his praise. This way is taken by Christ with some, according to his charge from his Father, John vi. 39. *And this is the Father's will which hath sent me, that of all which he hath given me, I should lose nothing, but should raise it up again at the last day.*

5thly, This knowing of them who are given to him, is the ground of the confidence of Christ as Mediator, as to the success of his work; both of his work of redemption of them by his blood, and of the work of his Spirit, in applying it to the souls and consciences of the redeemed. So he proclaims it, John vi. 37. *All that the Father giveth me, shall come to me.* "I am sure, would he say, of every one of them, "sooner or later." As long as there is one given, not yet come to Christ, there is one yet to believe on him. Christ might well promise this to himself; for the Father had promised it, Isa. liii. 10. 11. *He shall see his seed, he shall prolong his days, and the pleasure of the Lord shall prosper in his hand. He shall see of the travel of his soul, and shall be satisfied: by his knowledge shall my righteous servant justify many; for he shall bear their iniquities.* The latter part of John vi. 37. is Christ's promise to us, *Him that cometh to me, I will in nowise cast out.* Why do none but the given come to Christ? Because none can come unless they be drawn by the Father, John vi. 44, 45. Behold this blessed order. The Father gives the elect to his Son, to be redeemed; the Son, in love, lays down his life for them, and redeems them. The Father draws them to Christ, and makes them believers: Christ receives them as given, redeemed and drawn; and thus are they saved. Christ knows them well, and therefore welcomes them.

APPLICATION. 1. This truth, That Christ knows all that are given to him, should feed and strengthen our faith, as to all the elect. Christ knows them; therefore they shall be saved. The apostle 2 Tim. ii. 18, 19. brings in this as a ground of faith, even when damnable errors creep in, and *overthrow the faith of some: Nevertheless, the foundation of God standeth sure, having this seal, The Lord knoweth them that are his.* The Lord-giver knows who are his, and whom he gives; and the Lord-receiver knows who are his; and whom he receives. The Lord knows better who are his, than the devil knows who are his, for many that the devil had as his, (as all natural men are, Eph. ii. 2, 3),

2, 3), and thought he was sure of as his, have been rescued by the Lord. But never did the devil prevail fully against any that are Christ's. It is a happy parenthesis in Matth. xxiv. 24. when our Lord is warning of dangerous times, by false christs, and of their great success in deceiving, he saith, that *they shall deceive (if it were possible) the very elect*. But it is impossible, because they are elect. There are two cases of the elect that this truth should strengthen our faith in. 1. As to the uncalled elect. Many of them are yet uncalled, and lying in the common pit of nature; but they shall be called. The gospel will be taken away from that place where none such are. All God's pains in the gospel are taken *for the elects sakes*, as Paul's pains were, 2 Tim. ii. 10. The Lord encouraged Paul to stay and labour in Corinth, by this argument, *For I have much people in this city*, Acts xviii. 9, 10. Some are converted already, and many more are to be converted. 2. In case of backsliding and apostasy: a sad, but no very rare case. Some that have given great witness of the truth of the grace of God in them, have, through the power of corruption, the prevalency of temptation, and the Lord's leaving of them, fallen foully, and lain long. Yet, if they be Christ's, his mark is on them, and they shall be recovered.

2. Believers, from this truth, have ground of strong consolation, both in praising and in praying: Heb. vi. 17, 18. The *immutability of his counsel* is declared, *that we might have a strong consolation, who have fled for refuge to lay hold upon the hope set before us*. Have you fled for refuge to Jesus Christ? Do you know it? Hath the Lord revealed it to you, that you have sought your only refuge in the shadow of Christ's wings? Then how should you rejoice and give thanks for your election? Thus the apostle did usually, Eph. i. 3, 4. 2 Thess. ii. 13. I dare not say, that no believer can be heartily thankful for Christ's grace, before he fully and surely know its highest spring: but I am sure that that believer praiseth best, that knows

best that he was given to the Son. The receivings of the glorified will be the greatest; their praises will be the highest; and their knowledge of eternal love as the spring of all their grace and glory, will be the clearest. And as this doth raise praise, so doth it raise mighty prayer. Our Lord prays for his people under this name, *Thine and mine*, John xvii. 9, 10. David prays for himself, under this name, Psal. cxix. 94. *I am thine, save me.* The clearer your knowledge be of your interest in God, and in his love, the more mighty will your pleadings with him be.

And so much for the second point.

OBSERV. 3. *Christ's heart is set on the bliss of all that the Father hath given to him.* And this he expresseth in this desire.

On this point, I would, 1. Give some proofs of this truth. 2. Show whence this heart-concern for their bliss doth flow.

I. *Proofs of this truth, That Christ's heart is set on the bliss and eternal salvation of his people,* are these five.

1. Christ's covenanting for them proves this. In that day (if a day may be talked of in eternity; but we are time-creatures, and have no fit words for eternity) when this blessed company were given by the Father to the Son, the Son did undertake to do all things needful to be done, to bring them to eternal glory. He undertook and promised to take on him their natures; and in that nature to bear their sins; and, by the sacrifice of that nature for their sins, to make an expiation of their sins. In a word, he promised to do all he was required to do, and he did all he promised to the Father, for the salvation of his people. Whenever we look to this treaty, we must gather, Surely the Son of God had a great mind to the happiness of his people.

2. Christ's

2. Christ's chearful laying down his life for their redemption, proves how his heart was set on their salvation. It was his errand in coming into the world: John x. 10. *I am come that they might have life, and that they might have it more abundantly.* Believers get a greater, higher, and more noble life by the second Adam, than they lost by the first Adam. This is the meaning of that *much more* twice mentioned by the apostle when comparing these two heads, Rom. v. 15. 17. But how doth Christ give, and his people receive this life? Even by his death. He *laid down his life for his sheep*, John x. 11. 15. *Therefore his Father loved him*, ver. 17. And thereby he proved his love to the salvation of his people, John xv. 13.

3. He proves his love to their salvation, by his sealing and confirming the covenant, the charter of their salvation, with his own blood. Compare Gal. iii. 15, 16, 17. with Heb. ix. 15, 16, 17. It is called *the blood of the everlasting covenant*, Heb. xiii. 20. Christ's blood was not only redeeming and purchasing blood, a just and full price both for the heirs and for the inheritance; but it was sealing blood, and confirming of that covenant, in and by which the inheritance was secured to the heirs, and the heirs secured for the inheritance. Alas! many have the Bible, and use it but little; and many use it amiss, because they know not its right name. It is well and warrantably, from its contents, called, in its title-page, in all languages and translations, *The Old and New Testament of our Lord and Saviour Jesus Christ*. But how few, in reading this title, mind the use and virtue of the blood of Jesus, which turned the covenant of God's grace into the testament of Christ, and thereby sealed and confirmed all the good words and good things in that covenant? It was a happy word we find in the *Book of martyrs*, that some in the dawning of the light of the gospel in this land, near two hundred years ago, used, in calling the New Testament (a great rarity in those days) *The blood of Christ.* You never rightly read

the

the gospel, nor do you understand the design of it, nor rightly believe one promise in it, till in heart you can say, "This gospel is the only charter of my sal-"vation, sealed with the blood of my only Saviour." If any be for another Saviour than Christ, and for another security and charter for salvation than his thus sealed testament, on their eternal peril be it. Let them try, and perish. For, as God is true, perish they shall, even all that take that course, Acts iv. 12.

4. Christ proves his love to his people's salvation by his intercession for them. Of which this chapter is a great instance. And whereof we have so much spoke in Rom. viii. 34. Heb. vii. 25. and ix. 24. and 1 John ii. 1. This is his business in heaven. By this he *prepares their place for them*, John xiv. 2, 3.; and on it assures them of their possessing of it.

5. Christ gives his Spirit to his people, to prove his concern about their salvation. And we may allude to Isa. v. 4. *What could have been done more?* He covenanted with the Father from eternity about their salvation. He bought it for them, and them for it, in the fulness of time. The day of Christ's redeeming his people, was the flower of time, the greatest and noblest thing done since God set the clock of time a going; for his glorious return is to be at the end of time. He turned the covenant of their salvation into a testament by his blood; and did in that testament leave all the grace and glory bought by his blood as a legacy to his people. He, when he had done this, went to heaven with his blood, Heb. ix. 12. that it might speak before God, Heb. xii. 24. for all blessings to his people. And till they get full possession of glory, he gives to them his Spirit. All that are his have his Spirit, as surely as it is, that *if any man have not the Spirit of Christ, he is none of his,* Rom. viii. 9. 15. Gal. iv. 6. This gift of the Spirit is a marvellous gift. None can know it, but they that receive it: John xiv. 17. *The Spirit of*

of truth, whom the world cannot receive, because it seeth him not, neither knoweth him: but ye know him; for he dwelleth with you, and shall be in you. 1 John iv. 13. *Hereby know we that we dwell in him, and he in us, because he hath given us of his Spirit.* This gift is always given in mere love and grace, and is a sure proof of God's special love. This gift of the Spirit is an earnest of heaven, 2 Cor. i. 22. *God hath sealed us, and given the earnest of the Spirit in our hearts;* and 2 Cor. v. 5. And Eph. i. 13, 14. he is called *that Holy Spirit of promise, which is the earnest of our inheritance, until the redemption of the purchased possession, unto the praise of his glory.* He is called *the first-fruits of the Spirit,* Rom. viii. 23. This gift is an enriching gift. How great things doth he in and on the man! How much good doth he bring along with himself! He reveals Christ to the soul, John xvi. 14, 15.; draws the soul to Christ, unites him with Christ; dwells in the believer, and *seals him to the day of redemption,* Eph. iv. 30.; comforts him till that day comes. Hence called the *Comforter* by our Lord, John xiv. 16, 26. xv. 26. and xvi. 7. Yet for all the richness of this gift of the Spirit, this you must know, that as soon as a man receives this gift, he sees and finds himself to be a poor, empty, and needy creature. When this eye-salve of Christ anoints a man's eyes, then he seeth what he did not before; that he is *wretched, and miserable, and poor, and blind, and naked,* Rev. iii. 17, 18. Therefore is the Spirit of Christ in believers a *Spirit of grace and of supplication,* Zech. xiii. 10.; *a Spirit of adoption, crying, Abba, Father,* Rom. viii. 15. and Gal. iv. 6. If *no man can say, that Jesus is the Lord, but by the Holy Ghost,* 1 Cor. xii. 3.; surely no man can call the God and Father of our Lord Jesus Christ, *Abba Father,* but by the Holy Ghost. The first word of the new creature is *Abba.* But many believers live long ere they can say *Abba* confidently. They do not consider duly, that as this relation is granted by the Lord; so it should

should be pleaded by believers, without any regard to worth in us, but only to his own free grace and love in Jesus Christ. The Spirit of Christ in believers is a Spirit of prayer, a Spirit of begging in a child at its heavenly Father's door. The believer finds manifold daily wants; he knows none can relieve and supply his wants, but his *God by Jesus Christ*, Phil. iv. 19. He hath an instinct, and some ability by the Spirit to beg and wait. The operation of the Spirit in believers, the communion of the Holy Ghost, is a great mystery. He works more on them, than they feel and know; and they feel more than they can express in words; and they express more, than any that have not received *the same Spirit of faith* (2 Cor. iv. 13.) can understand. But this we know, that whensoever the Spirit of Christ applies his grace and power to the heart of a sinner, there is something wrought that day, that shall last to eternity. There is, by that finger of God, that impression made upon the soul, and that mark left upon it, that shall never wear out, and that sin and Satan shall never be able to blot out again; but it shall remain, and grow, and be seen at the coming of Christ at the last day, Phil. i. 6.

II. *Why is Christ's heart so set upon his people's glory in heaven?*

1. Because of his near interest in them. His interest in his church and people, is greater and closer than we can conceive. The Holy Ghost useth many similitudes to help our thoughts. Of them I would name only two of the plainest and most common. One is, of Christ's being the head, and the church his body and members; Eph. i. 22, 23. iv. 15, 16. and Col. ii. 19. Another is, the marriage-union of man and wife; and especially of the first married couple, Adam and Eve, our first parents, Eph. v. 25.----32. And you may well think, that it was a fit match. When the first man was made, God took a part of

this

this man's body, and made of it a woman to be a wife to him. So is the church, Christ's bride, taken out of Christ's side; not in a sleep, (as it was with the first Adam, Gen. ii. 21, 22.) but in and by his death. As Eve was made a most excellent woman, both for endowments of body and mind; so Adam in innocency did doubtless love her perfectly. She was of him, from him, for him, and made to be with him. All this is but a shadow of the church, Christ's bride. The first Adam's love to his rare wife, was nothing to Christ's love to his bride. Yea, Christ is not only the head of the body, and the husband thereof, but Christ is to the church, as our souls are to our bodies, 1 Cor. vi. 17. All the life, power, and ability of our bodies, naturally flows from the soul dwelling in it. If the soul be never so happy, (as *the spirits of just men made perfect* are, Heb. xii. 23.), yet it hath a happy longing in its glorified state for its re-union with the body. So Christ, *the quickening Spirit*, (as Paul calls him, 1 Cor. xv. 45), hath a great happy desire of having his glorified body with him where he is.

2. Christ is much concerned about glory to his people, because of his engagements for and to his people. There is a treble engagement of Christ that he lieth under for bringing his people to heaven. 1. The command of his Father, John vi. 38, 39, 40. And this *commandment is eternal life;* and this Christ knew, and revealed it, John xii. 49, 50. 2. His promise to his Father in the everlasting covenant. 3. His promise to us in the gospel, 1 Joh ii. 25. He hath engaged to his Father, that none that are given to him shall ever perish; and he hath promised often and plainly to us in the gospel, that none that believe on him shall ever be ashamed. And wofully would a believer in Christ be ashamed, if he came short of heaven.

3. The greatness of Christ's love to his people, makes him so much concerned about their compleat salvation.

salvation. Christ's love is so great, that it passeth knowledge; and some Christians love to Christ is so weak, that it is hardly seen and felt by them. It is not every one that can give Peter's answer unto Christ's question, John xxi. 15, 16, 17. *Lord thou knowest all things, thou knowest that I love thee.* Now, we know concerning love, that it natively lieth in wishing well to the beloved. Doth Christ love his people? How can he but wish them well? And how can he wish them better, than to be with him where he is?

APPLICATION. 1. Is Jesus Christ so much concerned for the glory and blessedness of his people? Then see how sweetly we come to heaven. It is by Christ's blessed will; his blood paying the price, and giving us the right and title to glory; and his heart and good-will giving possession of it. Thus are we saved, both surely and sweetly.

2. How firmly should we believe on Jesus Christ, and trust him for salvation? It is no small reproach to him, that is so often done by that unbelief and doubting that is so usual to some Christians. Christ minds our salvation heartily, and we believe feebly; he saying, *I will have them with me where I am;* and we often saying, *Lord, thou wilt not bring me where thou art.* Is it not sinful in us, and dishonourable to Christ, for us to be saying, *Thou wilt not,* when he is saying, *I will?* We should trust our salvation on Jesus Christ, not only as on him that only can save, and that is able to save perfectly; but as on him that hath more good-will to save, than we can have willingness to be saved by him. None had ever been saved by him, none had ever been brought to heaven, unless Christ had had more willingness to bring them thither, than they had to be led thither by him. *He must in all things have the pre-eminence,* Col. i. 18. and in this especially. Unbelief is in all doubtings of Christ's good-will to save. Whatever may be said of the le-
per's

per's faith, in Matth. viii. 2. *Lord, if thou wilt, thou canst make me clean;* no perishing sinner can be quite excused, that shall put an *if* on Christ's willingness to save one that employs him in his office of saving, wherein his glory is so concerned, and his heart so deeply engaged. We should give him the glory that is due to him; to believe that the willingness to save is greater in the Saviour, than willingness to be saved is in the sinner. For Christ's good-will to save, is the cause of any desire of salvation in any: Psalm cx. 3. *Thy people shall be willing in the day of thy power.* When he hath a mind to save, he doth work this willingness in men to be saved by him; and they will own it to proceed from his willingness, when they become strong believers; and will see it and know it perfectly, when they get full salvation.

3. How strongly should believers love the Lord Jesus Christ? Is his heart so set on thy heaven? How filled with love to him ought thy heart to be? Woe to them that love him not, 1 Cor. xvi. 22. And in no better case are they that think they love him enough, and such as love any thing as well, and that hate not all things in comparison with him, Luke xiv. 26. To love Christ as thou dost thy life, will not be enough. It is higher and greater love that Christ doth deserve and require, and will only accept.

4. How patiently and quietly should we submit to Christ's conduct and guiding us in the way to heaven? Is his heart set on bringing you thither? Let him guide you in the way as he pleaseth. Doth he say peremptorily, *I will have them with me where I am?* Let him guide you as he will, while you are in the world. When a believer is satisfied by faith, that Christ wills glory to him in the end, he will find it easy to submit to Christ's conduct by the way. He may indeed, in some trials of his faith, be put to say, " This is a dark path I am led to walk in:" but faith will say, " But I am in Christ's hand; this is his way " of leading me; every step that Christ leads the be-

"lieving traveller in, must lead to heaven." He best knows the way; and the wisdom of the Christian lieth in following Christ whithersoever he goeth, and leadeth him. Though thou seest not heaven, the end; though thou knowest not the path he leads thee in; though the path, to thy sense, looks liker the way to hell, than to heaven: yet if Christ leadeth thee, and if thou be in his hand, it is impossible, but that Christ thy guide will bring thee to heaven, as thy home.

SERMON IV.

JOHN xvii. 24.

Father, I will that they also whom thou hast given me, be with me where I am; that they may behold my glory which thou hast given me: for thou lovedst me before the foundation of the world.

THIS chapter contains the best part of the gospel. If the gospel be good news from heaven, (as surely it is), the best part of those good news is what the Saviour sends up to heaven in this prayer. And what he sends up in this prayer, he brought down from heaven, from his Father, John vi. 38. I have made some entrance on this verse 24. the sweetest of this prayer, if comparison may be made, where every word is most sweet and excellent. I have spoke unto the manner of Christ's praying, *I will*. The manner is singular, and the matter most excellent. The manner of Christ's praying here, is more like a commander, than a supplicant. What specialties there were in the person that made it, and in

the

the season that drew forth this high word, you have heard.

The matter of Christ's prayer in this verse, I took up in four; and have spoke to the first of them, to wit, the description of the party he prayeth for. In this chapter, our Lord not only describeth them he prayed for, but expresly denieth that he prayed for any besides them, ver. 9, 10. *I pray for them: I pray not for the world, but for them which thou hast given me, for they are thine. And all mine are thine, and thine are mine, and I am glorified in them.* From this description of them Christ prayed for in this verse, and in other parts of this chapter, I have spoke unto these three points. 1. That there is a select determinate company of men, that were given by the Father to the Son, to be redeemed and saved by him. 2. That this company was particularly and exactly known by Jesus Christ. 3. That Christ's heart was fixed and resolved on the eternal salvation of all them that were given to him. And here he expresseth it highly, in this *I will*.

The *second* thing in the matter of Christ's prayer, followeth to be spoke unto; and that is, *the blessing he prayeth for unto them.* It is, *that they may be with me where I am.* There are three things here, that I would first take notice of and explain; and then speak to the words themselves; and give you from them, the doctrines which I intend to insist more largely upon.

1. The first thing I take notice of, is this *also*, and what is its signification. 2. What is this *to be with Christ*, as distinct from other scripture-words about Christ and his people. 3. What it is *to be with Christ where he is*.

I. Concerning this word *also*. It doth not in the least hint, that there are any that he desires may be with him where he is, besides those that were given him: but it is only his praying for another, and greater blessing, to them that were given to him. Our Lord had prayed for many and great things for them before in this chapter and prayer. He had prayed his Father to *keep them*, to *sanctify them*, and to *make them all one in the Father and in the Son*. "But "(would our Lord say) there is something more than "all this I would have for them;" I would have them *to be with me where I am.* Hence

Observ. *Nothing short of, nothing less than heaven, and eternal glory in it, doth stint and limit Christ's heart and prayers for his people.* For all he hath done for them, for all he hath given to them, (and there is a great deal of both), there is still this *also* in his heart for them. *I will that they also may be with me where I am.* "I will not only go where they are, but I will "also have them where I am." Nothing less than "everlasting blessedness to his people, doth limit "Christ's will and prayers for them. He prays for every thing to them, and for this *also*. When the apostle is speaking to believers in Heb vi. 4,----9. he gives a very gracious insinuation, after a most fearful alarm. When he had spoke some of the most terrible words in the scripture, upon a supposition of an utter apostasy from Christianity, after great attainments: If *such as have been enlightened*, &c. *do fall away*, their case is desperate; they are soil that *bring forth nothing but briers and thorns, are near unto cursing, and their end is to be burned.* But, beloved, (faith he, ver. 9.), *we are persuaded better things of you, and things that accompany salvation, though we thus speak.* All the grace that Christ giveth, all the grace that believers receive and act in this life, are but things that accompany salvation, that do pertain unto the state of salvation, and prepare for the full enjoyment of salvation in heaven.

There are several sorts of gifts that Christ gives, and believers receive, in this life, that pertain to salvation. As,

1. Their

1. Their right and title to heaven. And that is Christ himself possessed by faith; *dwelling in their hearts by faith,* Eph. iii. 17.; *Christ in them the hope of glory,* Col. i. 27. That day that Christ entered into their hearts, the hope of glory began to dawn. And the deeper he enter into the heart of any, the greater is the hope, so as to make the believer *rejoice in hope of the glory of God,* Rom. v. 2.

2. The Lord giveth also meetness for heaven; and that is wrought by his Spirit and grace on his people: Col. i. 12. *Giving thanks unto the Father, which hath made us meet to be made partakers of the inheritance of the saints in light.* This meetness for partaking is inseparable from a right and title to glory; at least so far, that no believer can have a comfortable view of his right, without some experience of his meetness for enjoying the inheritance. This same apostle saith to this same purpose in 2 Cor. v. 5. *Now he that hath wrought us for the self-same thing, is God; who hath also given unto us the earnest of the Spirit.* He hath been at great pains on us, and hath used many means and methods with us. And what hath all this been for? It hath only been the Lord's gracious and wise way of polishing and framing us for heaven.

3. There is *the earnest of the inheritance* that Christ gives, and Christians receive sometimes, Eph. i. 13, 14. This pertains to glory nearly. It is like *the first-fruits of that good land,* frequently spoke of in the word; and might be more often tasted by believers, were it not for their laziness and unbelief when they want it; and their bad guiding of it, when at any time they enjoy a little of it.

APPLICATION. Imitate our Lord Jesus Christ in your praying for yourselves. Imitate him,

1. In all your askings. There are some spiritual blessings that believers are very desirous of. Conscience terrifies you, and then you cry, O for the sprinkling

ling of the blood of Jesus, and for peace with God thereby, and peace within! O for victory over sin, and for strength to walk worthy of the Lord unto all pleasing! All good prayers. But if all this were granted you, remember to pray on this *also* for glory. Beg pardon and heaven *also*, holiness and heaven *also*. Ask any good thing which you want, and which he hath promised. Ask every thing, and heaven *also*. Let your prayers for yourselves be as large as Christ's are for you.

2. Remember this *also* in all your receivings, as well as in your askings. His fulness is infinite, his bounty is great; but his people are but narrow vessels, and cannot receive much: and are leaky vessels, and cannot keep long what they receive. Is he kind, large-hearted, and open-handed to you? (as no believer dare deny). Bless him, and beg heaven *also*. Jacob was a meek, lowly, humble man, and saith, Gen. xxxii. 10. *I am not worthy of the least,* (or, *I am less than the least*) *of all the mercies, and of all the truth which thou hast shewed unto thy servant.* This man looks on the least mercy as a great mountain, and on himself as a little mole-hill. You would think, surely this humble man will not stand with God for any thing; yet he will *weep and make supplication,* as in Hof. xii. 3, 4. and wrestle all night, and say, (doubtless with his eyes full of tears, and his heart full of faith and love), *I will not let thee go, except thou bless me.* Receive all his grace and bounty with all the sense you can reach, of your own unworthiness; yet still remember this *also*. Be not satisfied so as not to desire eternal glory. Make use of all experiences of his grace to you, to quicken both your desire and your faith of eternal life. Let that *well of water in you,* which Christ's grace hath made in you, *spring up into everlasting life,* John iv. 14.

II. The second word that is next to be explained, is, *with me: I will that they be with me.* It may be some of them were with Christ when he prayed
thus;

thus; it may be all the eleven apostles were there: But their being with Christ in the garden, was but a small matter. Christ was then at his lowest; then was the cloud thickest, and the eclipse darkest on the Son of God. It is another, and better place and case, that Christ prays to have them *with him* in, than this.

There are three words concerning Christ and his people, in the scripture, that are very good and gracious; but this in the text is beyond them all.

1. We find, that his people are said to be *in him*, 1 John v. 20. and 2 Cor. v. 17.

2. Another word is, that Christ is said to be *in his people*, 2 Cor. xiii. 5. We are in Christ by faith; and Christ dwells in our hearts by faith, Eph. iii. 17. So John xvii. 23.

3. And Christ is said to be *with his people*. This was amongst the last words of Christ, when going to heaven, Matth. xxviii. 20. *And lo, I am with you alway, even unto the end of the world.* " Though ye " shall never see my face any more, till I bring you " to heaven, yet I am with you always." But this " word of being *with Christ*, is above all those three, for as great as they are. This is *far better*, Phil. i. 23.

III. The third word to be explained in the text is, *where I am: That they may be with me where I am.* Where was Christ when he said these words? He was either in the garden, or going to it. For what is in these four chapters, xiv, xv, xvi, xvii. was, in all appearance, spoken by our Lord, partly at his last supper, partly immediately after it; as may be gathered from John xiv. 31. *Arise, let us go hence.* Christ was on the earth when he said this; but surely he meant heaven in this word, *where I am.* He was just upon leaving the world, and on going to heaven; as he speaks, John xvi. 28. *I came forth from the Father, and am come into the world: again, I leave the world, and go to the Father.* And John xvii. 11, 12. he speaks as if no more in the world: *And now I am no more*

more *in the world, but these are in the world. While I was with them in the world, I kept them in thy name.* So like is this blessed prayer to the intercession of our great High Priest in heaven. Now let us consider how far this blessing of *being with Christ where he is*, is above and beyond all he had done for, and said before to his people; and yet they were very considerable.

1. Our Lord Jesus Christ was made what his people are. He was made all that we are, except sin. There was no difference betwixt Christ and another man, as he came into the world, but only in this, (and it was his glory, and our salvation), that he was sinless. But all his people are *shapen in iniquity, and in sin did their mother conceive them*, Psalm li. 5. *Are the children partakers of flesh and blood? He also himself likewise took part of the same. He took on him the seed of Abraham. Wherefore in all things it behoved him to be made like unto his brethren*, Hebrews ii. 14, 16, 17.

2. Jesus Christ was not only made what his people were, but he came where they are. He came into the world, their dwelling-place, and came down from heaven into the earth, John vi. 38. Never did any person come down from heaven but Jesus Christ. Neither could he come down from heaven, if he had not been God; for that body he took to himself, was formed *in the lowest parts of the earth*, Psal. cxxxix. 15. (as well as the body of other men), though in a singular manner. What marvellous grace and love was here, that the eternal Son of God would not only take on him his peoples nature, but would come and dwell where they dwelt, and that with delight? See Prov. viii. 30, 31. *Then I was by him, as one brought up with him; and I was daily his delight, rejoicing always before him*, as the Son with the Father. It is very like to that in John i. 1, 2. *In the beginning was the Word, and the Word was with God, and the Word was God. The same was in the beginning with God.*

Ver.

Ver. 14. *And the Word was made flesh, and dwelt among us.* But see farther what is said, Prov. viii. 31. *Rejoicing in the habitable part of his earth, and my delights were with the sons of men.* When was this? *From everlasting, or ever the earth was,* ver. 23. *While as yet he had not made the earth,* ver. 26. How marvellous is this expression, that God's Son, the eternal Wisdom of the Father, did eternally *rejoice in the habitable part of the earth,* when there was no earth; and that *his delights were with the sons of men,* when there was no man, nor son of man, in the earth? But *the habitable part of the earth,* though not yet made, was the place he was to come into, for redeeming his people. And as he delighted in it from eternity, he came triumphantly into it, in the fulness of time: Heb. x. 7. *Lo, I come (in the volume of the book it is written of me) to do thy will, O God.* He also loved the ground his bride was to tread on, the earth where they were to live in, and where in time he was to court the heart and win the love of his people.

3. Our Lord went where his people deserved to go. There is a good sense of that harsh-like word, *He descended into hell.* It is a popish fable, to imagine, that Christ, after he died, went down into the place of the damned, either to suffer, or to do any thing there. His humiliation was accomplished in his dying, and lying in the grave for a time. But if we take it in this sense, that that stroke of divine justice that his people by sin had deserved, Christ did feel and bear; this is the usual voice of the gospel. The sword of justice was roused, furbished, and drawn against Jesus Christ, and his soul pierced thereby, Zech. xiii. 7. He was apprehended, accused, arraigned, condemned, and executed, most unjustly and wickedly by men, but most righteously by God. Mens putting of Christ to death, was the most unjust and wicked act that ever was done in the world. But the Lord Jehovah's part in it, was most just and righteous. If you have ears to hear it, this is a sure truth, Never did a damned

sinner

sinner deserve hell more justly, nor was, or shall be sent into it more righteously, than the spotless Lamb of God deserved the stroke of divine justice for the sins of his people laid upon him. It was indeed infinite grace and love in the Father, to substitute his only begotten Son to be the Saviour of sinners, 1 John iv. 9, 10. It was infinite grace in our Lord Jesus Christ, to condescend to be the sacrifice for sinners, 2 Cor. viii. 9. But when both are done, justice was glorified in the execution of this sacrifice, Rom. iii. 25, 26.

4. Our Lord also went whither he had a mind to bring us; and that is, to heaven. And yet all this is short of *being with him where he is*. On this, consider, 1. How he went, and left his people: Luke xxiv. 50, 51. *And he led them out as far as to Bethany; and he lift up his hands, and blessed them. And it came to pass, while he blessed them, he was parted from them, and carried up into heaven.* A blessed way of going hence. Our blessed Lord came into the world, as the greatest blessing that ever it got. He blessed his people while he was with them, and blessed them at parting, and will return again to bless them more. The last use our Lord made of his lips on earth (*into which grace was poured*, Psalm xlv. 2.), the last use he made of his holy hands, was to bless his people; and the force and virtue of that blessing remains to this day, and will until his return. He went away blessing, and will come again blessing. He *ascended with a shout*, Psalm xlvii. 5.; and he *shall himself descend from heaven with a shout*, 1 Thess. iv. 16. 2. Consider what he went to heaven for. It was to possess heaven for us, as *the forerunner*, Heb. vi. 20.; to *prepare a place for us*, John xiv. 2, 3.; to *make intercession for us*, Heb. ix. 24.; to mind our concerns while we are here, and to welcome us to heaven when he calls us hence. You may think, that it is far more comfortable for believers now to die, having Christ in

in heaven before them, than it was for believers to die before he came into the world, as many did; or to die, and leave Christ in the world, as it may be some did: though his saving grace is the same in all the states he was in. But now we die to *be with him*, Phil. i. 23. to *be where he is*, John xiv. 2, 3.

5. Christ is with his people even while they are here in the world. This is also a great blessing, but short of this *being with him where he is*. There are two seasons when this presence of Christ with his people is known. 1. When they are at their best. When is a Christian at his best? Every one can answer, It is when most of Christ's presence is enjoyed. 2. When is he at his worst? When in great affliction, Isa. xliii. 2. Paul found this presence: 2 Tim. iv. 16, 17. *At my first answer no man stood with me, but all men forsook me.* He had never a friend then and there, but Jesus Christ. *Notwithstanding the Lord stood with me, and strengthened me.* When a believer is greatly tempted, then is he in a bad condition. Peter was warned both of his danger and relief, Luke xxii. 31, 32. Paul had this exercise, 2 Cor. xii. 7, 8, 9. and relief under it; and makes this use of it, *Most gladly therefore will I rather glory in my infirmities, that the power of Christ may rest upon me.* As if he had said, " I have got a troublesome visit from the " devil; but it hath been the occasion of a gracious " visit from Christ. And if the one come first, and " the other follow, the first is to be patiently borne, " and the other to be thankfully received." There is also a presence of Christ with his people, even in their stumblings. Though he be displeased with them for their falling, yet he hath a double care about them. One is, that they may not fall utterly: Psal. xxxvii. 24. *Though he fall, he shall not be utterly cast down; for the Lord upholdeth him with his hand.* Another care of Christ about his stumbling children, is, to take them up again. Lastly, Christ's people have his presence with them in dying. And it is a precious

precious and needful blessing. Will Christ withdraw his gracious help and presence from his people, when it is so very needful? Paul calls dying a sweet name, 1 Thess. iv. 14. *sleeping in Jesus*. It is a dark place, and a cold pillow, that this sleep is taken on. But it is the sweetest sleep that ever the believer took. The body is freed from all pain and trouble, and will be sweetly awakened at the last day. And till then the Spirit is not only with him that gave it, Eccl. xii. 7. but with him that redeemed it, Psal. xxxi. 5.

But now what Christ prays for here, is far beyond all those. He was made what we are; came where we were; suffered what we deserved; went to heaven for us; gives his presence with us here, in life and death. But more than all is this, *I will have them where I am*.

There are two points of doctrine that I would speak to from this word.

DOCT. 1. *To be with Christ where he is, is Christ's, and the believer's heaven; that heaven that Christ gives, and that believers receive.*

DOCT. 2. *That our Lord's will is set upon his people's enjoying of this blessedness.*

I would at this time conclude with three words of application of what hath been said.

1. Behold how greatly Christ loves his people. This prayer of his for them, flowed from his boundless love. He cannot be pleased without them, and they cannot be happy without him. All the glory and bliss that Christ is possessed of, doth not fully satisfy him, till he have all his people with him. His church is *his body, the fulness of him that filleth all in all*, Eph. i. 23.

2. Behold how happy are his people. Moses sung this of old, Deut. xxxiii. 29. *Happy art thou, O Israel! Who is like unto thee, O people saved by the Lord?* Much more may we say so, when *Christ hath appeared,*

ed, who hath abolished death, and hath brought life and immortality to light through the gospel, 2 Tim. i. 10.

3. Learn to pray moderately for the lives of Christ's people. There are some of the godly that are very useful by their gifts and grace; and, if spared, might be of great profit to the church of Christ. Such we should be loth to lose, and their lives we may pray for; yet it must be done moderately. Who can tell but Christ and we are praying counter to one another? He may be saying in heaven, " Father I will " have such a one to be with me where I am;" and we saying on earth, " Lord we would have him to " be with us where we are:" we saying, " We can- " not spare him as yet;" and Christ saying, " I will " be no longer without him." It is the force of this prayer of Christ, " I will have them to be with me " where I am," that is the cause of the death of the godly. It is the force of this prayer that carries away so many of the saints in our day. Christ is saying in heaven, " I will have them where I am. They are " despised in the world, and badly used on the earth: " Father, let us have them where we are." Should not we pray modestly for their lives, while we know not his secret will? and should not we believingly submit to his will, when he reveals it? Say, " Let " them go from us, since Christ calls them to be with " him." It is his will, and their great advantage, Phil. i. 23.

SERMON V.

John xvii. 24.

Father, I will that they also whom thou hast given me, be with me where I am; that they may behold my glory which thou hast given me: for thou lovedst me before the foundation of the world.

I Entered last day upon the second thing I took up in the matter of Christ's prayer in this verse; which was the blessing Christ prays for to his people, in these words, *That they also may be with me where I am.* In opening of them, I did speak a little, 1. To the force of this word *also.* 2. What it is *to be with Christ.* 3. What *to be with him where he is.* And then raised two points of doctrine. 1. *That the perfect blessedness of the church and people of God, is in being with Christ where he is.* 2. *That it is Christ's will that all his people should partake of, and possess this blessedness.*

To the first of these I would speak, *viz.*

DOCT. 1. *That the perfect and compleat blessedness of the church and people of God, stands in being with Christ where he is.*

Thus Christ expresseth it, John xiv. 3. *That where I am, there ye may be also;* and John xii. 26. *If any man serve me, let him follow me; and where I am, there shall also my servant be.* The apostle sums up the blessedness of the church at the last day in this, 1 Thess. iv. 17. *And so shall we ever be with the Lord.* So also in 2 Cor. v. 6. 8. it is called *being present with the Lord.* And in Phil. i. 23. it is called *being with Christ.*

There

There are four things I would premise concerning this matter, that may be of use to regulate your thoughts in hearing and studying the word of God about heaven.

1. This blessedness is greatly in the dark to us. It is an enjoyment *within the vail*, as Heb. vi. 19. And it is necessarily so. The thing we desire to be informed in, is, What it is *to be with Christ where he is?* And here every thing is dark and deep. What Christ is, where he is, what it is to be with him, who can tell or know? When the beloved disciple, who lay in Christ's bosom on earth, is speaking of this bliss, in 1 John iii. 2. he saith, *Beloved, now are we the sons of God, and it doth not yet appear what we shall be: but we know, that when he shall appear, we shall be like him; for we shall see him as he is.* Why! Did never John *see him as he is?* No. They that saw him in his humbled state, saw him under a vail, which his work rendered necessary for a time. And believers, that now see him by faith, see him not as he is; but only see him as painted forth to us in and by the gospel, as Gal. iii. 1. No man can know what it is to *see Christ as he is*, till he do *see him as he is;* and that is not till he appears. To this belongs that word, 1 Cor. ii. 9. *Eye hath not seen, nor ear heard, neither have entered into the heart of man, the things which God hath prepared for them that love him.* Heaven will be a blessed surprise to all that possess it. It will be found to be far beyond all the most large desires, and the highest expectations, that ever were raised in their hearts. So will hell be to all the heirs of wrath, vastly above all their fearful expectations, Heb. x. 27.; and the foretastes of it, that are great in some wicked men: Psal. xc. 11. *Who knoweth the power of thine anger? even according to thy fear, so is thy wrath.* No man can over-fear God's wrath; and no man can over-rate the glory to come. In that matter, the Lord *doth exceedingly abundant above all that we ask or think*, Eph. iii. 20.

2. There

2. There is some light about this in the word, that helps us to know somewhat of this bliss of *being with Christ where he is*. There are three special ends the Spirit of God designs, in making any mention of the heavenly state and glory. 1. To disparage this world, and all things either enjoyed or expected in it; and that both as to the worldling, as Psal. xvii. 14, 15. where the portion of the ungodly in this life, and the blessedness of the righteous in that to come, are expressed. So doth our Lord compare the two states, to disparage the present, and to prefer the future, Luke xx. 34, 35, 36. and Matth. vi. 19, 20. And heaven is also spoke of, in comparison with, and preference above the best state of Christians in this world, 2 Cor. v. 1, 2. and Phil. i. 23. 2. Heaven is spoke of in the word, to invite and allure men to seek it. It is *the prize of the high calling of God in Christ Jesus*. And all should *press towards this mark*, Phil. iii. 14. They should *run so as they may obtain it*, 1 Cor. ix. 24. as being the *one thing needful, and that good part, or portion*, Luke x. 42. 3. The word speaks of heaven, and the glory to come, to encourage the people of God, and heirs of glory, under all their trials and troubles in this life. If it had not been for this, the Lord might have kept the glory to come, amongst many other *secret things that belong to him*, Deut. xxix 29. But he knew, that *through much tribulation* his people *must enter into the kingdom of God*, Acts xiv. 22.; and that the hope of glory was a proper and needful cordial to support their hearts in all their sorrows. And be ye assured of it, that if ever ye be in the depths of distress, (and who is secured against them?), ye will find, that nothing short of the believing views and lively hope of glory, will be able to keep you from sinking. *I had fainted, unless I had believed to see the goodness of the Lord in the land of the living*, said David, Psal. xxvii. 13. And they have little of David's spirit, that think that David had no better *land of the living* in his eye there, than the land

of

of Canaan, in which he lived as a stranger, though he were the King of it. So also faith Paul of himself, and of all believers in Christ, 1 Cor. xv. 29. *If in this life only we have hope in Christ, we are of all men most miserable.* For these ends the Lord speaks of heaven in the word; and not to gratify the curiosity of men, but rather to check it.

3. This I would premise, that this light that shines in the word about heaven, is only a light to be seen by the eye of faith. None but a believer can know rightly what the word speaks of heaven. Unbelievers are blind, and cannot see far off, 2 Peter i. 9.; but the believer doth see afar off, Heb. xi. 13. The word is light in itself, and shines in that light, as the sun is light in itself: so that, if all the world were blind, the light of the sun would be no less in itself than it is; but it would be a light to none; for it is light to none, but to them that have eyes. Even so it is with the light of the word. It shines brightly in itself, but the blind unbeliever seeth nothing of it. He is both blind and vailed, 2 Cor. iv. 3, 4.

4. *Lastly,* This I would premise, that the experience of believers in this life, is a great help to them in knowing what heaven is. Now, let us join all these four together: There is no full and perfect knowing what heaven is, till we be in it; There is no right knowing of heaven, but in the light of the word; That light in the word can only be taken up and perceived by the eye of faith; And this faith is much strengthened by experience. If believers themselves had not somewhat of this experience and spiritual feeling, they would be much more in the dark about the glory to be enjoyed in heaven than they are.

On this head of spiritual experience, I shall not mention any great and extraordinary enjoyments which the Lord; in his grace and wisdom, is pleased in some special seasons to indulge some of his people with. But I would only speak of some ordinary ones, which lie level with the experience of all true believers, and are of great advantage to them, as in many other things, so specially to raise and keep up right and high thoughts of heaven. As,

1. The revelation of Jesus Christ. This works faith; faith, union with Christ; union works communion with him; communion is the believer's bliss. This spring of all, the revelation of Jesus Christ, is of two sorts. 1. The revealing of Jesus Christ in and by the gospel. This all that have the gospel have, and many have no more; and they all perish that have no more. 2. The revealing of Christ to the heart, by the Spirit of Christ, prayed for, Eph. i. 17. This Paul got, Gal. i. 16. He *revealed his Son in me.* It is certain, that a man may read oft all the new testament, and hear the most able ministers preach Christ all his days, and yet remain ignorant of Jesus Christ, and perish. The apostle in Eph. i. 17, 18. joineth the knowledge of Christ, and the knowledge of heaven, together. He prayeth, *That the God of our Lord Jesus Christ, the Father of glory, may give unto them the Spirit of wisdom and revelation, in the knowleage of him: the eyes of their understanding being enlightened: that they might know what is the hope of his calling, and what the riches of the glory of his inheritance in the saints.* Doth heaven stand in *being with Christ where he is?* How is it possible that that man should know what heaven is, who knows not who Christ is? And none can know Christ, without revelation, Mat. xi. 27. and that by the grace of the Spirit of Christ, working on the heart in and by the light of the word of Christ.

2. The experience of believing in Jesus Christ, and of living by faith on him, Gal. ii. 20. is a great help to the knowing of heaven. We know, that there is no faith of this sort in heaven. Faith is the traveller's, the runner's looking to Jesus, while the race is not yet finished, Heb. xii. 2. But the glorified above look on, and behold him so as we cannot distinctly apprehend, 2 Cor. v. 7. *For we walk by faith, not by sight.*

sight. And they above *walk by sight, not by faith*. You may say, that since there is such a difference betwixt the two states, of *faith* and *sight;* how then can the experience of believing afford any light and help to know what heaven is? In answer to this, I would have you consider, 1. That *faith*, though opposed to *sight*, yet is it, in its exercise, a sort of spiritual seeing. So is it oft expressed, both with respect to the author of it, and the actings of it. See how it is wrought by its author, 2 Cor. iv. 6. *For God, who commanded the light to shine out of darkness, hath shined in our hearts, to give the light of the knowledge of the glory of God, in the face of Jesus Christ.* And as it is wrought by light, faith acts in seeing. Thus the great old-testament believers are said by their faith to have *seen the promises* (*i. e.* the blessings promised) *afar off*, Heb. xi. 13. And it is a *looking at things not seen*, 2 Cor. iv. 18.; that is, things not presently possessed, nor fully known. Faith is indeed described in Heb. xi. 1. to be *the evidence of things not seen*. And that description, (rather than definition), as it doth determine what the nature of the objects of faith are, *things not seen;* so doth it plainly express, that the act of faith is drawn forth by an *evidence* of these unseen things. And this evidence and demonstration is in the word of God, which the believer seeth, is persuaded by, and rests upon. " I know not, saith " he, all the great and good things that God hath " promised ; but I know God hath promised them ; " and though they be hidden in the promise, yet be- " cause they are secured thereby, I will embrace them " in the promise, until performance come." As it is expressed in ver. 13. *These all died in faith* (But how lived they? By faith also.), *not having received the promises*, (*i. e.* in their accomplishment ; but the promises themselves they had, for on them their faith stood); *but having seen them afar off, and were persuaded of them, and embraced them, and confessed that they were strangers and pilgrims on the earth.* Here is an account of old testament believers faith, that is enough to shame and humble most new testament believers. If we be helped at any time to set our Amen of faith to the promise of eternal life, we think it is a good length. But alas! when do we find this *seeing afar off*, this *persuasion*, this *embracing*, this *confessing and declaring plainly that we seek and look for this heavenly country?* as in ver. 10, 14. 2. Consider, more particularly, faith in Jesus Christ. It always, (1.) Riseth from a discovery of him. (2.) Acts in an approach to him. Hence so oft by himself faith is called *coming to him*, John vi. 37, 44, 45. (3.) And in that act intends and seeks eternal life in and by him. 3. Consider the native and immediate effect of faith. It is union with Christ. He draws to bring them near, they believe to be near to him. His *drawing* and their *coming*, makes it up. Is then the state of glory, in *being with Christ where he is?* Surely, then, such as are united to him by faith, and have him *dwelling in their hearts by faith*, Eph. iii. 17. and are *living daily by faith on him*, Gal. ii. 20. must have a great help to know better what it is to *be with Christ where he is*, than any unbeliever can.

3. There is the experience of communion with Christ, that is a farther and nearer help to believers to know what it is to *be with Christ where he is.* When Christ is revealed, he is believed on; when he is believed on, Christ and the believer are united; when the union is made, communion follows. This communion stands in these four.

1*st*, In a mutual interest of the persons united. Communion is that whereby Christ is ours, and we are his; as Cant. ii. 16. *My beloved is mine, and I am his.* All that Christ is, is ours for our salvation; and all that is ours, is his for his glory and service: that as Christ hath all right to dispose of us, and of all that is ours, because we are his; so we have a right to partake of Christ, and of all that is his, for our salvation,

vation, becaufe he is ours. Communion is in the improvement of this mutual right and intereft. I would name fome of the bleffed fruits of this intereft.

(1.) By virtue of this intereft, Chrift's righteoufnefs is a believer's for his perfect juftification. The righteoufnefs is perfect, and fo is the juftification. No glorified faint was more perfectly juftified, than Paul was in the day he was made a believer on Chrift. If perfect righteoufnefs be the ground on which a believing finner is juftified, (as the gofpel plainly declares), the juftification muft be perfect alfo. If juftification be fought by the law, and by works, the feeker of juftification muft ftill be doing, and can never have done; but is indeed undoing himfelf, difhonouring Chrift, Gal. ii. 21. and *fruftrating the grace of God;* and not only rendering his juftification imperfect, (for *the law made nothing perfect,* Heb. vii. 19), but impoffible, Rom. viii. 3. It is impoffible for God's holy law to juftify a finner; and never was appointed for that end, but rather to condemn, Rom. iii. 19.; to ftop finners mouths, and to bind them over to the judgment of God; till the righteoufnefs of God, without the law, come on them, to abfolve them, Rom. iii. 20, 21, 22.

(2.) By virtue of this intereft in Chrift, the believer receives the Spirit of Chrift for his fanctification: not indeed for his perfect fanctification, but for the perfecting of fanctification. Chrift's righteoufnefs is never applied imperfectly; for to whomfoever it is imputed, it is made over wholly, and to all the intents and purpofes it was wrought out, and brought in, by Chrift for. But the Spirit of Chrift is imparted to believers, in meafure, and in various degrees, as he feeth good: Eph. iv. 7. *Unto every one of us is grace given, according to the meafure of the gift of Chrift.* By this potent principle, the Spirit of Chrift, fanctification is even, at firft, univerfal in the whole man, and compleat in parts: 2 Cor. v. 17. *If any man be in Chrift, he is a new creature: old things are paft away;*

way; behold, all things are become new. He is a new man; is born again; hath a new nature, a new mind, a new understanding, a new conscience, a new heart and affections, and a new life. But though all be new in the believer, there is nothing in him that is perfectly new. He needs daily to pray, as Psalm li. 10. *Create in me a clean heart, O God; and renew a right spirit within me.* Yet, notwithstanding of all the weakness of this new creature, the mixture and neighbourhood of the flesh, its contrary, and of all opposition it meets with from it, and of the low state it is oft brought into by the captivating power of sin; yet doth the power of Christ's Spirit not only preserve the holy seed in the heart, but doth raise it up again, and will certainly perfect it. There was never a saving work of Christ wrought in the heart of a poor sinner, that Christ ever left to be matter of triumph to the devil. Christ is a wise builder: when he lays the foundation, he knows what the perfecting of it will cost him, is provided with it, and resolved to lay it out, and to finish his work: Phil. i. 6. *Being confident of this very thing, that he which hath begun a good work in you, will perform* (or *finish*) *it until the day of Jesus Christ.*

(3.) By virtue of this interest in Christ, believers have all Christ's fulness for their supply. He is *all in all* to them, Col. iii. 11. *It pleased the Father, that in him should all fulness dwell,* Col. i. 19. And surely this lodging of all fulness should please, and doth highly please all believers: John i. 16. *And of (*or *out of) his fulness have all we received, and grace for grace.* Eph. iv. 7. *Unto every one of us is given grace according to the measure of the gift of Christ.* Whence had Paul and John all their grace? Out of Christ's fulness. Whence was it that they received so much grace beyond others? It was *according to the measure of the gift of Christ.* But the stock and treasure is common to all believers. They are *partakers of Christ,* Heb. iii. 14. and *called to the fellowship of his Son Jesus Christ*

Christ our Lord, 1 Cor. i. 9. The apostle in Col. ii. 8, 9, 10. giveth a needful warning, *Beware lest any man spoil you through philosophy and vain deceit*. But how shall we know and discern the snare? It is *after the tradition of men, after the rudiments* (or *elements, or principles*) *of the world, and not after Christ*. His argument to inforce this warning, is deep and strong, verse 9. *For in him dwelleth all the fulness of the godhead bodily*. It dwelleth really, substantially, in this one man, Jesus Christ. So that they do deceive you, that direct you to any for supply but to him. If ye would *be filled with all the fulness of God*, as Eph. iii. 19. you must seek it, and find it in him, *in whom all the fulness of the godhead dwelleth bodily*. And this shall not be in vain: *And ye are complete in him*, verse 10. Never did, never could a believer use this fulness suitably to all its worth in itself, and to the gracious right he hath to use it.

But what is there in believers that Christ hath communion with? All good is in him, and this is the believers all; and therefore it is easy to understand what their communion with Christ is, and what his communications to them are. He clothes and covers them with his righteousness, sanctifies them by his Spirit, and supplies them out of his fulness. But is there any thing in his people that Christ hath communion with? I answer, Yes, there is; and that it is all in them, that either is consistent with their union with him, or that flows from that union.

(1.) Of the first sort is all the bad that is remaining in them. For as the grace of union with, and relation to Christ, was not suspended and delayed till they were faultless; so this grace when dispensed, doth not presently remove faultiness, as it will when this union and communion is perfect, which Christ here prays for. Christ's body is made up of sinful members; and they are, even while sin and infirmity cleaves to them, united to a sinless, glorious head. And it is the great glory of his grace, that he takes such members into

union

union with himself, and maintains that union by communion with them as their need requires, till the blessed day comes that is here prayed for, when this union shall issue in that communion that shall quite remove fault and infirmity in his people. To deny that Christ hath any interest, and concern, and work about what is bad in his people, is to deny our fellowship with him, in those things wherein we are most needy of it, and most sensibly benefited by it: for our own sinfulness and infirmity is better known to us, and sensed by us, than his righteousness and perfect fulness; neither is the latter so well known to us, as by its gracious application to our relief under the former. So our sinfulness (I mean, that that remains in believers, even in the best of them) serves for magnifying his forgiving grace. He that bids us *forgive our brother that sinneth against us, not only seven times, but seventy times seven*, Matth. xviii. 21, 22. doth forgive his people many more times, and many sins, even *all* of them, Psalm ciii. 3.; *all our trespasses*, Col. ii. 13. And how blessed is that communion, when the blood of sprinkling speaks peace and pardon to a troubled conscience! Our corruptions and spiritual diseases are the subjects of Christ's care. And his care about them, is to cure them, and to keep his people from dying under them. The greatest hand is used by tender parents, about their sick and wounded children. That man never knew the guilt of sin rightly, that thinks that any thing less or else than *the blood of the Son of God can cleanse from it*, 1 John i. 7. And that man never saw the corruption and plague of his heart rightly, that is not persuaded, that only the great physician, Christ, can cure it. And no man can employ him rightly for the one, and not for both. And they do but deceive themselves in their religion, whose main heart-exercise is not with Christ for both. Alas! there are many disquieted consciences, and many defiled hearts and lives, in many that are called Christians; and some of them are oft complaining,

and

and sometimes sinking in their complainings; and that because they do not believe, and lay this truth to heart, that the cleansing and purging the conscience from the guilt of sin, and the purifying of the heart and life from the dominion of sin, are Christ's proper works. The first he doth by the sprinkling of his blood, the other by the power of his Spirit, 1 Cor. vi. 11. Tit. iii. 4.----7. And all that use any other means for these ends, not only labour in vain, but sin greatly against God, who hath *made Christ unto us wisdom, and righteousness, and sanctification, and redemption; that no flesh should glory in his presence; and that he that glorieth, might glory in the Lord,* 1 Cor. i. 29, 30, 31.

Not only are our infirmities, sinfulness, and diseases, under the gracious care and cure of our Lord Jesus Christ; but our persons, our souls, our bodies, and all our lots and concerns, are at his disposal, to his glory and service. And every believer, in every distinct acting of faith, doth yield up himself, and all he is and hath, unto Christ's dominion. " Grant me " thy salvation according to thy promise, and guide " me in the way according to thy will:" Psal. cxix. 94. *I am thine, save thou me.*

(2.) Christ hath communion with his own good in them. All that is in us that is our own, is bad: and all that is good in us, is of his giving and working. All our graces, are his fruits, Cant. iv. 16. and v. 1. They are all of Christ's planting, watering, and ripening: and he feeds on them as *his pleasant fruits.* All the spiritual services and duties that believers perform, are all of them fruit growing from their abiding in the vine, Christ, John xv. 4, 5. and are pleasing to him. And surely when it is so, the believer finds sweet profit by it: Rev. iii. 20. *I will sup with him, and he with me.* It is easy to conceive how we may feast with him; for he hath all. But how can he feast with us, who are nothing, and have nothing? He doth it two ways. 1. He feasts with his people on his own store of grace he brings with him. As David said, 1 Chron. xxix. 14. *Of thine own have we given thee;* so doth Christ say, "It is of mine own "I feast with thee, O believer. All thy faith, love, "repentance, service, are my gifts, my grace, that "I bring with me, and am delighted in." 2. Christ may be said to feast with his people, in and by that pleasure he hath, not only to give, but to see them feed on what he brings with him. Would you feast Jesus Christ, believers? Feed on him with holy hunger. Is a kind mother delighted with her hungry babe's sucking at her breasts? Is it not as a feast to a charitable man, to see a person eat heartily of the food he gives him? Much more is it a feast to our Lord, to see starving sinners feeding on the bread of life, and drinking of the water of life? Hear his voice, Cant. v. 1. *I am come into my garden, my sister, my spouse; I have gathered my myrrh with my spice, I have eaten my honey-comb with my honey, I have drunk my wine with my milk: eat, O friends, drink, yea, drink abundantly, O beloved.* "It is all mine, all of my prepar- "ing; use it freely, feed plentifully; you are high- "ly welcome." But, alas! most Christians may give the answer that follows, ver. 2. *I sleep, but my heart waketh.* Christ's gracious offers and invitations are heard by us, as betwixt sleeping and waking: and so is it seen in the sorry entertainment we give them, and hence follows the poor life that many of us lead.

So much for the first thing in communion, mutual interest.

2*dly*, This communion hath converse in it. It stands, not only in the mutual interest that each hath in another, but also in converse one with another. This is what the apostle hath in 1 John i. 3. where we have two *cummunions* or *fellowships* spoke of; the fellowship of Christians with one another, and the fellowship that Christians have with the Father and Son: and that this second fellowship is mutual as hinted in ver. 7. *If we walk in the light, as he is in the light,*

light, we have fellowship one with another, and the blood of Jesus Christ his Son cleanseth us from all sin. They then that know best by experience, what it is to be with Christ on earth, in walking with him and in him, will know best what it is to be with him where he is. The greatest enjoyments of Christ here, are the best helps to conceive of what is to be received in heaven.

3dly, This converse breeds likeness to Christ. The nearer a man is to Christ, the more converse he hath with him; the more like he grows to Christ. Compare 2 Cor. iii. 18. with 1 John iii. 2. Paul speaks of Christians in this life, John of the same persons in the next life; and both speak of likeness to Christ, and as wrought the same way, by *seeing and beholding of his glory.* Perfect likeness to Christ, flows from a perfect beholding of his glory; and a begun likeness to him, from a begun beholding of his glory by faith. The apostle in 2 Cor. iii. 7. speaks of *the glory of the countenance of Moses, which was such, that the children of Israel could not stedfastly behold his face, which glory was to be done away.* In this, the apostle respects that passage in Exod. xxxiv. 29.----35. It is this, that Moses, returning from the mount, after his second forty days abode there, had, by his long converse with God, a beam of heavenly glory impressed on his face. Whether it continued all his life after, or not, the word is silent about it; and therefore we should not be positive. But this may safely be drawn from it, that the more near and continued that our converse with Christ on earth be, the more heavenly likeness to Christ is impressed on the soul. Hath not this been known to many, that when they had been long struggling and striving with, and bewailing of a body of death, and of strong corruptions and distempers, that rendered them unlike to Christ, and lothsome in their own eyes; if he be pleased (as oft he doth) to draw near to them, and *to cause them to approach to him,* as Psal. lxv. 4. how

suddenly

suddenly and how sweetly is likeness to Christ wrought in the soul! True nearness to Christ, and converse with him, hath always this effect. Communion with Christ, if real, is always the life of grace, and the bane of corruption. And let all examine and judge their enjoyments, by this sure and plain test. Have you any thing that you call communion with Christ? Doth it not, in some measure, mortify your lusts, and enliven the grace of God in you? If it do not work both in you, it is not of the right sort.

4*thly*, This converse with Christ, and this likeness to him, breeds love and delight. It is not possible it should be otherwise. So great mercies in themselves, so great blessings to us, and so much of God's love to us, shining in the giving of them, must raise love and delight. This is one of the fruits of communion with Christ; Cant. ii. 3. *I sat down under his shadow with great delight, and his fruit was sweet to my taste.*

The tree of life, Jesus Christ, hath a refreshing shade to the weary scorched traveller; and he hath fruit for the hungry soul. Sit down under his shadow, eat of his fruit, and you must find it sweet to your taste. *O taste and see that the Lord is good,* Psal. xxxiv. 8. *If so be ye have tasted that the Lord is gracious*, 1 Pet. ii. 3. See how the same apostle speaks of the communion that believers have with Christ, 1 Pet. i. 8, 9. *Whom having not seen, ye love; in whom though now ye see him not, yet believing, ye rejoice with joy unspeakable, and full of glory.*

So that ye may perceive, that what the Lord is pleased to afford to his people here, in communion with Christ, gives a great help to believers to know better, what it is *to be with Christ where he is*, than any unbeliever can; and that they who have the greatest experience of these things, have an advantage in this matter beyond ordinary believers.

So much of these four things that I thought fit to premise. That the glory of the heavenly state is
greatly

greatly in the dark to Christians while on earth; That the only light wherein any thing of it can be known, is the light of the word; That this light of the word is light only to the eye of faith; and, lastly, That faith is helped in this discovery, by experience.

It now follows, to speak unto this that heaven stands in, in *being with Christ where he is*. And this I would give in these four things.

1. It stands in perfect immediate presence with Christ. All the presence that Christ affords, and his people now enjoy here, is, in regard of this, but *absence from the Lord:* 2 Cor. v. 6. 8. *Knowing that whilst we are at home in the body, we are absent from the Lord. We are confident, I say, and willing rather to be absent from the body, and to be present with the Lord.* I am sure, that there are few Christians, but think, that if they did but enjoy that of Christ that Paul did often, they would think it a great presence. But Paul counts, that as long as he dwelt in the body, he was but absent from the Lord. Perfect presence is, when all on both sides is present; all of Christ, and all of the Christian. But now all of Christ is not with us; and all of us is not with him. On his part, we have Christ's Spirit, word, and grace. On our part, there is present with him, our hearts, and the workings of our faith, and love, and desire, towards him. But this presence is imperfect, and mixed with much distance and absence. And this sort of presence with Christ, is but mediate. There are some midses, glasses, and helps, which, though useful now, will be useless one day, 1 Cor. xiii. 10, 11, 12. Yet this imperfect presence, and mediate, is more excellent in itself, and more valued by every one that hath tasted it, than the utmost that this world, and the things of it, can give to a worldling, Psal. iv. 6, 9.

2. This *being with Christ where he is*, hath in it perfect and full fruition and enjoyment of Christ.

And here, words and thoughts shrink far below the greatness of this matter. What it is to enjoy Christ, who can tell? Believers are partakers of Christ, are in him, and he in them. Faith, when strong, grasps at him, and cleaves to him. Love, when flaming, embraces him straitly; *holds him fast, and will not let him go,* Cant. iii. 4. When Christ's love to us burns and shines, and our love to him is kindled thereby, how sweet is this enjoyment? But all this is far short of what shall be enjoyed, when we *shall be with him where he is.* The difference is far greater betwixt these two, than there is betwixt the loving husband and the beloved wife, entertaining correspondence by letters to one another, in different and far distant countries. Thereby they communicate their heart, and love, and mind, to one another. And this is very comfortable; especially when this intercourse may be speedy, and in an instant, as it is betwixt Christ and believers: Isa. lxv. 24. *And it shall come to pass,* (and blessed be he that this often comes to pass), *that before they call, I will answer; and while they are yet speaking, I will hear.* There is no length of time required to carry the believer's mind to Christ in heaven; and as speedily can he send his mind to them again. But this is far short of the comfort of seeing face to face.

3. This presence, this enjoyment, is in the best state and place. It is *where he is.* And surely our Lord is well lodged above. All the presence we have with, and enjoyment we have of Christ, is not where *he is,* but where *we are.* And here we are on the dunghill of this earth; having sin cleaving to us to provoke him, and misery on us to grieve us. Hence it is both amazing grace in him to grant any thing of his presence and fellowship to us; and hence all that we enjoy of it, is attended with manifold imperfections, inseparable from our state while we are where we are, and not to be removed from us till we are *where he is.*

4. This

4. This is to be for ever. The greatest blessing hath the longest duration; if duration were a proper word to be used of eternity, which is justly called a *perpetual now.* Christ's presence now where we are, is a choice blessing. Believers would fain have it, when they are without it; and would fain have more of it, when they have a little of it; and when they have much of it, they would fain keep it. But they cannot always have his presence when they would; nor can they always keep it, when they have got it. It may please him to *awake, and leave them,* Cant. iii. 5. and viii. 4. even when they are best pleased with his company. And even then he is our beloved, and his love to us the same, when *standing behind our wall,* when *looking forth at the window, shewing himself* (or *flourishing*) *through the lattice;* as when *his left hand is under our head, and his right hand doth embrace us,* Cant. ii. 6. 9. Christ's sweetest visits to his people *where they are,* are oft imbittered (to say so) with the thoughts and fears of his withdrawing. "Now, saith the believer, I have a clear sky; but "how soon may the weather change, and clouds re- "turn again!" But in the state of glory above, when we *shall be with him where he is,* no fears, no ground, or suspicion of any such thing, shall ever enter into the heart of any of the glorified. The state of grace is a sure state, of God's making. No vessel of grace and mercy shall ever be emptied of it. But it is not a sure state to every believer's thinking; for fears of miscarrying may be, where no real danger is. But the state of glory is not only sure and unchangeable, as it is of God's gracious making, but it is so as to every glorified person's thinking. No pillars in the upper house can shake, Rev. iii. 12. Pillars in the lower house may shake, but never are removed. But in heaven, there is no danger, no fear, nor any cause of either, to eternity. *We shall be ever with the Lord,* 1 Thess. iv. 17.

APPLICATION. 1. See how great Christ's interest is in our salvation; how justly he is called *our Saviour*. He hath bought and redeemed the kingdom for the heirs, and the heirs for the kingdom. He as slain is made the way to it, Heb. x. 19, 20. He is the guide to heaven, and *captain of our salvation*, Heb. ii. 10. He wills it to them in his testament, Luke xxii. 29.; welcomes them to heaven, when he calls them by death, Acts vii. 59.; and he, as fully enjoyed, is heaven itself.

2. Wonder not at this, that few are saved. From his doctrine you may see the causes thereof. We find Christ teaching this doctrine of the fewness of the saved, in Matth. xix. 23. 26. Mark x. 23.----27. and Luke xviii. 24.----27. It is thrice recorded, and on the same occasion, and with the same sense of it, in his disciples. The occasion of Christ's teaching it, was the great zeal of a young rich man, in asking of our Lord the way to heaven, and his sudden recoiling when Christ touched his idol. On this occasion Christ teacheth, *How hardly shall they that have riches, enter into the kingdom of God! His disciples were astonished at his words. But Jesus answereth again, and saith unto them, Children, how hard is it for them that trust in riches, to enter into the kingdom of God!* Mark x. 23, 24. Upon Christ's repeating and explaining his words, it is said, ver. 26. *And they were astonished out of measure, saying among themselves, Who then can be saved?* Why were they so astonished, and *exceedingly amazed?* as it is said in Matth. xix. 25. Were there not many poor people, that had no riches, nor any temptation to trust in them, (and such the disciples themselves were), who might be saved? Their amazement seems to have its rise from this, that if one snare, as that of riches, did so endanger a man's salvation, what greater danger were all men exposed to, by manifold temptations, and disorders of their arts? But as to the doctrine before us, that *being with Christ where he is, is heaven*, I may justly confirm

firm from it what Christ taught, that few shall be saved. For few know what it is, nor the way to it; and indeed no natural man can know what they are. When our Lord is again preaching this doctrine, in that noted place, Matth. vii. 13, 14. he faith, *Enter ye in at the strait gate; for wide is the gate, and broad is the way that leadeth to destruction, and many there be which go in thereat: because strait is the gate, and narrow is the way which leadeth unto life, and few there be that find it.* According to the frame of mens spirits, they frame thoughts of heaven, and of the way to it. The Turks paradise is brutish; the Popish paradise is little better. The natural philosophers conceptions of heaven are more manly, though carnal. Only a true Christian can have a right thought of heaven; because he knows Jesus Christ, and communion with him. Christ himself is the way to heaven, as he is a slain Redeemer; and Christ himself is heaven itself, as he is a glorified, enjoyed Redeemer. All this is unintelligible and incredible to every natural man. Can ever that man count it blessedness to be with Christ above, who counts it a piece of misery to be in his company on earth? And is it possible that such can be saved, that neither know what heaven is, nor the way to it, and do dislike and hate both the way and the end, as revealed in the word, and as impressed on the hearts of all the godly in all ages?

3. Lastly, Would you secure heaven to yourselves? See to get into Christ by faith; seek acquaintance with him, press after communion with him. Let all your thoughts of heaven, all your care to secure your possessing of it, and all your exercise in pressing towards it, let all center in this one person, Jesus Christ. Alas! how many poor Christians are there, who go aukwardly to work about salvation? how poorly they fare? how sorrowfully they live? and how many of them die in darkness? and all because they mind not
Christ

Christ rightly, as *the way, the truth, and the life!* They do attend on all the ordinances of the gospel; they would fain be in heaven; they often muse and think on it; and wonder at the greatness of the prize; and sometimes have some good hope, through grace, that they shall possess it. But with many these are but like *the morning-cloud and the early dew;* and their doubts and darkness return upon them; because they do not remember Jesus Christ, and live by faith on him, as the only way to heaven, and as he enjoyed, is the Christians heaven, and as he brings all the sons to glory. You need no more to secure your right to eternal life, than to be possessed of Christ by faith; and you need no better eternal life, than *to be with Christ where he is.* He himself describes it by this, *that they may be with me where I am.* And surely Christ best knows what heaven is; since he bought it, prepared it, and possessed it, for his people. And he knows the way to it; for he is both the way and the guide to it. *Hear his voice,* therefore, *and follow him, and he will give you eternal life; and ye shall never perish, neither shall any man* (or devil, or thing) *pluck you out of his hand,* John x. 27, 28, 29. Rom. viii. 35,----39.

SERMON VI.

John xvii. 24.

Father, I will that they also whom thou hast given me, be with me where I am; that they may behold my glory which thou hast given me: for thou lovedst me before the foundation of the world.

THERE are four marvellous things about salvation, that should be often thought on by us.

1. That there is so high a Saviour as Christ is, and so great a salvation as heaven is, provided for fallen man. There was no such provision made for standing Adam, to keep him from falling; no such provision for the fallen angels, to restore them to their first estate. But for fallen man this provision is made; not for all, but for a numerous remnant, according to the election of grace; and that to bring them to a far better estate than that Adam fell from by sin.

2. That the knowledge of this Saviour, and of this salvation, is kept from multitudes as needy thereof as any that have it. The Pagans, Indians in the east and west, are as needy of the gospel as you, and no more unworthy and undeserving than you; yet you have gospel-light, and they live and perish in gross darkness. This is only from his sovereign pleasure, as our Lord owns it, Luke x. 21. And that sovereignty shines, and is by us to be owned equally, both in dispensing and with-holding the outward means of salvation, and also in dispensing and with-holding the inward effectual grace, and blessing of the means.

3. It is marvellous, (though both very sinful and usual), that this Saviour and his salvation are so greatly despised, by the most part of them who need him and

and it extremely, and have the gospel-offer made daily to them. Alas! few mind him, and few care for the great salvation he brings with him, and offers so freely to men. No man under the gospel miscarries eternally, no man or woman perisheth, without Jesus Christ, but such as do not in heart care for him and his salvation. And justly do they deserve to perish, and dreadfully shall their perdition be.

4. It is marvellous, that this blessed Saviour and his great salvation are yet given to a multitude of refusers. All by nature are unworthy, many reject the offer often; yet grace prevails at last on some of them, and makes them willing. There are many in the world (but they were thought on by him before the world was made) from whom Christ will take no refusal, though they give him many; as Jer. xxii. 21. *I spake unto thee in thy prosperity, but thou saidst, I will not hear: this hath been thy manner from thy youth, that thou obeyedst not my voice.* Yet to many such there is a time of love fixed; and when it comes, they are spoken for, spoken to, dealt with, and prevailed upon. I cannot say, but they that are early brought to Christ, have some special advantages, both in their being prevented from gross sins, and sad wanderings, and in the opportunities of serving Christ by his grace given them. But I am sure, that the longer any stand out in rebellion against Christ, when they are subdued, they should most of all men admire the grace of their conqueror. Paul, though called when a young man, yet counts that Jesus Christ *did shew forth in him all long-suffering, for a pattern to them which should hereafter believe on him to life everlasting,* 1 Tim. i, 16. Yet, doubtless, Christ hath drawn forth more long-suffering to many sinners, than he did on Paul in his unregeneracy.

Of this Saviour and of his salvation I have been speaking from this part of this excellent prayer. I have been often commending this chapter to you: and though I hope none are so foolish as to think
that

that when they have got this chapter by heart, (and I know not any chapter in God's word more worthy of a room in the heart and memory, than this), they may make a prayer of it, as of one of David's psalms; yet I am sure we may pray upon it; for though many of the words in it be only fit to be uttered in prayer by the blessed mouth that first spoke them; yet all of them may be food for the faith of every believer.

I have spoke of the manner of this prayer; *Father, I will.*

I have also entered upon the matter of it; and have taken up four things therein. 1. The description of those he prays for: *Those whom thou hast given me.* None but Christ can describe those they pray for, this way. He only had the book of life before him in prayer. It is a great mercy, if we get spiritual light to read our own name in that book; but it is not allowed us, either to desire or expect to read any other name therein, but our own. 2. The blessing that Christ prays for to such persons. And it is expressed thus, *That they may be with me where I am.* Whence I did draw two points of doctrine.

OBS. 1. *That the perfect blessedness of the people of God, stands in being with Christ where he is.* On this I spoke last day.

OBS. 2. *It is Christ's will to have his people possessed of this bliss of being with him where he is.*

Thus saith our Lord, *Father, I will that they whom thou hast given me, be with me where I am.* Thus he saith of all them, without distinction or exception. This prayer is universal, for his whole body of the elect; and particular, for every individual member of that body. As they cannot be perfectly happy, till *they be with him where he is,* (and that they all know); so our Lord gets not all his will and mind about them, till they are thus with him. And this we should believe. The meaning of this will of Christ about his people's bliss, is in these. 1. It is our Lord's heart's desire.

desire. 2. It is his delight to have them with him. 3. It is his fixed purpose and resolution. His heart is fixed in this, that he will have them all with him. 4. It is his will declared to his Father, in such a manner and season, and with such circumstances, as add great weight to it. 5. It is his will revealed unto us in his written word; and therefore is of great use to believe and rejoice in it. But who can tell (even when Christ hath told us it) what this his *will* is? The *will* of the Son of God, the *will* of a dying Redeemer, the *will* of a man personally united to the Son of God; how far doth it exceed all our thoughts?

In handling of this point, I would,
1. Prove that it is Christ's will.
2. Shew why it is so. And then,
3. Apply it.

I. That *it is Christ's will to have his people with him where he is,* appears from these two. 1. The price he paid for them; and, 2. The pains he takes on them.

1. The great and dear price he paid for them. The price was of infinite value, and the purchase was great. He bought the heirs for the inheritance, and the inheritance for the heirs. Christ in redeeming had respect unto both; and himself, as slain, was the price for both. He bought us and our forfeited inheritance, as he oft declares. And this doth prove, that it is his will and mind that they should possess it. What wise or honest man is at cost to purchase that for another that he will not let him possess? When our Lord laid down his life, yea staked down his crown and glory, and bore so much distress, and all for this, that he might at last have all his people *with him where he is;* sure we must conclude, that Christ's heart and mind was greatly set upon it. The grand view of the good-will of Christ to the saving his people, and having them in heaven, is to be had on his cross.

cross. The death of the Saviour proclaims his goodwill to save. He knew he must save us by dying, and we know that we are saved by his death. Therefore he had a desire and delight to die for his people. *It pleased the Lord to bruise him,* Isa. liii. 10; and Christ was pleased to be bruised, Heb. x. 5,---10.

2. The second proof is: The great pains that Christ takes on his people to bring them to heaven, proves that his heart is set on their possessing of it. On this proof I would insist in a few particulars.

1*st*, Christ draws them to himself whom he minds to save. By nature they are far off from Christ, and from salvation. By his grace they are brought near, Eph. ii. 13. Christ and salvation are inseparable. When Christ entered into Zaccheus's heart by faith, then *salvation came into his house,* Luke xix. 9, 10. Christ's drawing of a sinner, is his working of faith; and the sinner's believing on Christ, is his coming to Christ. Thus the nearness is obtained. Christ is *the author and finisher of faith,* Heb. xii. 2. But this way of working of faith is a great mystery, John iii. 8. Believers themselves find their own faith a great mystery to themselves. They often know better the fruits and effects of their faith, than they know the actings of it. And again, they may know better what they do, and what way their hearts act towards Christ, when they believe, than they know what Christ was doing with them, when he was working faith in them, and making them believers. For usually Christ's work in drawing men to himself, is so terrible, that they cannot think that any good is meant to them. Little did Paul know what Christ meant by his first visit and words to him, Acts ix. 3,---9.; but well knew he afterwards, Gal. i. 15, 16. and oft did he tell it, Acts xxii. and xxvi. The sum of all he said was this: " I was a bitter enemy to Jesus Christ; yet he was " pleased to make me a believer on him, and called " me to preach him, and faith in him, to the perish- " ing world." When Christ is drawing his chosen by *the cords of love*, (as Hosea xi. 4.), usually they are jealous that these cords of love are but the gins of an enemy. How is it possible that the charge of sin on the conscience, the discovery of the abominations in the man's heart, and the binding of him over to the righteous judgment of God, (Rom. iii. 19.), can be looked on as gracious methods of Christ for drawing men to him? Yet afterwards they know, that all this was done in love, and for their good. Of all the sins the Lord's people are guilty of, this is the greatest, and should be deeply repented of, even the rebellion against, and resistance they made to the saving grace and drawing arm of Jesus Christ. That we walk after the imagination of our own hearts, that we love to wander, that we live in sin, and love and commit it; all these things are proper and natural to sinners; so that tho' all should abhor it, yet none should wonder at it. But when Christ is drawing perishing sinners to himself, that he may save them; when he is plucking them out of the fire that will burn them, and out of the water that will drown them; then for men to oppose and resist him, (as all do till his grace make them willing), hath somewhat in it beyond the common sinfulness of men: yea it is a sin beyond the possibility of the devil, the father of sin and of sinners; for the grace of God was never in the offer of the fallen angels, nor did it ever make any assault upon them. Yea the reprobates, though many of them sinfully resist the general drawing of Christ by the gospel, and his Spirit's dealing with them, as in Acts vii. 51. *Ye stiff-necked, and uncircumcised in heart and ears, ye do always resist the Holy Ghost: as your fathers did, so do ye;* by which they draw on dreadful guilt, and destruction, and are made inexcusable; as our Lord tells them, John xv. 22, 24. *If I had not come and spoken unto them, they had not had sin: but now they have no cloke for their sin,* viz. their sin of unbelief: yet they never resist the saving arm and design of Christ to save them; as many of the elect do for a while, till the

Lord's

Lord's day of power come, which always prevails over all refiftance. For, fure, another fort of grace was applied unto blafpheming Saul, than on the traitor Judas; and on Peter ftumbling, than on Judas falling. Herein Chrift abundantly proves his mind and good-will to fave his people, in his drawing them to himfelf, that he may fave them. So faith he in John xii. 32. *And I, If I be lifted up from the earth, will draw all men unto me.* And this he faid in one of his faddeft hours, as ver. 27, 28. The devil, and wicked world, (that lieth in his arms, as in 1 John v. 19. *The whole world lieth in wickednefs,* or *or in that wicked one*), they thought, that if they could once get rid of Chrift, and flay him, that they fhould never more be troubled with Chrift, nor with believers on him. But they were utterly difappointed: and this Chrift foretels; and it was bleffedly fulfilled, and will be till his fecond coming. It is as if he had faid, " They defpife the virtue and grace of a living Saviour; and " think if they had flain him, there would be an end " of him and of his intereft on earth. But when " they have done what they would, they fhall find " themfelves farther from their purpofe; for I will " put forth the virtue of my death, in drawing mul-" titudes unto me." And it is not unlike, but that within a few weeks after his death, and within a few days after his afcenfion, there was a greater multitude of finners drawn to Chrift by faith, than were in all the few years he lived and preached on the earth.

So much for this firft proof of Chrift's will and mind to fave his people, from his drawing them unto himfelf, or his working faith on him in them.

2*dly*, Another proof of this is from his making them meet to poffefs heaven, Col. i. 12. Take heed in this matter. No man is meet for Chrift till he be in him. But he that is in Chrift, is meet for heaven; and none fhall poffefs it, but he that is made meet for it; and that is a divine work. Chrift is meet for sinners, to save them. See how meet he is made of God, 1 Cor. i. 30. He is made all we want for salvation. Christ had no work in the world but for sinners. And none will employ Christ in his saving calling and office, but convinced and sensible sinners. None but such can see their need of Christ; and such as see no need of Christ, can never employ him by faith: for believing is nothing but a needy lost sinner's trusting this able Saviour with his salvation. *Christ came to seek and to save that which was lost*, Luke xix. 10. And the lost man comes to, and seeks salvation from Christ, and gets it. If a man disown his own name, *a sinner*, he therein disowns Christ's name, *a Saviour of sinners*. If men pretend to use Christ as a Physician, and subscribe not their true name to their petitions, *a lost, sick sinner, bleeding to death by the sting of sin and of the law*, he will have nothing to do with them. He will say to them, "I came to save sinners; but you are whole and righ-"teous folks, and think you can save yourselves. "It is but a little that ails you, and you think you "can soon cure it. But if you try your own art, you "perish; and your wound is deadly, and no balm "can heal it but mine." Now, no man is meet for Christ, till he gets Christ. But a man must be made meet for heaven, before he gets it. No man can get this meetness but by Christ; and Christ's working of this meetness, is the proof I give of Christ's mind to give glory to them in whom he works it.

A little on this, What this meetness for heaven is; wherein it stands; and how Christ works it in his people.

This meetness to possess heaven, is twofold; a meetness as to the state of the person; and a meetness as to his nature and frame, that is to be the possessor of heaven. And the apostle in that scripture named, Col. i. 12, 13, 14. hints at both plainly enough.

(1.) Meetness in the state of the person for possessing of heaven, stands in two things. He must be reconciled

conciled to the Lord of this good land of heaven, and he must be related to this inheritance. Both come by Jesus Christ. Enemies and strangers are unmeet to possess it; and none such shall, to eternity. Yet all men by nature are both enemies to God, and unrelated to heaven. But Christ changeth the state of them whom he minds to save, and thus maketh them meet to possess the inheritance. They are made friends, and reconciled to God, by the grace of justification; they are made children and heirs, and so related to the inheritance, by the grace of adoption. And both are by Jesus Christ; as in Rom. v. 8, 9, 10. and viii. 14. 17. Gal. iii. 26. and iv. 5, 6. Can an enemy expect an inheritance from his enemy? And this is the natural state that God and man stand in to one another. Can a stranger expect an inheritance in a strange country, where he hath no friend nor relation to leave him any thing, and when the man is so poor that he can purchase nothing? The apostle in Eph. ii. 12. tells them what they were by nature, and what they should remember still: *That at that time ye were without Christ;* and what followed on it? *They were aliens from the commonwealth of Israel, and strangers from the covenant of promise,* (Israel's peculiar right, Rom. ix. 4. *Who are Israelites; to whom pertaineth the adoption, and the glory, and the covenants, and the giving of the law, and the service of God, and the promises*), *having no hope, and without God in the world.* How came the blessed change from this woful state? *But now in Christ Jesus, ye who were sometimes far off, are made nigh by the blood of Christ,* ver. 13. *Now therefore ye are no more strangers and foreigners; but fellow citizens with the saints, and of the houshold of God,* ver. 19. So that all that pretend to the hope of heaven, should search well, and make out that they have a right to it, and friends there. And the great friend in heaven is Jesus Christ; who bought the kingdom dearly, and conveys the right unto it freely, to all that believe on him.

(2.) There

(2.) There is a meetness for heaven in the nature and frame of the heart of the heir of it. This meetness is necessary: Heb. xii. 14. *Without holiness no man shall see the Lord.* And it is wrought by Jesus Christ in the grace of sanctification. Thus the apostle discourseth plainly in 1 Cor. vi. 9, 10, 11.; where he expresly shews the equal necessity of justification and of sanctification, unto the inheriting of *the kingdom of Christ, and of God,* and of the interest that Christ hath in giving them both. It is very remarkable in Rom. viii. 30. one of the deepest, and yet one of the clearest scriptures (deepest for matter, and clearest for faith) about God's method of salvation: *Moreover, whom he did predestinate, them he also called: and whom he called, them he also justified; and whom he justified, them he also glorified.* It seems to some to be strange, that there is no mention in it of sanctification. Only there is predestination, calling, justification, and glory. The obvious reason of this is, that sanctification is included in glory. It is not so much the way to glory, as it is a piece, and part, and beginning of it. Now, this great work of Christ in sanctifying his people, is seen in all his work on them, and way with them, from their regeneration, until their welcome to heaven. About this meetness for glory by sanctification, these three things are well known. 1. That they that study sanctification the right way most diligently, do attain most of it. The only way is by faith in Christ Jesus, Acts xxvi. 18. 2. That they that attain most of it, think least of their attainments. They see so much evil remaining in them, as Rom. vii. and so much good before them, Phil. iii. 12, 13, 14. that they still press forward for more sanctification. If any man do think himself to be very holy, any Christian may not only justly question the truth of that pretence, but also his having any holiness at all. For true gospel-holiness is a frame of heart and soul wrought by the Spirit of Christ, that works in believers a holy hatred of all sin; a

lothing

lothing of himself in whom so much of it still remains; and a pressing after that perfection in holiness, which only can be attained when he is where Christ is. 3. That all sensible and wise believers, in their building their faith and hope of possessing glory, and in their believing and pleadings with God for that possession, do lay far greater (yea another sort of) weight on what Christ hath done for them, and hath promised to them, than on that small begun holiness he hath wrought in them; though that also be to be thankfully owned, tenderly cherished, and used as food to their faith.

So much for this second proof, That Christ proves his mind to have his people *with him where he is*, when he not only draws them to himself when they are on the earth, but makes them meet to be with him in heaven. All he hath done for his people when he was in this world, is applied to them for the change of their state; and all he doth in them by his Spirit, is for the change of their frame. And thus by both he makes them meet for heaven.

3*dly*, Another proof of Christ's will to have his people *with him where he is*, is, That he by his Spirit, works in the hearts of his people, desires, faith, and hopes of this bliss. This is both a proof that they shall possess it, and that Christ hath a mind that they should have it. Christ raiseth no desires, raiseth no faith and hope of that which he hath no mind to give. So the apostle argues, 2 Cor. x. 1.----5. *We know* what heaven is, ver. 1. *We groan earnestly*, ver. 2. *We groan*, as *being burthened*, ver. 4. *We are confident always* in these groanings, ver. 6. 8. The reason of all is in ver. 5. *Now he that hath wrought us for the self-same thing, is God; who hath also given unto us the earnest of the Spirit.* So doth the apostle reason in Heb. xi. 16. speaking of the ancient believers before the law: *But now they desire a better country, that is, an heavenly;* (and this desire they declared plainly, ver. 14. by word and deed);

wherefore God is not ashamed to be called their God: for he hath prepared for them a city, i.e. heaven. Their desiring of it is not the cause or reason of God's preparing of it; but God's preparing of it was the cause of his revealing of it; and his revealing of it by his promise to them, was the ground of their believing of it; their faith was the cause of their desire of it; and this desire, thus raised and thus grounded, was a demonstration to them, that they should surely possess it. And so should it be to every believer in all ages. Hath Christ raised desires in your hearts *to be with him where he is?* Do ye feel them in your souls? And are you daily expressing them to him in prayer alone, and in all your attendance on him in gospel-ordinances? If he hath yet farther opened to you the door of hope, as the day-dawn to thy heavy darkened heart; *lift up your heads* and hearts, *your redemption draweth near*, Luke xxi. 28. *Now is your salvation nearer than when you believed*, Rom. xiii. 11.; nearer than when *you first trusted in Christ*, Eph. i. 12.; nearer than when you first begged it of him. Gracious Jesus will never baulk the desires of heaven which he himself hath put and kept up in thy heart: Psal. x. 17. *Lord thou hast heard the desire of the humble: thou wilt prepare their heart, thou wilt cause thine ear to hear.*

4*thly*, Christ's good-will to give eternal life to his people appears in the earnest he gives to them. This is oftener spoke of in the word, than known and felt by the readers and hearers of the word. It is called *the earnest of the Spirit*, from its immediate author, 2 Cor. v. 5.; *the earnest of the Spirit in our hearts*, for therein it is put, 2 Cor i. 22.; *the earnest of our inheritance*, Eph. i. 13. for unto that it refereth. It is something of heaven given to believers on earth; some special presence of Christ manifested to them; some special fellowship with him, filling them with joy, and peace, and likeness to him. How well is this known to them that have it? And how

sure

sure is it, that no words can make any other to know it? It is *the hidden manna, that Christ gives his people to eat of,* (and no man knows its taste, but the eater of it, and while he eats of it); and *the white stone* Christ gives, *and in the stone a new name written,* (If it be written, may it not be read by any? No), *which no man knoweth, saving he that receiveth it,* Rev. ii. 17. Why is this earnest given? It is to secure the bargain of the new covenant to the believer, and to secure him of the possession of glory. Therefore is it called *the first fruits of the Spirit,* Rom. viii. 23.; *sealing of believers,* 2 Cor. i. 22. and *to the day of redemption,* Eph. iv. 30. This earnest must be a rich jewel, when the devil that great thief and robber, sets himself so against them that have got it. It was more than an earnest that Paul got in 2 Cor. xii. 1, 1, 3. The devil hated Paul from the day that Christ took him out of his arms; he hated his gifts, grace, and service; and that Paul knew well, and felt often: but he never fell on him fiercely, as when Paul came down enriched with extraordinary enjoyments. No believer shall get this earnest, if the devil can hinder it; and none can keep it, without a battle with hell. But though Satan by his malice and craft, and our unbelieving hearts, join together (as too oft they do) to rob us of this earnest, and the sense of it; yet Christ will never take it away, nor break the bargain of our salvation, Psal. lxxxix. 33, 34, 35. *Nevertheless, my loving-kindness will I not utterly take from him, nor suffer my faithfulness to fail,* is the voice of God in the new covenant. It may be a question with some, If this earnest be an universal blessing to all, or only a special kindness to some believers? On the one hand, the discouraged complaining mood of some Christians seems to say, that they have it not; on the other hand, many have this earnest, and that frequently repeated to them. What shall we say to this question? These things we may be sure of; that it is a choice mercy, and a great advantage to a believer to have it; (as the contraries are as sure, to such as have it not); that it is a great duty to press after it; that there are ways and means of God's appointment for reaching it; that there are gracious promises of a blessing on those means; and that faith and diligence in seeking this blessing in God's way, is usually successful. It seems far safer for us, to lay our want of it on our own unbelief, than to reflect upon his word and way.

So much for the first thing in this doctrine, Wherein appears Christ's will and mind to have his people where he is?

II. *Why it is, and must be his will and mind?* Take these two accounts of it. 1. Because of his faithfulness in the covenant. And, 2. Of his love to his people.

1. Because of his faithfulness in the covenant of grace. The clearest and surest view of our salvation, is to be had in this covenant. Therein we see, 1. The elect are given by the Father to the Son, to be redeemed by him, and that he may give them eternal life; as John xvii. 2. *thou hast given him power over all flesh, that he should give eternal life to as many as thou hast given him.* This charge the Son accepted from eternity, and, in the fulness of time, came into the world to fulfill, John vi. 38, 39. They were given to him, on condition of his coming, and redeeming of them by his blood; which condition he fulfilled. 2. They are promised to him as his purchase by the Father, when the Son hath bought them as he promised: Isa. liii. 10, 11. *When thou shalt make his soul an offering for sin, he shall see his seed, he shall prolong his days, and the pleasure of the Lord shall prosper in his hand. He shall see of the travail of his soul, and shall be satisfied,* &c. 3. The bringing them safe to glory, is charged on the Son, and promised by him again to the Father: John vi. 38, 39. *For I came down from heaven, not to do mine own will, but the will of him that sent me.*

And

And this is the Father's will which hath sent me, that of all which he hath given me, I should lose nothing, but should raise it up again at the last day. John xii. 50. *And I know that his commandment is life everlasting.* Christ stands engaged by this covenant, to give a good account of all his charge; and he will do it fully one day, when he presents his people to his Father; and will say of all, as Heb. ii. 13. *Behold, I, and the children which God hath given me;* and as he said of a few of them in this chapter, ver. 12. *While I was with them in the world, I kept them in thy name; those that thou gavest me, I have kept, and none of them is lost.* And surely Christ is as good at keeping of his people when he is in heaven, as when he was on earth: for *he is with them always, even unto the end of the world, Amen,* Matth. xxviii. 20. 4. Christ yet further promiseth eternal life to his people: 1 John ii. 25. *And this is the promise that he hath promised us, even eternal life;* as it is the grand comprehensive promise. Yea, Christ himself is called *eternal life,* 1 John i. 2. and verse 20. When Christ came into the world, eternal life came into it; when Christ is shown and revealed, eternal life is made known; when Christ is embraced by faith, eternal life is got: 1 John v. 11, 12. *And this is the record, that God hath given to us eternal life: and this life is in his Son. He that hath the Son, hath life.* O that all men did but know, how closely, how inseparably, and how eternally, Christ and eternal life are linked together! No eternal life without Christ; no Christ without eternal life. He also promiseth it, as well as contains it: John x. 27, 28. *My sheep hear my voice, and I know them and they follow me. And I give unto them eternal life, and they shall never perish, neither shall any man pluck them out of my hand.* It is this, and such like promises of eternal life, made by Jesus Christ, that every true believer builds his hope of heaven upon. And thus Christ's faithfulness and truth is concerned in bringing all his people to glory.

2. Con-

2. Consider Christ's wonderful love to his people. True love cannot bear long parting, much less everlasting parting. Christ loves his people so well, that he must have them with him; otherwise he should lose his love, and his beloved; and that cannot be. The love of Christ to his people may well be their delight, and their wonder. There is both pleasure and profit in studying of it. But all our thoughts can never reach to its infinite dimensions; for it hath *height*, and *depth*, and *breadth*, and *length*, and in all *passeth knowledge*, Eph. iii. 18, 19. And because of the sweetness of this theme of Christ's love, and because all I shall say in the application of this doctrine at this time, is to require love to him again; I would speak a little of this blessed love of Christ to his people, as it is the cause of his willing to have them with him where he is.

1*st*, Christ's love to his people hath no cause nor reason for it, but itself. Love is the only cause of his love. Our love to him hath good cause, and strong reason for it. His own worth in himself, his love to us, and the great things he hath done for us, and hath promised to us, justly deserve more love than we can give him. But none of these things are with us to engage his love to us.

2*dly*, This love of Christ not only hath no cause in us to raise it; but it is a love that acts and moves against all things that may justly quench love and raise lothing. There is not only no worth nor *beauty in us that he should desire us*, (as the unbelieving world thought, and thinks falsely of Christ himself, Is. liii. 2.) but there is a great deal in us to make us justly hateful and lothsome in his eyes. There is enmity to him in our heart and nature; there are provocations in our conversation and walk; there are vileness, lothsomeness, poverty, and all misery, in our state; yet Christ's love overcomes all: Ezek. xvi. 6, 7, 8. *Thy time was the time of love, saith the Lord.* A strange time of love

love, and a strange love! A wretched, naked polluted infant, *cast out in the open field, to the lothing of its person*, as ver. 5. Was that a time of love? Was that a time for the Prince of heaven to fall in love with the filthy perishing brat? Unto any but to the heart of a God, this would have been a time of lothing, and not of love. The same thing the apostle teacheth without a parable, Eph. ii. 1, 2, 3, 4.

3*dly*, It is a love that sets Christ on work in all his saving work. And hard, and dear, and costly work to him it was: yet love made him to do it all; and delightfully he did it. He died for us in love; he called us in love; he planted his grace in us in love; he visits us in love; and when he corrects and rebukes, he doth that in love too, Rev. iii. 19. And though we do not like it, he likes it, and it is for our good. All that Christ doth for, and in, and with, and on, and about his people, (and who can tell all?), he doth all in and from his love to them. And this shews us both the nature of his love to us, and the debt we are under to love him again.

4*thly*, This love of Christ to his people, both designs and effects the greatest good to them he loves. Among creatures there is a deal of love to little purpose. Either they intend but little by their love; or if they do design it, their love cannot reach it. But the greatest good, eternal life, is not only intended by Christ in his love to his people, but it is surely attained. All that Christ loves, are saved: why? because his love is saving. Salvation is designed by this lover, and is perfected by his love.

APPLICATION. Let me therefore exhort you to love Jesus Christ. Is his heart set upon the having all his people with him where he is? Surely we ought to return love to him back again. Most of them that pretend to the name of Christian, think they make some conscience of it, as being a most just debt and
duty

duty to him: and will be ready to say with Paul, 1 Cor. xvi. 22. *If any man love not the Lord Jesus Christ, let him be Anathema, Maranatha.* But as the love that Christ bears to his people, is not so well known and believed as it ought to be; so the love his people owe to him, is not so well paid as it ought to be. I would therefore advise you in five things about your love to Christ.

Advice 1. Take a serious view of the lover, and of the beloved, and of the love he bears them; of Christ that doth love, and of his people whom he doth love, and of the love he bears to them. When these three are seen by the eye of faith in the light of God's word, his glory and greatness who loveth, the vileness of them he loveth, the greatness of the love he bears them, two thoughts will rise in the heart. 1. How marvellous is it, that such a person as he should love, in such a manner, such persons as we be! 2. How great should our returns of love be to him again! What is the cause of this usual and sad remark, That carnal, secure sinners count it an easy thing to believe that Christ loves them, though they never tasted of his special love; when many sincere Christians find the faith of Christ's love to them so difficult, though they dare not deny their *tasting* sometimes *that he is gracious?* as 1 Peter ii. 3. Yea they find it hardest to believe it in such times, when either the divine dignity of Christ, or their own wretchedness, are seen by them; (and usually they go together). This is the cause of it, because this love of Christ is so mysterious and wonderful, (as the lover is, Isa. ix. 6.). We cannot easily think, that Christ doth love any, but such as are some way like him; nor do we rightly know, that Christ can, and doth love them that are not like him, so as to make them like to him by his love; for his love hath always this blessed effect in all them that it falls upon.

Advice 2. Learn to believe Christ's love. Usually, we would fain have his love proved and manifested

ted to us. But I advise you to take this way, of getting your faith to fix on Christ's love. Think not that I would persuade you rashly to conclude in yourselves, that Christ loves you. But what I design, is only this: Take Christ's love-letters and Christ's amiable picture in the gospel, (and the new testament is full of them); and believe, and love them, and him by them. Behold *Christ crucified*, Gal. iii. 1.; behold him dying, and redeeming by his blood, and that in mere love to the redeemed. Read his love-letters filled with gracious calls, offers, and promises: and all these letters sealed with his blood, shed in love. A blessed exercise, that you would soon find the advantage of.

Advice 3. Then pray much for his manifested love to you in particular. You are to give him glory in believing his love-letters and his beautiful picture in the gospel, and in raising faith and love by those helps: But you may also beg his manifesting his love to you. See his promise, John xiv. 21, 23. words more precious than fine gold, *He that hath my commandments, and keepeth them, he it is that loveth me: and he that loveth me, shall be loved of my Father; and I will love him, and will manifest myself to him.* " I will love " him, and make him know it." And when one of his disciples asks, either in ignorance or wonder, *How this could be!* verse 22. our Lord answers, *If a man love me, he will keep my words: and my Father will love him, and we will come* (i. e. my Father and I) *unto him, and make our abode with him*, ver. 23. Very like his words in Rev. iii. 20. *Behold, I stand at the door and knock: If any man hear my voice, and open the door, I will come in to him, and sup with him, and he with me.* Thus he manifests his love; 1 John iv. 12. *God dwelleth in us, and his love is perfected in us.* Ver. 15. *Whosoever shall confess that Jesus is the Son of God, God dwelleth in him, and he in God.* Ver. 16. *And we have known and believed the love that God hath to us;* (and so must we know and believe the love that his Son hath to us). *God is love; and he that*

dwel-

dwelleth in love, dwelleth in God, and God in him. Ver. 17. *Herein is our love made perfect.* But how did it begin, and how is it advanced? Ver. 19. *We love him, because he first loved us.* Alas! what are Christians doing? and how poorly they do? Where is the man who is sick of love for Christ? This blessed disease (or soul's health rather) is twofold; either in pining hunger for the manifestation of his love, as Cant. v. 8.; or in the overwhelming sweetness of his manifested love, Cant. ii. 5. If you know nothing of neither of these, your carcases may be well, but your souls do not prosper. I do not think that there ever was a poor believer, that did long breathe after Christ's love, but he felt it. Most people do not care for it: and therefore they seek it not, and therefore they find it not; and some of them may say, (as they in Acts xix. 2. *We have not so much as heard whether there be any Holy Ghost).* "We have not felt any " of the love of Christ; we know nothing of it, but " as it is spoke of in the scriptures, and as it is to " be enjoyed in heaven." But how it doth burn as a hot fire in the heart, Cant. viii. 6, 7. even on earth, alas! few feel.

Advice 4. When Christ hath manifested his love, then light your torch of love at the warm beams of the Sun of Righteousness. I mean, kindle your love to him at the fire of his love to you. No other fire will kindle true love to Christ, but the faith and feeling of Christ's love to you. What made Paul such a fervent lover of Christ, but that he knew so well how Christ loved him? *He loved me, and gave himself for me,* Gal. ii. 20. No wonder he said, Acts xxi. 13. *I am ready not to be bound only, but also to die at Jerusalem for the name of the Lord Jesus.* "Christ died " at Jerusalem for my redemption; and shall I not " die there for his glory, if he call me?"

Advice 5. When you have kindled your love to Christ at his love to you, then let it burn and spend (but it cannot spend, but grows by burning) in his service,

service, and to his praise. Use and act that love in all holy worship, and in all gospel-obedience. That is the best worship, and the most acceptable obedience, that is performed from love to Christ. This *love constrained* Paul, 2 Cor. v. 14. unto his excellent living to Christ. That working and running that only the spur of the law in mens consciences constrains some unto, is of no account in the sight of God. Faith in Christ raiseth love to Christ; and faith and love enlivens to all holy obedience, and spiritual worship. Then the Christian reads and hears the word of Christ, because he loves to hear his voice. He prays; for he loves to speak, and to pour out his heart to his best friend. He sits down at the Lord's table, because he loves to see, and draw virtue from his slain Saviour. He hates evil, because he loves the Lord, Psalm xcvii. 10. He keeps Christ's commandments, because he loves the commander, John xiv. 15. Sirs, be assured of this, that you are not yet got into the right road of Christianity; you are not yet in that path, wherein you can be hearty and sincere, and wherein you will be constant, and never faint; until you get once into the power of the love of Christ. Then you will be sweetly carried on in all your way, and in his ways. Then may the believer in, and lover of Christ, say, " Let the Lord lead me whither he pleaseth; I
" am still going to heaven, and am in the river of life,
" the love of Christ, that begun (if I may say so)
" from eternity, and carries me through time, un-
" to the eternal enjoyment of the same love in hea-
" ven."

SERMON VII.

John xvii. 24.

Father, I will that they also whom thou hast given me, be with me where I am; that they may behold my glory which thou hast given me: for thou lovedst me before the foundation of the world.

MENS hearts are best known by their prayers. And by the same way we may know Christ's heart. Whosoever would know how deeply his heart is concerned in the saving of his people, let them read and believe this prayer. And indeed, unless people do know how Christ's heart stands affected to their salvation, their hearts will never stand well affected towards him, in their employing him for salvation. A clear and strong persuasion of Christ's hearty concern in and about saving of sinners, will make a poor sinner hearty in trusting him with his own salvation.

Of this I have been speaking from these precious words. The manner of this prayer I have spoke to. In the matter of it I took up four things. 1. The description of the party he prays for: *They whom thou hast given me.* 2. The blessing he prays for to them: *That they also may be with me where I am.* On this part I observed, 1. *That the perfect bliss of believers stands in their being with Christ where he is.* 2. *Christ's will is to have them possessed of this bliss.* This latter doctrine I did last day open and confirm; and began to apply it in one instance, of the debt of love to Christ that lies on all Christians.

I would now proceed to a more large application of both the doctrines, and that in four exhortations.

Exhort.

Exhort. 1. Is it not Christ's will to have all his people *with him where he is?* Then we are called to admire this wonderful will of Christ. This will hath its causes and springs, as you have heard. But these are so far from making it less, that they indeed make it more wonderful. For helping you to admire this will of Christ, I would give you a few things to consider.

1. Jesus Christ knows himself best. We hear these words of *being with Christ:* but little do we know what they contain and mean; because we know so little, who, and what Christ is. But Christ knows himself fully and perfectly; and therefore he knew what a great blessing he willed for his people, when he uttered this suit to his Father. It is the wise constitution of God, that the knowledge of Christ, and the enjoyment of Christ, and the knowledge of that enjoyment, are inseparable. We alas! know little of Christ, we enjoy little of him; and therefore know very little, what perfect enjoyment of him is. But Christ knew himself perfectly, and what bliss his company would be to his people. This is one thing that may make us admire this will of Christ. As if our Lord had said, " My poor people know not ful- " ly wherein their greatest bliss consists; but I know " it well, and will to them."

2. Our Lord Jesus knew best where he was to be. I told you where Christ was when he made this his will, even near the lowest step of his humbled state. He was just going to the garden of agony, and from that to the death of the cross. But he prays as if in heaven already. And well did he know whither he was going, and what a high and happy state himself was going to, unto which also he meant to bring his people; as he commends it, and encourageth his disciples from it, in John xiv. 2, 3. But we, when we pray for heaven, we pray in the dark. We pray for a blessing, that we do not know, but in a very small part. See 1 Cor. ii. 9. 1 John iii. 2. If it were possible that any believer, out of heaven, did fully
know

know what heaven is, that man would either be as in heaven, or would pray wonderfully for it. But well did Christ know what heaven was; and therefore prays for it unto his people.

3. Christ knew well where his people were; in an evil world, ver. 11.; and what bad entertainment they had, and were to have in it. In love and pity to them, therefore he wills this blessed lodging for them in heaven.

4. Christ knew well what their frame of heart and desires were. He knew what a heart he had put in them; that nothing less than being with him where he was, could content, satisfy, and make them happy. Would you know, when Christ begins to do good to a poor sinner? what is the first thing Christ doth to one he minds to save? It is plainly this: He makes such a hole in the man's heart, that nothing but Christ and heaven can fill. None but Christ, nothing but being with him where he is, can satisfy this man. Christ's grace given, *springeth up into everlasting life*, John iv. 14. And he that created this spring, will neither divert nor stop it. But as their hearts, by his grace, spring up to heaven; Christ's heart, in this prayer, springs up to that same everlasting life for them.

Exhort. 2. Love this blessed willer. Love Jesus Christ, who wills to have all his people in heaven with himself; and love him for willing it. But some will say, "I know not that Christ wills this for me. "If I did but know it, I would then love him." *Ans.* 1. Though you do not know it, you doubt not, but he deserves thy highest love. No darkness as to your interest in Christ, can dissolve the obligation of duty to love Christ, nor excuse thee from the sin of not loving him. 2. All the devils in hell, or out of hell, or in thy heart, cannot prove, that thou art one that Christ hath no mind to have with him. If any of them suggest it, you have reason to say, they lye, and cannot possibly prove it. I will suppose thy
state

state to be as bad as thou imagines; that thou hast no light, nor knowledge, nor ground to believe and hope that thou art in Christ's will and prayer; yea, that thou hast many fears of the contrary, and appearance of grounds for them. Yet it is certain, that it is impossible to prove, that Christ hath no mind to save thee. 3. Is it not some considerable encouragement to you, that it is certain that many just such as you, are in this will of Christ? This prayer was put up, and hath been oftentimes answered, for many just such as you be. There is not so great a difference betwixt men in their natural state, as many imagine. There is indeed some difference in their outward conversation. Some wander strangely; and some are, by education, and restraining common grace, kept within tolerable bounds. But still as to the substance of an unrenewed state, all in it are alike. They are *swine still*, whether *washed*, or *wallowing in the mire*, 2 Pet. ii. 22. till Christ's grace change them. 4. You that doubt that you are not in Christ's will for glory, can you bless him, and love him, for willing salvation to so many others? It is a sad supposition, I own. And I think it sinful for any to lay it down as to himself, that Christ hath no mind to save him. Yet sad suppositions laid close to the heart and conscience, do sometimes produce and draw forth some good thing that lay hid in the heart. Let me therefore argue with such. You fear, or conclude, that Christ hath no mind to save you, that he hath no thoughts of love to you. Well. Though this thought be sinful in all such that daily hear the voice of his love in the gospel, I would say to such, 1. Is it not righteous with him? Do you not own that you deserve not his love, and that you justly deserve his hatred? Proud quarrelling with his justice, is very unsuitable to a pleader for his mercy. 2. Is not this sad case very afflicting to your souls? Alas! many have bitter complaints in their mouths, when there is little sense in their hearts of that they complain of. Surely, ly, there are complaining hypocrites, as well as boasting hypocrites. 3. Is there any inclination in your spirits to admire, love, and praise Jesus Christ for saving so many? I am persuaded, (and that with good warrant from Christ's gospel), that person that admires Christ's grace in saving others, shall never be lost himself. Yea, there is some heavenly fire in this *smoking flax*, or *wick*, that tender-hearted Jesus *will not quench*, Isa. xlii. 3.; nor will he let the *many waters quench it, nor shall the floods drown it*, Cant. viii. 7. although they be the floods of hell.

Exhort. 3. Search and try whether you are in this will of Christ. Blessed be the Lord, that no man can know that he is not in Christ's will; yet any Christian may know that he is in it. It is a matter of the vastest concern, and calls for suitable diligence, 2 Pet. i. 10. Christ's prayer, and Christ's blood, are of the same extent; and both have an everlasting voice and virtue. This prayer of our Lord's was put up in the same night he was taken; and its force and virtue is still as great as when it was first uttered. So it is with the voice and virtue of his blood. It speaks to this day as precious things as when he shed it. Alas! our prayers have but little virtue and force when they are first put up, and that little is quickly spent; and were it not for *our Advocate with the Father*, 1 John ii. 1. they would all come to nothing, and never be more heard of. But it is far (O how far!) otherwise with Christ's prayers. They have infinite virtue when first put up, and that virtue is of eternal duration. Here we have our Lord praying to have all his people with him where he is. His prayers were always heard: John xi. 41, 42. *And Jesus lift up his eyes, and said, Father, I thank thee, that thou hast heard me; and I knew that thou heardst me always.* And surely he was heard in his last and main prayer for his own glory, and his people's blessedness, in this text. Christ did all the Father's will, in working out the redemption of the elect; and the Father will do do all the Son's will, in giving the bleſſings bought to the redeemed. It is then of the higheſt importance to us, to know we are in this will of Chriſt, that always is effected; and in this prayer of his, that is, hath been, and will ſurely be anſwered. And, for your help in this inquiry about your intereſt in Chriſt's will and prayer, I would look into this bleſſed chapter, and Chriſt's prayer in it; and from it ſhow you ſome marks of them Chriſt prays for; and let your conſciences judge of your intereſt in them.

Mark 1. Of them Chriſt prays for, is in ver. 6. *I have manifeſted thy name unto the men which thou gaveſt me out of the world.* Would ye know if you be in Chriſt's prayer and will? Then ſee if Chriſt hath manifeſted to you the Father's name. It is his work, and his only; Matth. xi. 27. *All things are delivered unto me of my Father: and no man knoweth the Son but the Father: neither knoweth any man the Father, ſave the Son, and he to whomſoever the Son will reveal him.* Now, what is the Father's name? Many think they know it, to whom Chriſt never revealed it. If you aſk them, if they know Chriſt's Father's name? they have a ready anſwer, Is he not the firſt perſon in the Trinity? Is he not God the Father, the Almighty, the Maker and Ruler of heaven and earth? Yes. But this is the name of God only, and that in general. The name of Chriſt's Father, is that name and diſcovery of God wherein he ſtands related to the Son, and the Son to the Father, with the power and virtue of this name; as in ver. 26. of this chapter, *And I have declared unto them thy name, and will declare it: that the love wherewith thou haſt loved me, may be in them, and I in them.* In comparing ver. 6. and ver. 26. I would remark two things. 1. One is in Chriſt's way of his expreſſing his work in revealing his Father's name to his people. In ver. 6. it is, *I have manifeſted;* in ver. 26. it is, *I have declared thy name.* But though there be ſmall difference in the Engliſh, there is a conſiderable one in the Greek;

as any acquainted with the original do know. I never looked on the inscription on Christ's cross, written by his enemies, in Hebrew, Greek, and Latin, as a warrant to preachers of Christ's gospel to stuff their sermons with shreds of those, or any strange tongues; nor that criticisms on the words in the original languages are proper for the pulpit: and if the preachers had as little pleasure in them, as the people have profit by them, they would be quickly laid aside. But sometimes the penury of the vulgar tongue doth not answer the fulness of the original; and in that case it must be supplied by farther explication; as in these two verses before, in ver. 6. and ver. 26. In ver. 6. our Lord tells the Father, that he had *manifested his name* to them; in ver. 26. that he had *declared his name* to them. As the words run in the English, they seem to us to be much the same; but as in the Greek, there is a remarkable difference. In ver. 6. Christ's *manifesting the Father's name to them*, respects the clear and glorious discoveries Christ had made to them of the Father's name in and by Christ's incarnation, words, and works. In ver. 26. his *declaring to them the Father's name*, respects the light and knowledge of the Father's name, which Christ had wrought, and was farther to work in them. The *manifesting*, speaks the discoveries of his Father's name that Christ made to them; the *declaring* it, speaks forth the fruit of the former in his disciples. It is as if he had said, " I have made thy name known " to them, I have made them know thy name; and " they do know it;" as he saith, ver. 25. 2. Another remark I make in comparing ver. 6. and ver. 26. is this, That the fruits and effects are the same in both. Whatever difference there is in the words expressing this work of Christ, the fruit produced thereby is the same. In ver. 6. the fruit is said to be in two. 1. *They have kept thy word;* expressing their faith and obedience. 2. *Now they have known that all things whatsoever thou hast given me, are of thee*, ver. 7. " My
" person

"person, my calling, my furniture, my words and "works, are all of thee." This they knew. And it seems to relate to what they say, chap. xvi. 29, 30. In ver. 26. the fruit of Christ's *declaring the Father's name to them*, is said to be, *That the love wherewith thou hast loved me, may be in them, and I in them.* The Father's name is a special discovery of the love of the Father unto his Son first, and then through the Son unto perishing sinners. See if you have had any thing of this. Christ teacheth the Father's name, and the Father teacheth Christ's name by his Spirit, when he draws men: John vi. 45. *Every man that hath heard, and hath learned of the Father, cometh unto me.*

Mark 2. Is in ver. 8. (And it is a sad thing if people cannot find their own name in no part of this prayer): *And I have given unto them the words which thou gavest me.* Search if Christ hath given you any of his words. He hath *the tongue of the learned* from the Father, Isa. l. 4. and useth it on all he saveth. We are saved by words; not by the words which men speak, but which Christ speaks: John vi. 68. *Lord, to whom shall we go? Thou hast the words of eternal life.* So here Christ saith, " I have given them these " words of love, and life, and power." Hath Christ at no time spoke to your heart, so as you have been made to say, *This is the voice of my beloved;* as Cant. ii. 8.? Men must hear Christ's voice, before they open the door to him, Rev. iii. 20. His voice makes the dead to hear, and live, John v. 25, 26.

Mark 3. Of one in Christ's prayer, is in ver. 14. 16. Such are not of the world, as Christ is not of the world. They are *in the world*, but *not of it;* as the apostle distinguisheth, 1 John ii. 19. speaking of apostates. They were for a while in the church, and with it; but never of it, as appeared by their apostasy from it. Our Lord was in the world, as never any man was. *He was in the world, and the world was made by him, and the world knew him not*, John i. 10. The world knew neither its Maker, nor Saviour. His people are in the world, but not of it. They have neither *the spirit of the world*, 1 Cor. ii. 12. nor their heart on it, nor their treasure and portion in it, Matth. vi. 21. There is something sown and planted in their hearts, that came from another world than this, and draws them to heaven as their home; and this world is but their passage and thorough-fare unto it. Are your hearts on heaven, and off this world? Conclude you are in Christ's prayer and will.

Mark 4. Christ prays for believers on him, ver. 20. Every one that can make out his faith in Christ, may lay claim to this prayer, (though he be but a weak believer), and to an interest in it.

5. *Lastly*, I shall give one mark in general from the whole prayer. Can you say Amen to all of it? Can you set your seal and Amen of faith and love to all that Christ prays for here? a hearty Amen to all Christ prays for his own glory, and the happiness of his body the church? Do you daily desire with the heart the same things that Christ here prayed for, especially as to this ver. 24.? When you hear Christ's desire of having his people with him where he is, doth your heart echo to it, " I would, O that I were " with thee where thou art!" If it be so, you have part and portion in this good matter. If Christ's will and thy will jump together for the same blessing, then art thou in Christ's prayer and will; and there will be a performance of the Lord, when he shall get all his will on thee, and thou all thy desires from him.

Exhort, 4. Believe on this blessed willer of salvation, and on this will. You are not called at first to believe your interest in Christ, and in his will to save you in particular: but you are, on the peril of your souls, to trust this Saviour with your salvation; and the rather, because of his declared ability and good-will to save. Saving faith in Christ, is not a bare assent unto any proposition of truth concerning Christ the Saviour; for that is but an act of the mind, and it is in devils and in many ungodly men: but it is an act
of

of the heart on the person of the Saviour. *Men believe with the heart unto righteousness*, Rom. x. 9, 10. It is a trust on this divine person, as revealed to us by his names in the gospel. So faith is called so oft *believing on his name*, John i. 12. 1 John iii. 23. There is one name of Christ in Isa. lxiii 1. *I that speak in righteousness, mighty to save;* where we have a taking description of the object of faith. All he speaks is true; and you may trust him, and take his word. And he can do all, any thing, every thing, in and about salvation, that a sinner can need to be done. He is *mighty to save*. Never did a sinner perish thro' Christ's want of might to save. Remember these two names of Christ in all your employing of him about your salvation. The truth of his saving word, and the might of his saving arm, ought never to be out of the eye of faith. How strong would faith grow in us if our faith did duly fix on both?

There is one scripture I would open a little to you to this purpose. It is a place well known, (O that it were as well used!), in 1 Tim. i. 15. *This is a faithful saying, and worthy of all acceptation, that Jesus Christ came into the world to save sinners, of whom I am chief.* A text that ought to be in the memory and heart of every Christian. There are three things in it that I would glance at, to show you what I drive at in pressing you to believe on this great willer of eternal life to his people. Here you have three things. 1. The sum of the gospel: *Christ came into the world to save sinners.* 2. Here is the commendation of the gospel: *It is a faithful saying, and worthy of all acceptation.* 3. Here is the believer's application of the gospel: *Of whom I am chief.*

1. We have a sum of the gospel: *Christ Jesus came into the world to save sinners.* In this short sum we have three things. 1. His name who is the Saviour, *Jesus Christ*, the Son of God. It looks rather like the devil's gospel, than God's gospel, that hath not Christ's name in it. 2. What this Saviour did:

He

He *came into the world*. Never did man come into the world but Jesus Christ. The first man and woman were made in the world by their great Maker; and all their posterity are *born in the world*, as Christ calls it, John xvi. 21. Only Christ *came into the world*. And this word comprehends, not only his incarnation, but all the work he did in the world, and all the entertainment he met with from God and man, angels and devils, when he was in the world. 3. His errand and business he came into the world for and upon: *To save sinners.* A strange errand, and a hard work! If there had been no sinners in the world, Christ had had nothing to do in the world. They therefore that deny themselves to be sinners, they do what they can to turn Christ out of his office of a Saviour. He came not to *condemn the world*, for that was past already, John iii. 17, 18.; neither did he *come to judge the world*, John xii. 47.; *but to save the world*. For at his second coming *he will judge the world*, Acts xvii. 31. There was never a sinless man in the world, but the first and second Adam. The first was such for a little time, and by his fall made all the world sinners. The *second man, the Lord from heaven*, (as 1 Cor. xv. 47.), was always sinless; and *by the sacrifice of himself, put away sin*, Heb. ix. 26. and saved sinners. How frequently did he assert, and prove it by word and deed, that this was his errand into, and his business in the world? How frequently did his enemies, the scribes and Pharisees, stumble at his person, doctrine, and kindness to sinners; and that because they neither knew him, nor his errand into the world? If he was gracious to sinners, they call him a *friend of publicans and sinners*, Matth. xi. 19.; if he forgave a sinner, as Matth. ix. 2. they say, *he blasphemeth*. When the great sinner approacheth him with faith and love, Luke vii. 39. even his host, that was no open enemy, (since he invited Christ to his house and table), yet *he spake within himself, saying, This man, if he were a prophet, would know who, and what*

what manner of woman this is that toucheth him: for she is a sinner. And belike he thought, if Christ had known it, he would not have suffered her to do so. Poor man! he doubted Christ's being a Prophet; but he had no thought of Christ's being God's great High Priest. Brethren, Christ is not changed from what he was when he was in this world, now he is in heaven. He hath the same kind heart to sinners, and the same business with them, to save them. And the world is not changed from what it was when he was in it. Christ's acts of grace to sinners, from the Father's right hand, are as much maligned by such as are ignorant of him, and enemies to him, this day, as what of this sort he did on earth, (when he was in their streets, fields, and houses), was maligned and reproached by the scribes and Pharisees. Men change in every age; but the seed of the serpent, the children of the devil, and the spirit of unbelief, never changes. And all that hath been, is, or shall be, in the world, of this enmity to Christ's grace to sinners, flows from mens gross ignorance of Christ's main business in the world.

Now, this was Christ's errand into the world, to save sinners. But how doth he save them? Some say, by shewing them the way of salvation, and by his doctrine, and by his example. The devil said this of Paul and Silas, Acts xvi. 17. *These men are the servants of the most high God, which shew unto us the way of salvation.* But who can think, that God sent his own Son, and that the Son came into the world, to do no more, than a prophet, an apostle, or an ordinary gospel-minister, doth, or can do? Some will tell you, that Christ saves sinners, by teaching and helping them to save themselves. What a gross perverting of the gospel is this? How plain is it, that Christ came not to help us to save ourselves, but to save us by himself? He alone did all the work, and he alone was able to do it. And the glory of saving is so rich a jewel in Christ's crown, that no man, without pride

and

and blasphemy, can offer to wear it. To be the Saviour of sinners, is Christ's property; and no creature in heaven or earth, can share in it. The holy angels are humble adorers of this name, and all the redeemed of the Lord are the happy partakers of the virtue of this name of Christ, Rev. v. 9,---14. The Papists will tell you, that Christ saveth sinners indeed by his death; but that all the application of the virtue of his death he hath left with the church; that he left Peter to be the head of the church; and that Peter left his power with his successors, the bishops of Rome. And, by those delusions, Antichrist hath usurped Christ's throne of salvation, and hath deceived the world, and damned it; and, instead of saving sinners, hath been *destroying the saints of the most high God*. Nothing but the wrath of God on despisers of Christ and his gospel, would have brought in, and kept up so long this abomination of desolation, 2 Thess. ii. 10, 12, 12. Rev. xiii. 8. and xvii. 8. But what saith Christ, and the apostles, about Christ's saving sinners? How plain is it, that he, and he alone, and by himself, doth all?

2. We have the commendation of this gospel: *This is a faithful saying, and worthy of all acceptation.* 1. The gospel is a *saying*, a *report*, Isa. liii. 1. Rom. x. 16. But it is a *testimony of God*, 1 Cor. ii. 1.; a *record of God*, 1 John v. 10, 11. *Faith comes by hearing* of it, Rom. x. 17.: and is built on this divine saying. 2. It is a *faithful saying;* because it is *the record that God giveth of his Son*, 1 John v. 10.; and it is given by *him that cannot lye*, Heb. vi. 18. Tit. i. 2. 3. This faithful saying is *worthy of all acceptation*. And this extends to all persons; all and every sinner should accept it: and also to the acceptation itself; it is worthy of all manner of acceptation; of all sorts, degrees, and measures of acceptation. No man is excepted, and no sort of acceptation is excluded. No man can exceed in his accepting of this saying. So that the apostle commends the gospel by two things,

that commend any saying of God or man. 1. It is true; and any man may trust it. 2. It is good; and every man should accept it.

3. We have the application of the gospel: *Of whom I am chief.* You and I make no doubt but that Paul was, when he wrote this, one of the greatest believers in Christ that ever was; and that from that faith he was one of the holiest men on earth; and that from both he was one of the humblest saints; (as strong faith, and true holiness, never fails of producing this effect): and therefore he saith, *Of whom I am chief.* He had said just before in verse 14. *The grace of our Lord Jesus Christ was exceeding abundant, with faith and love, which is in Christ Jesus.* Yet for all this grace he counts himself the chief of sinners. Why doth he say so? Surely, because he thought so. But why did he think so? I may say, Paul would never forget his own name, *chief sinner*, though he was not a condemned, but a pardoned sinner. But wherein lieth the force of this way of his applying the gospel to himself thus? The saying is general, *Christ came into the world to save sinners.* How could he say, *Of whom I am chief?* Did Christ come into the world to save all sinners? No: John ix. 39. *And Jesus said, For judgment* (or *discrimination*) *I am come into this world: that they which see not, might see; and that they which see,* (that think they see), *might be made blind.* Like what Simeon said of Christ, in Luke ii. 34. *Behold, this child is set for the fall and rising again of many in Israel;* and 1 Peter ii. 7, 8. Are all sinners alike? No. Well did Paul know it, who judged himself to be the greatest of sinners. But Paul applies it to himself warrantably thus, as any other sinner may. "Because Christ's
" business in the world is to save sinners, though I be
" the chief of sinners, I am but a sinner; and greater
" or smaller sinners are all one to Christ; his errand
" is for both sorts, and his saving skill is for both
" sorts. All diseases are alike to Christ's art. All

" of them are desperate, and incurable to any, but
" Christ; and all alike curable by him." Would
you know, then, by the example of this great sinner,
by the practice of this great believer, and by the teaching of this great apostle Paul, (whose heart and pen
was guided by the Holy Ghost), what faith in Jesus
Christ is, and in what manner you should act it? Then
do four things.

1 Take God's holy and righteous law, and read it,
and think on it with faith and fear, and sign it. Study
it in a clear light; and bring it to your conscience,
and your conscience unto it. When God's law, with
its spiritual light and power, and your conscience meet
together, it will fare with you as it did with Paul,
Rom. vii. 8, 9. *Without the law sin was dead. For I
was alive without the law once,* (and then he was dead
in sin): *but when the commandment came, sin revived,
and I died.* How could Paul be without the law, who
was so zealous a Pharisee? I may say, he was indeed
busy with the law, but the law was not busy with
him. He sought righteousness and life by the law;
and little dreamed, that sin and death would come upon him, when the law came to him. Now, when
you and the law meet thus, seal to the law and subscribe your name, " I am the chief transgressor of this
" law;" as Paul doth in Rom. vii. 12, 14 *Wherefore
the law is holy, and the commandment holy, and just,
and good. For we know that the law is spiritual: but
I am carnal, sold under sin.* The truly convinced sinner thinks well of God's law, while he thinks worst
of himself. He *speaketh not evil of the law, nor judgeth the law,* James i. 11. when he judgeth and condemns himself. One of these is in the heart of every
sinner: He either condemns God's law for its strictness, (as the wicked servant did his lord and master,
Matth. xxv. 24.); or he condemns himself for his sinful breaking of it. And if a sinner's conviction be not
found and thorough, then the poor sinner's heart is
divided; and his frame is made up of reflecting, partly

on

on the strictness and righteousness of God's law, and partly on some of his own breaches of it. But such a man is far from sealing the law with Paul's name, *the chief of sinners.* Nay, he can name and call many others, greater sinners than himself, as the Pharisee did, Luke xviii. 11.: not like the publican, ver 13. who, in his plea for mercy, calls himself, *me the sinner*, (so it should be read); " me the great, the sin-" gular sinner;" the same word, another Pharisee called the forgiven believer by, Luke vii. 39. If there be therefore any allowed grudge against God's law, and a readiness to judge other sinners greater sinners than yourselves, you are not like to write after Paul's copy.

2. Next, turn to the other side of the Bible, the gospel; and sign the same name, *chief of sinners*, to it also: *Christ came into the world to save sinners.* The greater the sinner be, the greater is his need of a Saviour; and the saving of the chief of sinners, brings the chief honour and glory to the Saviour. Therefore doth Paul both seal to the truth of the gospel-saying, and to its being worthy of all acceptation: he believes it, and welcomes it, as chief of sinners. And so must you, if you believe to the saving of the soul. Tho' there be greater and smaller sins and sinners; yet no man ever did, or can believe, as a little sinner. *Least,* and *less than the least of all saints*, we find in a great saint's mouth, Eph. iii. 8. But never did any true saint either think or call himself *a little sinner.* For as no man that seeth sin truly, can call any sin small or little; so no man that seeth himself to be a sinner really, can count himself a small or little sinner. Nor can it ever be, till there be a little law to break, a little God to offend, a little guilt to contract, and a little wrath to incur. All which are impossible to be, blasphemy to wish, and madness to expect.

3. Would ye put forth and act faith on Jesus Christ? Come to Jesus Christ on the same errand he came into the world for. He came into the world to save sin-

ners; come to Christ to be saved by him. This is believing. Christ came into the world, to get glory to his grace in saving sinners; and the believer comes to Christ, to give Christ employment in his calling of saving, and to get the benefit of his calling. A sinner's giving of Christ employment in his office of saving is proper believing. The physician came for the sick, to heal them; and the sick seek to the physician, that he may heal them, Matth. ix. 12, 13. *The great and good Shepherd of the sheep* (as he is called, John x. 11. and Heb. xiii. 20.) *came to seek and to save that which was lost*, Luke xix. 10. When he hath found them, and caught them in the arms of his love, and layeth them on the shoulders of his care and strength, as in Luke xv. 4, 5.; then they by faith, bleat, as it were, after his care and protection, till he bring them safe into the blessed fold in heaven, John x. 16. You may hear the blessed bleating of one of Christ's flock, Psalm cxix. 176. *I have gone astray like a lost sheep,* (as all his flock have done, Isa. liii. 6.), *seek thy servant.* And surely, when the shepherd seeks the stray sheep, and the stray sheep seeks the shepherd, they will quickly meet. If Christ come into the world to save sinners, and if sinners come to him, to be saved by him, he will save them, and they shall be saved by him.

4. *Lastly,* When you have given employment to Christ in his office of saving, leave it to him, and trust it with him. Are we commanded to *cast our burden upon the Lord,* Psalm lv. 22.? to *cast all our care upon him,* 1 Peter v. 7.? May we not, must we not cast our main care upon him? And is not *the keeping of our souls* our main care, 1 Peter iv. 19.? If we cast this care on Christ, must not we trust him quietly with it? It is a great, but common fault with many Christians; they say they cast their care upon him, when yet, through unbelief, they keep the burden still on themselves. Remember, that on thy casting thy burden

on the Lord by faith, if he take it not quite off thee, he will either take off the weight of thy burden, or he will make it as wings to thee in thy journey to heaven. How many can seal to this in their experience? Hast thou with thy heart committed thy greatest care of thy salvation to Jesus Christ? Then say in thy heart, "My main care is over; I have put it in a good, "strong, and sure hand." See how Naomi saith to Ruth, chap. iii. 18. *Sit down my daughter, until thou know how the matter will fall: for the man will not be in rest, until he hath finished the thing this day.* So say I, Sit down quietly, and with confidence: leave the care of thy salvation on Christ, for that is his province; and set about the work of thy salvation, for that is thine, wherein also he will help thee, Phil. ii. 12, 13. When you are once come to Christ, all your remaining duty is to abide in him, and bring forth fruit, John xv. 4, 5. But it is indeed a large one.

But, alas! for as plain as the call of faith is in the gospel, there are two thoughts in mens hearts that defeat all, and send thousands of gospel-hearers unto hell. 1. Some do not, will not believe, that they are sinners. Who think so? may ye say. I answer, All the secure world do think so. They may say, that they are sinners, as all are; and it may be some profane lips may swear it, as in that idle asseveration, *As I am a sinner.* But do they know what it is to be a sinner; what dreadful vileness is in a sinner; what a lothsome creature every sinner is in God's sight; and what wrath hangs over their heads, which will surely fall on them, unless mercy prevent it? Do men believe this as to themselves in particular? No, surely; as is undeniable by their backwardness to search their hearts and ways, their enmity against the searching light of God's word, and by their rebelling against any glances of light that force in themselves upon their conscience. They believe not that they are lost, undone

done sinners: and they cannot endure to be persuaded of so plain and damnable a condition. They will not own themselves to be sick, though a sovereign physician is at hand.

2. Even these, when awakened, or others to whom their being sinners is discovered with divine light and power, cannot be persuaded, that Christ hath any business with them, or that they should make application to him. Most of awakened sinners say and think, much as the devils did, Mark v. 7. *What have I to do with thee, Jesus, thou Son of the most high God? I adjure thee by God, that thou torment me not.* I may say, that the devil hath better cause and less sin in saying so, than an awakened sinner: for Jesus Christ came into the world to save sinners; but he came also *to destroy the works of the devil*, 1 John iii. 8. To awaken a secure sinner's conscience, and to speak peace to an awakened conscience, are proper and mighty works of God.

I would conclude at this time, with a few exhortations to some duties of believers, from this doctrine of Christ's willing of eternal life to all his people.

1. Mourn moderately for the death and departure of believers out of this world. They are well where they are, and far better than they were when here, Phil. i. 23.; and we shall quickly meet again, in a far better world than this. This last is the apostle's argument to the same duty, 1 Thess. iv. 13, 14. Yea, this Christ himself useth in comforting his disciples, in their sorrow for his own death, John xiv. 2. 3. And surely Christ's death was a more trying providence to his disciples, than ever any, or many, or all Christians death, can be to us. If the glorified spirits of saints above did hear and know the mournings of their friends whom they have left behind; would they not say, as Christ going to die said, *Weep not for us, but for yourselves, and for your children?* Luke xxiii. 28. (Christ had still a kind heart to children, and expressed

sed it when going to the cross). They would say, "Fools, do ye mourn for us, who are got beyond mourning? You will never be well, till you be with us. You are but mourning over the rotten rags of mortality, that we have cast off. You are but mourning over our tent, while we are in the King's palace. We could not be in both at once. Judge which is best. You are mourning over our grave when it is empty, as they did over the empty grave and grave-cloaths of our Lord, when he was risen, and alive for evermore," John xx. 5, 6, 7. and Matth, xxviii.

2. Pray moderately and modestly for the lives of believers. We should pray for their lives; we should thankfully own the Lord's mercy to them and us, when he answers our prayers, as Phil. ii. 27.: but yet we must pray with deep submission. It may be that Christ in heaven is desiring at that time to have them with him where he is, when we on earth are praying, that they may be kept with us where we are.

3. Learn to look Christian-like on your own death. Learn both to kiss death as a friend, and to defy it as an enemy, 1 Cor. xv. 55, 56, 57.; and to triumph over it, as conquered and destroyed by Christ, Heb. ii. 14. and abolished by Christ, 2 Tim. i. 10. You all know you must die. It is a more common than godly word with many, *As sure as death*. I would not have men talk much, when they think little, of death. Nor ought any think of dying, and going hence, without thinking whither they are going. But for believers, you know that death is that dark trance that you must pass through, in order to the fulfilling this prayer of Christ. You must cease to be where you are, before you can be with him where he is. This world, and your condition in it, must be mean and low in your eyes; and Christ's world, and that condition in which you shall be, when in it, must be high to your faith, ere you can look on going hence, without amazement. Therefore climb by faith, as

to the top of Pisgah, and take a large view of this good land of glory; as the type of it, Canaan, was, at God's command, beheld by Abraham, Gen. xiii. 14,-----17. though he was but a pilgrim in it, and did not possess it, but in his seed; and as it was beheld by Moses, Deut. iii. 27. xxxii. 52. and xxxiv. 1,----4.; though the sight of it was all, and possession was denied him. But it is not so with us, as to the true Canaan. All that behold it by faith, shall possess it; and this makes the beholding of it to be the more sweet to us.

I have commended this scripture to you, in 1 Tim. i. 15. specially to help and direct you in the work of faith. That which we should daily act, and that which we live by; that we should daily hear of, and that without wearying. As Christ hath no other business in the world, but to save sinners; so sinners should have no other business with Christ, but to believe on him. Remember and believe this truth, There is no thing a man can do with Christ, there is nothing a man can do for Christ, that can either please Christ, or profit the man, except he first trust Christ for salvation. The faith and trust of the heart on him for salvation, is the main service, and the first, he craveth. If a man shall pretend to worship, to obey and serve, yea to love Christ, and suffer for him; yet if he do not trust Christ by faith, all is a provocation to Christ, and all is unprofitable to the man. Believe this, you can do nothing that will please him, or save you, but trust in him. And if this faith were more diligently acted, all the blessed fruit of peace within, and sanctification, and holy walking, and patience in tribulation, would exceedingly abound in you, 2 Thess. i. 3, 4.

SERMON

John xvii. 24.

Father, I will that they also whom thou hast given me, be with me where I am; that they may behold my glory which thou hast given me: for thou lovedst me before the foundation of the world.

I Have spoke to the first two things in the matter of Christ's prayer in this verse. 1. His naming of the persons he prayed for: *Those which thou hast given me.* 2. His name of the blessing he prays for to them: *That they may also be with me where I am.* Christ would not be in heaven alone; he cannot be without his ransomed ones. He had sent many to heaven by his grace, before he came into the world, Acts xv. 11. He hath been still drawing multitudes of them, since he went back to heaven, John xii. 32. And he will shortly return again from heaven, to gather them all and every one, in soul and body, and carry them all home to his Father's house, John xiv. 2. 3.

It follows to speak of the *third* thing in the matter of this prayer. And that is, *The end for which Christ desires this blessing for those persons.* It is, *That they may behold my glory which thou hast given me.* Deep words! and deeper matter! What is rendered, *my glory*, is in the original, *the glory that is mine*, with a special emphasis. This being the main and deepest thing in these words, I must insist the more upon it.

There are three expressions in this prayer of Christ's glory. 1. In ver. 5. *The glory I had with thee before the world was.* This he prayeth for. This glory that the Son had from eternity with the Father,

ther, was that glory which he had as the eternal, natural, and essential Son of God, which far passeth created understanding. But now this Son of God had taken on man's nature, and in that nature had done his work of redemption, and fulfilled his Father's will and commission to him: (for our Lord speaks as if he had done all, when it was so near finishing): now, I say, when he is going again out of the world to his Father, as John xvi. 28. he prays, that he, as man, and successful Mediator, may be admitted to, and possessed of that glory, which he, as the Son of God, from eternity possessed with the Father; and which was not interrupted, but vailed only, in and by his humbled state on earth. But this is too deep for us; but well understood by him that prayed for it, and who hath been long possessed of it.

2. In ver. 22. We have another expression of Christ's glory: *And the glory which thou gavest me, I have given them.* This is another glory than the former. This was given to him by the Father, and given to his people by the Son. It was given to him, that it might be given to others by him; as his *receiving gifts for men*, Psal. lxviii. 18. is called his *giving gifts to men*, Eph. iv. 8. He received, that he might give. And great is Christ's glory, both in the fulness he received, and in his giving, and our receiving out of his fulness. All *fulness dwelleth in him*, Col. i. 19.; and all the receivings of his people are *out of that fulness*, John i. 16.

3. In our text we have the third expression of Christ's glory. And it is spoke of in three words. 1. It is *my glory;* " mine specially and properly." 2. It is *my glory which thou hast given me.* 3. It is a glory to *be beheld by his people.* And this is what I would speak unto.

This prayer of Christ, *that his people may behold his glory*, doth respect three things; which I would first dispatch.

1. It

1. It respects Christ's glory in itself. It wants (if I might say so) to be displayed and seen. This *Sun of Righteousness* (as he is called Mal. iv. 2.) wants a dark world to shine upon, and would have eyes to look to his glorious light. He calls men to behold him: Isa. lxvi. 1, 2. *I said, Behold me, behold me, unto a nation that was not called by my name.* He at last *will be glorified in his saints, and admired in all them that believe;* and he cometh in his glory for that end, 2 Thess. i. 10. And all he doth in and for his people, is, ver. 12. *That the name of our Lord Jesus Christ may be glorified in you, and ye in him, according to the grace of our God, and the Lord Jesus Christ.* What a vast difference is there betwixt the glory that Christ gives us, and the glory he gets from us! We have nothing to give; or if we had, and gave, we can add nothing to his glory; but he not only gives to us, and adds to us, but he is *all in all* to us, Col. iii. 11. Yet so gracious is he, that if you put a perishing soul into his hand to save, if you bring your vile sores to him to be healed, therein he will be glorified. Christ is honoured in his calling specially.

2. This word respects his people and their happiness. Not only is Christ glorified in his people's beholding of his glory, but in this beholding of it they are made happy. There was never a believer that ever had so large a faith, or a heart so enlarged and inflamed with love, as to be able fully to take up what warm love, and what a high and great design was in our Lord's heart in putting up this petition for them. Believers on Jesus Christ, make no doubt but that he means well for you. Great things are designed by him for you, and more than you can imagine, in this prayer for you, that *you may behold his glory when you are with him where he is.*

3. This word respects the eternal work and employment of his people, when they are with him where he is. If any ask, What shall they do? how

shall they be employed through the ages of eternity? Christ answers it here, *They shall behold my glory;* work that they shall never come to an end of; work they shall never weary in; and work that they shall have as little mind to weary of, as they shall have cause or reason to be weary in: for every view of his glory will dart in fresh bliss unto the beholders of it.

There are two things to be discoursed on from this part of the text. 1. What is the glory of Christ given to him to be beheld in heaven? 2. What is the beholding of this glory by his people in heaven?

I shall not enter on any of them this day; but would prepare your hearts to think of them. These two questions, *What Christ's glory is?* and, *What the beholding of it in heaven is?* are neither of them to be fully answered in this life. Christ's glory would be but a small glory, if either the heart of man could conceive it fully, or the tongue of man could express it all. If the glory that Christ hath prepared for his people be such as 1 Cor. ii. 9. how much more must Christ's own glory be? There was a man as able to tell as ever any was; and that was Paul. He had been long exercised in the study of Christ, and in preaching of him: yet he, when an old man, and in bonds for Christ, Eph. vi. 20. speaks thus, Eph. iii. 8. *Unto me, who am less than the least of all saints, is this grace given, that I should preach among the Gentiles the unsearchable riches of Christ.* And surely the riches of Christ are both those riches of grace and glory that he is possessed of, and the riches that he enricheth his people with here and in heaven. Is not this a strange text? and is it not a strange preaching that is made on an unsearchable theme? Yet for all he knew, and for all he taught, Christ's riches were still unsearchable even to Paul; though it is just to think, that he did dive deeper in them than any man since. Christ's riches, in Paul's eyes, were like a vast heap of gold, that no man could count; or like the

the vaſt ocean, whoſe drops none can meaſure or tell: and Paul did preach them the better that he ſaw them to be unſearchable. But if this man ſhould be caught up to heaven, and come again to the earth, would he not be able to tell ſtrange things then? So it was with Paul, 2 Corinth. xii. 1,----7. But what ſaith he of it? verſe 4. *He heard unſpeakable words, which it is not lawful for a man to utter.* Any Chriſtian may ſafely think, that though there be a vail caſt on theſe *viſions and revelations of the Lord* to Paul, as he calls them, verſe 1. yet the main thing revealed, was the glory of Chriſt. But it was revealed in ſuch a light, as was not fit to ſhine on earth; and therefore the apoſtle ſaith no more of it, but only tells us what he felt after it; both his great danger, and his ſharp cure, ver. 7, 8, 9.

But though Chriſt's glory in heaven, and the beholding of it, be things within the vail, and cannot be fully known by us till we be there; yet we muſt not lay aſide all thoughts and inquiries about them while we are here. There are means and ways that God hath appointed, that we ſhould uſe for knowing them. By his bleſſing ſome knowledge of them is got: and this knowledge is neceſſary to all, and of great advantage to them that attain it.

I would therefore give you a few things more remotely about this great ſubject.

1. There is a diſcovery made to us in the word of the glory of Chriſt. And there only are we to ſtudy it. It is the glory of the written word of God, that the glory of Chriſt is revealed in it, and to us only in and by it. We muſt not ſtudy to know Chriſt, we muſt not ſearch into his glory, but in that light. There are three ways that ſome uſe, that are vain and unprofitable. 1. One is, by the works of God's creation and providence, Pſalm xix. 1,---7. Theſe do diſcover plainly the *being* of God, and *his eternal power and godhead*, Rom. i. 20. and declare his wiſdom and goodneſs. But nothing of Chriſt's glory is, or can be

learned

learned in and by the old creation. Such as talk of a gospel preached to the heathen by sun, moon, and stars, give them an office their Creator never made them for, or put them in. And if they that teach such doctrine, pretend to be Christians, surely they must have both a low and a false scheme of *the glorious gospel of the blessed God*, as it is called, 1 Tim. i. 11. 2. Another way is, by mens wisdom. That noble power in man is quite dark, and dull, and blind, about Christ and his glory. It can do somewhat in its own sphere and orb; it can search into the earth and mount up to heaven, and can contemplate God's glorious works. But it can never find out Jesus Christ nor see his glory: 1 Cor. i. 20, 21. *Hath not God made foolish the wisdom of this world? for after that, in the wisdom of God, the world by wisdom knew not God,* (that is, savingly), *it pleased God by the foolishness of preaching to save them that believe.* The gospel is *the hidden wisdom of God in a mystery,* 1 Cor. ii. 7; and the substance of it, Christ, is the main and greatest part of this mystery, 1 Tim. iii. 16. Both these are weak, vain means to know Christ by. 3. There is another way, that is not only unprofitable, but wicked; and that is the way of idolatry. And the whole of Popery is of this sort. They use many crafty devices to discover Christ's glory to the blind people. They have pictures of Christ, as on the breasts, as on the cross, as in glory in heaven. But instead of making Christ's glory known to men, they, by these cursed devices, darken his glory, disgrace the Lord Christ, *crucify him afresh, and put him to an open shame.*

The word of God then is the only light in which Christ's glory shineth; and in this only light must we inquire into it. In other matters, there are many truths and things that are demonstrable by nature's light, as well as they are asserted in the word of God. But about Christ and his glory, nature's light, God's works of creation, and man's natural wisdom, can give no help; and therefore we should not call in their assistance. It is only God's word that can help in this great inquiry, and it we should use.

2. The only eye wherewith Christ and his glory can be seen, is the eye of faith. The only mental eye by which the spiritual glory of Christ can only be seen, is faith. *Faith* is sometimes opposed to *sight*, as *sight* is taken for full enjoyment, 2 Cor. v. 7.; and *faith* is sometimes expressed by *sight*, as *faith* is a real apprehending of its object; as Heb. xi. 1, 13, 27. 2 Cor. iii. 18. and iv. 18. and in innumerable places, both in the old and new testament. And this eye is simply needful, even where the light of God's word shineth most. The Jews had the old testament; and yet knew not Christ, and saw no glory in him, as was foretold of them, Isa. liii. 2, 3. They saw him, and yet believed not, but hated him. So it is with all men to whom the gospel cometh, until faith be given. No eye but that of faith, can see and take up Christ and his glory; for two causes. 1. Christ and his glory is out of our sight now. And, 2. It is always beyond the reach of any power in us, but faith given by God. Christ's glory did once pass before mens eyes; but none saw it but believers, John i. 14. and 1 John i. 1, 2. Could any thing but faith take up Christ's *glory, as of the only begotten of the Father, full of grace and truth?*. Could any but a believer see him, and call him *eternal life*, when he was made of no reputation? At the last day Christ and his glory will make a great appearance, *when he comes in his glory, and sits on the throne of his glory*, Matt. xxv. 31. But at that day (though all the nations be gathered together) there will be no faith, neither on his right nor left hand. What a strange word is this? and what a strange day will that be? All the saved will have no faith, nor have any need of it, nor use of it. Sight and love puts an end to their faith. And all the damned shall be no more unbelievers; for sight and fear of Christ's glory will eternally remove their unbelief;

belief: Rev. i. 7. *Behold, he cometh with clouds; and every eye shall see him, and they also that pierced him: and all kindreds of the earth shall wail because of him; even so, Amen.* But from Christ's going to heaven, till his return to judge the world, faith is the only eye that can savingly take up Christ and his glory.

3. This eye of faith is only of Christ's giving. No man is born with it; it grows up in no man by nature; no means, nor minister, nor any creature, can give it. It is only Christ's gift; it is by his Spirit, Eph. i. 17, 18.; it is the fruit of his *eye-salve*, Rev. iii. 18. All men are darkness, till made *light in the Lord*, Eph. v. 8. There are two things always done by Christ together, when he works faith. 1. He manifests and reveals himself, and, 2. Gives an eye to see him and his glory. No man can see Christ by his own power, nor can he see Christ against Christ's will: *If he hide himself, who then can behold him!* Job xxxiv. 29. If the sun shine, and the man have eyes, and them opened, he doth and must see, and never until then.

4. This eye of faith that Christ giveth, is of great advantage and use to them that receive it; as 1 John v. 20. *And we know that the Son of God is come*, (how do you know it?), *and hath given us an understanding that we may know him that he is true;* (that understanding, and the knowing of Christ, is faith): *and we are in him that is true, even in his Son Jesus Christ. This is the true God, and eternal life.* I would name some advantages that attend the gift of faith, to the praise of the giver, and the profit of the receivers of this gift.

1*st*, The first life comes in this way. When Christ works faith in the heart, the new life is begun in the soul. The man that gets faith, and is made a believer, *hath everlasting life, and shall not come into condemnation; but is passed from death unto life*, John v. 24.: and this life is from *the hearing of the voice of the Son*

Son of God; and they that hear, shall live, verse 25. Christ hath a voice to send forth, that can make the born deaf hear, and the dead live. But how is it in the acting of this faith wrought by Christ? We have a notable place for this in John iii. 14, 15. *And as Moses lifted up the serpent in the wilderness, even so must the Son of man be lifted up: that whosoever believeth in him, should not perish, but have eternal life.* Our Lord is here teaching Nicodemus, a weak but honest beginner: and he teacheth him wisely, and teacheth him great things. He teacheth the corruption of nature, the absolute necessity of regeneration; that this regeneration is from the Holy Spirit of God, who therein works sovereignly, secretly, and effectually. He then preacheth himself to him, as he that came down from heaven, and was in heaven, ver. 13. He did not understand Christ's doctrine of regeneration: Christ puts him to greater mysteries about his person, and his mission from heaven. We may think, that he that said about the former, *How can these things be?* might be more puzzled to know how Christ was to save sinners, and how they were to use him for salvation. Both these Christ teacheth him in ver. 14, 15. and more fully afterwards in that chapter to ver. 22. And this he doth by a type, that no Israelite was ignorant of, tho' few masters in Israel did rightly understand it. The plain and full sense of it is this: As Moses (at God's command and appointment lifted up the brazen serpent in the wilderness, that every Israelite stung by the fiery serpents, might look to it and live, as in Numb. xxi. 6,---9.; so Christ, the Son of man is lifted up upon the cross, that every sinner stung by sin, and the curse of God's law, might look to him by faith, and live for ever. The Israelites were to use the lifted-up serpent, by looking on it, as the only ordinance of God for their healing; and were to use neither salve nor plaister for the fiery serpent's deadly stings. So the stung sinner must use a crucified Christ, as the only ordinance of God for life, and eternal life; and that life comes to him only by this look of faith.

2*dly*, All the believers growth and increase in grace and life, is by believing beholding of the grace and glory of Christ. When the apostle is exhorting to growth in grace, as the sure preservative against apostasy, 2 Peter iii. 18. he adds, *Grow in the knowledge of our Lord and Saviour Jesus Christ.* As if he had said, " If you would grow in grace, you must also " grow in the knowledge of Christ." Yea, when he is speaking of the greatest attainments in grace, 2 Pet. i. 8. he tells this is the fruit of them; *They make you that ye shall neither be barren nor unfruitful in the knowledge of our Lord Jesus Christ.* But more directly Paul teacheth us, how faith advanceth the Christian in his new life; 2 Cor. iii. 18. *But we all with open face, beholding as in a glass the glory of the Lord, are changed into the same image, from glory to glory, even as by the Spirit of the Lord. We all :* it is not only I Paul, whom you may think singularly priviledged: but all we, who, under the dispensation of the gospel, have had the vail taken off our hearts and eyes, we all behold the same glory of Christ, and with the same sort of fruit. Though we do not all behold it in the same clearness and brightness, nor with the same measure of fruit; yet all that do truly behold his glory, are truly made comformable to him. If no likeness to Christ's image be wrought in you, you make it to be justly suspected, that it is either not the right Lord you behold, or not the right eye you behold him with, or that it is not a right glass you behold him in. For where all three are right, the fruit of likeness to Christ never faileth.

3*dly*, All the peace, and comfort, and joy of heart, which believers have in this life, come in by believing beholding of Christ, and of his grace and glory. Joy and peace fills the heart by believing, Rom. xv. 13. What can distress a believer when Christ's glory is seen? and what can quiet his heart, when a dark cloud

cloud and vail is on his glory? No storm can be on a Christian, and no fear can disquiet him so, but that word spoke with Christ's power will comfort, Matth. xiv. 27. *Be of good cheer, it is I, be not afraid.* Thus were they made to *rejoice with joy unspeakable and full of glory, who loved him, and believed on him they had not seen*, 1 Peter i. 8.

So much for this fourth thing, That the eye of faith and its exercise is of great advantage to a Christian.

5. The beholding of the glory of Christ by the eye of faith, is the greatest and surest test of mens state that can be. They that have it, are true Christians; for thus are they made such; as 1 John v. 20. They that never saw Christ's glory, remain still in the pit of condemned nature, where darkness and death do rule.

6. and *lastly*, The beholding of Christ's glory by faith, as it is revealed in the gospel, is a good help to understand what the beholding of his glory in heaven is: for it is the same Christ, the same glory of Christ, that is beheld in earth and in heaven. Only this glory shines in another manner in heaven, and is beheld with another and higher eye than faith; though faith is the best eye, and the gospel the best glass, on earth. On this I would shew how impossible it is, that an unbeliever that never saw Christ's glory in the gospel, can have any right apprehension of the beholding his glory in heaven.

1*st*, Consider what heaven is, The Lord of it tells us, it is in *being with him where he is*. Now, that man that never knew what Christ's company on earth is, can never know what his company in heaven is. Speak to him of heaven, as a state of rest and happiness, where no crosses, nor death, nor trouble, can be; this the natural man can know and relish. But Christ's true heaven, and Christ's picture of it in the word, are as dark and disgustful to an unbeliever, as Christ's yoke and burthen is. But to a believer, *whom the Lord hath chosen, and caused to approach to him*, Psal. lxv. 4.; who hath been oft made to say, Psalm. lxxiii. 28. *It is good for me to draw near to God;* and can say, as 1 John i. 3. *Truly our fellowship is with the Father, and with his Son Jesus Christ:* to such, I say, *being with Christ where he is*, hath another light in his mind, and another gust in his heart.

2dly, The work of heaven, to behold Christ's glory cannot be understood by an unbeliever, no more than a born blind man can know what pleasure and profit is in beholding the glory and light of the sun. And if such would and could search their hearts, they would find; and if they were ingenuous, they would own the truth, (as some of them in blasphemy do say), that the gospel-discovery of heaven is dark and disgustful to them; they neither know it nor love it. It is hid from their blinded eyes, and cross to their carnal hearts.

3dly, They know not the title to heaven; how a man comes by a right to it, and enters into the possession of it. And that is, by free grace in Jesus Christ. And this is no small part of Christ's glory, and of believers happiness, that it is so. This title is only to be perceived by faith. The same grace that we owe the forgiveness of sin to, we owe the possessing of glory to, Acts xxvi. 18. By that same grace that we are welcomed to Christ's house of grace on earth, Rom. v. 2. by the same grace we are welcomed into Christ's house of glory above. It is *grace brought to us*, 1 Peter i. 12.; it is *the mercy of our Lord Jesus Christ unto eternal life*, Jude, ver. 21. But an unbeliever, who hath no knowledge nor relish of this blessed tenure to glory by free grace, what fit and right thoughts can he have of heaven? All men are by nature ignorant of the true heaven, of the true way to it, of the true work and bliss in it, and of the only title to it, and tenure of it; and therefore need what the apostle prays for in Eph. i. 17, 18, 19.

APPLI-

APPLICATION. Although you may think it preposterous, to speak any thing in application, before we enter upon the doctrine itself; yet, as what hath been said, is but introductory to what I intend (if the Lord will) further to speak on this great subject, so what I say now in application, shall be accordingly managed.

The text we have before us, is about the beholding of Christ's glory in heaven. I have been shewing you, that it is simply necessary to any right understanding of this great bliss, that a man do know in his experience somewhat of the beholding of Christ's glory by faith in this life. Without this, no words that men can speak about this, can be understood by natural men: 1 Cor. ii. 14. *For the natural man receiveth not the things of the Spirit of God; for they are foolishness unto him: neither can he know them, for they are spiritually discerned.* I may truly say, that no natural man doth, or can understand this verse. It is grievous and shameful, to see and read what blundering confused work many wise and learned men, but destitute of that mind and Spirit of Christ that led Paul in writing of it, make of this verse; when it is plain and bright, though deep, to every ordinary Christian. Now, the glory of Christ, and the beholding of it, are of the deepest of *the deep things of God*, ver. 10. How then can a natural man receive them, know them, or discern them? He is without that spiritual faculty by which only they can be rightly entertained. It is a dangerous and hurtful practice to the church of God, and to the souls of men, and to the truths of God, (and not a few are guilty of it, and many smart by it), for men to endeavour to bring down the deep mysteries of the gospel unto the sense and gust of a natural unrenewed man. It is sure, that they that teach, should teach plainly; and they that write, should make *the vision plain, that he may run that readeth it,* Hab. ii. 2. But they must still *speak*, or write, *as the oracles of God,*

God, 1 Pet. iv. 11. and as *stewards of the mysteries of God*, 1 Cor. iv. 1. If, as it is undoubted, we cannot bring up the natural man's understanding unto the deep things of God; we must not essay to bring down the depths of God unto their natural blindness. This were to degrade the things of the Spirit of God, and to delude the sinner. But let us study to declare God's mind in his word, as plainly as we can, to natural men that hear us; and withal tell them, that the things themselves, of which we speak as plainly as we can, are beyond their reach; that they may know that the things of God are deep, and they themselves are blind, till the Spirit of Christ *open the understanding*, and *open the scriptures* unto them; as he did to his disciples, Luke xxiv. 32. and 45.

My work at this time shall be, to offer you some helps to try yourselves, and to find this out, Whether ever you have beheld the glory of Christ in the gospel? You have the gospel-glass, and most of you think you have the eye of faith also. My question that I put your consciences, is, Have you seen his glory in the gospel by faith? If you have, then you will find three things.

1. Where-ever Christ's glory is seen by faith, it is always seen as singular, transcendent, and matchless. So it is in itself, and so it is seen by all that do behold it. Paul calls his knowledge of Christ, *the excellency of the knowledge of Jesus Christ my Lord*, Phil. iii. 8. And that you may not think that he thought he had a great deal of it, and that you might know that Paul is rather commending Christ's excellency, than the measure of his attainments in the knowledge of Christ; he tells us in ver. 10,----14. how small an opinion he had of what he had attained, in respect of what he wanted, and followed, and pressed after. If ever you had a true view of Christ's glory, you will judge, that there is no glory like it. What you formerly thought glorious, you will then say of it, as 2 Cor. iii. 10. *For even that which was made*

made glorious, had no glory in this respect, because of the glory that excelleth. And the apostle is there speaking of the most outwardly glorious appearance that ever God made in the world, in giving the law. And as he saith again, of that that is most glorious in the eyes of one that knows not Christ, his own righteousness, in Phil. iii. 8, 9. he calls it, and all things else, *loss and dung*, compared with Christ. And so will every man that seeth Christ with any thing of Paul's eye. For illustration: Suppose a man blind from the womb, had his eye-sight given him by God, as it were in John ix. ; suppose that his sight were given him in the night, and in the house, he would doubtless wonder at the light of candles: but if he went abroad, and saw the stars in the firmament, or if the moon did shine, this would be more glorious still: yet when the morning dawneth, and when the sun riseth and shineth, would not the man think, " Surely I never saw such a glorious " light before?" Fire and candles on earth, and moon and stars in heaven, have no such light as the sun. So will it be unto them to whom *the Sun of Righteousness ariseth with healing in his wings*, Mal. iv. 2. with salvation in his beams. He will say, " No " glory like Christ's glory, no man like him; no an- " gel, no creature, like him." If Christ's glory hath not disgraced all other glory save his own, you have either seen little of it, or none at all.

2. When the glory of Christ is seen by faith, desires of seeing more of it rise in the heart. What the preacher saith in general about seeing in Eccl. i. 8. *The eye is not satisfied with seeing*, is justly applicable to this spiritual eye in beholding Christ's glory. It is not satisfied, nor ever will, till the believer is with Christ where he is, and beholds his glory there. Paul had many and singular views of Christ's glory, and yet is studying Christ still. If you knew Christ as well as Paul did, you would be of his mind; yes,

if you have any right beholding of his glory, you will still desire more.

3. He that beholds Christ's glory truly, he perceives his own darkness and blindness, and is humbled thereby. You may think this a strange mark; but it is a sure one. It is strange, but most true, that an unbeliever, who *hath never heard Christ's voice, nor seen his shape,* (as Christ saith to the Jews concerning his Father, John v. 27.), may, and many of them do think, that they know Christ, and many say, as Hos. viii. 2. *My God, we know thee;* " My " Saviour, I know thee;" when a true beholder of Christ's glory thinks, that he doth not know him at all, or next to nothing. And those thoughts are proofs, that the one is quite ignorant of Christ, and that the other is begun to know him. What the apostle saith, 1 Cor. viii. 2. *If any man think that he knoweth any thing, he knoweth nothing yet as he ought to know,* holds good specially in the knowledge of Christ. A proud conceit of a man's knowing Christ, is a demonstration that the man never saw his glory. Even as if a man should say, " I have seen the sun " in his noon-day glory, and I can stare upon it stea-" dily." Would not any man think, that either this man hath not right eyes, or that he hath not seen the right sun, but only a picture of it, that hath or can have nothing of the true sun's light, and heat, and influence; or that the man lyeth grosly? for all know, that the glory of the sun is too great and bright for the sharpest and strongest eye. When a man from the top of a high mountain looks round about him, he can see many miles, and many things, If this man have high thoughts of his eyes and sight, you cure him, or he cures himself, of that fancy, by trying his sight with the sun; then he seeth what a disproportionate faculty his eye is to this glorious object. So is it with men when they approach Christ's glory; then their darkness and blindness is discovered. As *in his light we see light,* Psal. xxxvi. 9. so by

and

and in this light we see our own darkness. A very wise and good man said, in Prov. xxx. 2, 3, 4. *Surely I am more brutish than any man, and have not the understanding of a man. I neither learned wisdom, nor have (or know) the knowledge of the holy.----What is his name, and what is his son's name, if thou canst tell?* It is impossible, that any ray and beam of Christ's glory can be rightly taken up by the eye of faith, but the beholder of it is humbled by the sight of it. And the brighter the discovery be, the more humble will it make the man to be. Perfect humility is only in heaven, where the perfect discovery of Christ's glory is made by him, and got by the inhabitants. What said Isaiah, *when he saw his glory, and spake of him,* John xii. 41.? *Wo is me, for I am undone,* Isa. vi. 5. Why undone? *Because I am unclean, and have seen the King, the Lord of hosts.* What did the beloved disciple when he had a vision of Christ's glory? *When I saw him, I fell at his feet as dead;* and he might have died quite at the sight, unless Christ had laid his right hand upon him, and spoke comfortably to him, Rev. i. 17, 18. What was the fruit of Job's *seeing of the Lord with the seeing of the eye,* far beyond all he had heard by *the hearing of the ear?* Was not this the fruit and effect of it, *Wherefore I abhor myself, and repent in dust and ashes?* Job xlii. 5, 6. Thus will it be with you, if you obtain any true discoveries of Christ's glory.

VOL. II.   T   SERMON

SERMON IX.

JOHN xvii. 24.

Father, I will that they also whom thou hast given me, be with me where I am; that they may behold my glory which thou hast given me: for thou lovedst me before the foundation of the world.

THERE is no greater theme in earth, nor in heaven, than the glory of Christ. There is no higher enjoyment here, nor above, than the beholding of this glory. Yet all the Lord's chosen shall surely partake of it, for here Christ prays for it. In explaining Christ's words in his prayer for that blessing, I proposed to speak to two things: What is Christ's glory; and, What is the beholding of it.

Before I enter upon either of them, there are yet three things I would observe from the connection and scope of these words, *I will that they be with me where I am, that they may behold my glory which thou hast given me.*

Obs. 1. Christ's presence, and his people's beholding of his glory, go still together. So it is on earth, so it is in heaven. When is it that a man begins to see any of Christ's glory, but when he is drawn to Christ? when Christ draws near to him, and manifests himself to him? Time was when Paul saw nothing of Christ's glory; he heard of him, and hated him, and persecuted him: but all this was from his *ignorance and unbelief*, 1 Tim. ii. 13. When he was first charged by Christ for his evil way, Acts ix. 4, 5. no wonder that his first word was, *Who art thou Lord?* " I do " not know thee, I never knew that I did thee any " wrong."

"wrong." But when once Christ reveals himself unto him, immediately he saw Christ's glory, and made it his all. So it is with all natural men, till Christ draw near to them, and bring them near to him savingly: Christ *hath no form or comeliness; and when they see* (or hear of) *him, there is no beauty that they should desire him,* Isa. liii. 2. This is as true of them that hear of, and see Christ crucified in the gospellight, Gal. iii. 1. as of the Jews that saw his humbled state on earth. They wonder what men see in Jesus Christ; what glory in him they behold by faith; what believers mean, when they say, as Cant. iv. 16. *His mouth is most sweet; yea, he is altogether lovely. This is my beloved, and this is my friend, O daughters of Jerusalem.* If you had ever heard his voice, or seen his face, you would know him from all the men on earth, or gods in heaven, (if I may say so). But, alas! there are many that bear the name of Christians, (and God knows well, and men may know pretty well also, how little they deserve that name), that never saw so much glory and desirableness in Jesus Christ, as they see in a heap of the white and yellow dust of the earth. They cannot afford a good word or thought to the Jews, (and justly), who did prefer Barabbas to Christ, when themselves daily do the like, in preferring the satisfying of their vile lusts unto the enjoyment of Christ's company. And what the Jews did, they do, from the same cause, (and a sad and sinful one it is). They neither of them did, or do see any thing of Christ's glory. He is far from them, they *know him not,* 1 Cor. ii. 8.; he hath not manifested himself unto them. This truth appears also, as in the beginning, so in the progress of Christianity. If the Christian *grows in grace,* it is also *in the knowledge of Christ,* 2 Pet. iii. 18. If the new creature grows, it is by and under the beams and shinings of *the Sun of Righteousness,* Mal. iv. 2. All gospel institutions are for this end, (and when blessed, reach it), Eph. iv. 13. *Till we all come in* (or *into*) *the unity of the faith, and of the knowledge of the Son of God, unto a perfect man, unto the measure of the stature of the fulness of Christ.* Every Christian's experience bears witness to this. Do you not sometimes see more of Christ's glory than at other times? Is not the light brighter, and your faith more quick and active? And when is it so, but when Christ draws nearer to you, and you are brought nearer to him, than usually? But for such poor creatures, that know nothing of Christ's presence with, or absence from them, save in and by his ordinances and providences, (in which also a true believer may find Christ's special presence, though others do not, nor can); I say not, that such do see more of Christ's glory, but rather that they never saw any of it. They *are blind, and cannot see afar off,* 2 Pet. i. 9. Christ is far from them, and they from him: he hath not yet looked on them in love, nor have they looked on him by faith. But for true Christians, if you should ask the question, When did you see most of Christ's glory? all would answer, That though it be little that ever they did behold of it, yet the best sight ever they had, was when he drew nearest to them; then he displayed his glory, and then they beheld it. And it may be that he did so, and they found it, when they were in the deep dungeon, in darkness and distress. No case is a believer brought into, but Christ's love will visit him in it; and the darker the place be, his sunshine is both the more needful, and the more glorious: Micah. vii. 8. *When I sit in darkness, the Lord shall be a light unto me.* Not only *will he bring me forth to the light, and I shall behold his righteousness,* as ver. 9.; but *when,* and while *I sit in darkness, the Lord will be a light to me;* and *enlighten my darkness,* as David sings by faith, Psal. xviii. 28. and thousands have felt it. So that it is undoubted, that most of Christ's glory is seen when he is nearest his people.

Thus also it is in the state of saints in heaven. They are brought near to Christ: they are *with him where he is*, and therefore *behold his glory*, and all above what we can conceive. Christians labour here under many humbling things within and without. They would fain see more of Christ's glory; they pray as Moses did, Exod. xxxiii. 18. *I beseech thee shew me thy glory.* But yet they cannot behold it as fain they would. Why? Because they cannot be so near to Christ as they would; and he will not draw so near to them as they would, while they are where they are, and not yet where he is. The greatest nearness to Christ, and the greatest visions of his glory, are both reserved for his people, when they shall possess *the inheritance of the saints in light*, Col. i. 12.

Obs. 2. Our Lord Jesus Christ is truly willing that his glory should be beheld by his people. He prays here for it in an extraordinary manner, *I will* it. Christ is a great deal better pleased, and more desirous, that his glory should be beheld by his people, than they are either willing or able to behold it. He hath a good mind to be looked upon, when he speaks so in Isa. xlv. 22. *Look unto me, and be ye saved, all the ends of the earth; for I am God, and there is none else; a just God and a Saviour,* ver. 21. (None can save a sinner, but a God. A mere man-saviour can save no sinner: and there is no God-saviour, but our Lord Jesus Christ, who is *over all, God blessed for ever,* Rom. ix. 5.). Christ is here calling men to look on him for salvation. Look to Christ, and you will see salvation in his heart and eye, and salvation will dart in upon your heart and soul. The brazen serpent was set up to be looked on by Israel. Though it could not speak, it could heal by God's ordinance. But the antitype, Jesus Christ, can both heal and speak; and the power of his voice can, and always doth give eyes to the man, and salvation by looking. It makes the *dead both to hear, and live,* John v. 25. Again, in Isaiah lxv. 1. he saith, *Behold me, behold me, unto a nation that was not called by my name.* Some quarrellers may say, If Christ be so willing to have his glory to be be beheld by men, why doth he not display his glory, and give all men eyes to see it by? I answer, That though this cavil savours of an ungodly, unhumbled heart; yet there are a few things that may stop such mouths. 1. It is a wonder of grace that he doth so to any: and they all admire it that do partake of it. Thomas seems to admire it, John xiv. 22. It were more hopeful work, and fitter for such, to admire that free grace falls on any, than to murmur and grumble that it passeth by so many. 2. Would you have this great blessing? have you sought it humbly and earnestly? have you turned his gracious call and promise into an earnest prayer? He saith to you, *Look to me, and be thou saved;* answer it, *Lord, look on me, and save me.* A better man than any of us prayed so, Psalm cxix. 132. *Look thou upon me, and be merciful unto me, as thou usest to do unto those that love thy name:* and to the same purpose more largely in Psalm cvi. 4, 5. Must not that man be both wicked and unreasonable, that quarrels with God for not giving that grace that himself is unwilling to receive, is careless to ask, and strives against with all his might? But nothing will fully stop the mouths of cavillers against free grace, but either some taste of this grace, or the judgment of the last day, *Out of their own mouth they shall be judged* by the Lord, Luke xix. 22.

But even Christians themselves are apt to say, That if Christ be so willing to have his glory to be beheld by his people, why then doth he stand so far off? why doth he hide himself so long? why do I pray, and am not heard? If he would as earnestly have it beheld, as I would fain behold it, why is this distance and darkness so long continued? We have many such complaints from eminent saints in the word, and they are too common in all times. We experience more the tremblings of unbelief in scripture-saints, than the vigour of their faith. The infirmities of saints are recorded in the word for our humbling and warning; and their graces for our imitation and encouragement.

Unto

Unto such honest complainers I would say, 1. That this mood cometh on you from the remnants of that natural enmity to the glory of his grace; which enmity, though it was subdued in its power in you, in the day of his power on you, yet hath its roots under ground, and doth sometimes spring up and trouble you. There is no evil perfectly rooted out of a sanctified man in this life, nor no grace planted in him that is perfect. 2. That the sovereignty of his grace appears as much in the times and measures of its dispensation, as in its being given at first to the sinner that never got any before. Let all believers remember that they are still under the dominion of the same free grace that at first subdued them to Christ. The greatest receivers of Christ's grace are not masters of it, but subjects and receivers. They must not say, as Jer. ii. 31. *We are lords, we will come no more unto thee.* The richest saint must be, and is a humble beggar at grace's door all his days; and Christ is the Lord of the house, and the dispenser of the alms; and as the alms is too good not to be patiently waited for, so the Lord is too good and too great to be quarrelled with: and never did a believer get any good by complaining of him. Complain to him, and pray, and ask largely, but still with faith and patience. Knock at his door; but stay, and bless him, that ever he gave you any crumb of his grace. Mix your prayers for new wanted grace, with praises for his old dispensed grace. Christ loves you, and hath proved it; believe it, bless him for it, and wait for his renewing his love to you; and in due time you will find, that he will not only answer, but outdo all your desires to him, and all your expectations from him.

Obs. 3. The beholding of Christ's glory in heaven, is the main part of the happiness of his people in it. So Christ expresseth it, (as I glanced at it before), as if he would explain what his people should get and do, when *they are where he is; they shall behold his glory.* This is that true beatific vision, that happy-making

making fight, that so many of the schoolmen (generally better philosophers than divines) do talk and write of. But poorly must all such talk and think of it, that are unacquainted with Christ and his grace in their own hearts. But this is sure, and plainly revealed, that the happiness of the glorified stands and flourisheth to eternity in the *beholding of Christ's glory*. The object is most excellent. The eye which they behold him with, and the light they behold him in are rare and singular. (No such eyes, and no such light on earth, or in the lower created heavens). And the fruits of this beholding this his glory in this blessed way, are inexpressible. There are two eyes that believers behold Christ's glory with; faith and sight. It is the same glory of the same Jesus that is seen; it is the same man that seeth his glory: but how vastly different are these two eyes, and the two beholdings! The one is for this life, the other for the other life. The glory of Christ, as it shineth in heaven, is not for the eye of faith. Faith may take it up in the promise, and believe and wait for it; but the glory of Christ in heaven is far above the eye of faith, Rom. viii. 24, 25. And, on the other hand, the glory of Christ, as it shineth in the gospel, and as seen by faith, is not for sight, and is unspeakably below it. For as needful and useful as faith is now to believers, yet when they come to *the end of their faith, the salvation of their soul*, 1 Peter i. 9. they have no more to do with it. There is no need of the shield of faith, when the war is ended, and the soldier of faith is made *more than a conqueror, through Christ that loved him*, Rom. viii. 37. Pictures of Christ, and love-letters from him, and love-tokens, (the glory of the gospel, and the necessary food of faith), are no more needed when the blessed beloved is present and enjoyed.

I. I would now come to speak of the first thing, *the glory of Christ*. And it is with reverence and godly ly fear that I should speak, and you should hear, of this great and awful theme. And what I mean to say of it, shall be under these two heads; 1. The glory of Christ as he represents God unto us: 2. His glory as he represents us unto God: As he is God's only true representative to his church; and as he is the only representative of his church unto God. Christ is both, and great is his glory in both. And this glory I would soberly speak of.

To begin with the *first* head, That Christ is the only representative of God unto his church: And great is his glory therein. And this glory of Christ is beheld by faith now, and to eternity by sight. There are many words about this, especially in the new testament, (where the old testament vail on Christ's glory is taken away; and yet the new testament light will itself evanish also, when the Lord returns in his glory, and hath his church with him where he is). I shall name a few of them. Col. i. 15. he is called *the image of the invisible God.* Heb. i. 3. he is *the brightness of his glory, and the express image of his person.* Who is the image? He that *upholdeth all things by the word of his power; who, when he had by himself purged our sins, sat down on the right hand of the Majesty on high.* Whose glory's brightness is he? whose person's character bears he? God the Father's, who spake in the old testament times by the prophets, and in the new testament times by his Son, ver. 1, 2. So in 2 Cor. iv. 6. *The light of the knowledge of the glory of God shineth in the face* (or *person*) *of Jesus Christ.* All deep words, and deep matter in them.

To prepare our way to enter on this theme, there are three things I would lay before you.

1. That a right and sound knowledge of God is simply and absolutely necessary unto true happiness, in this and in the other world. Our Lord in this chapter, ver. 3. saith, *And this is life eternal, that they might know thee the only true God, and Jesus Christ whom thou hast sent.* And 1 John v. 20. speaking

of Christ as known, the apostle saith, *This is the true God, and eternal life.* None know the true God, none can come by eternal life, but they that know Christ. No faith, love, worship, or obedience, can be performed and acted by him that knows not God. The Athenian inscription, *To the unknown God*, was ridiculous, but suitable enough for blind idolaters. This truth, of the necessity of the knowledge of God, in order to the pleasing and enjoying of him, and of his favour is ingraven on mens hearts by nature.

2. God in himself, and absolutely considered, is unknowable by men in this life, (to carry it no further now), unless he some way manifest himself to us. To this that seems to refer in 1 Tim. vi. 16. He *dwelleth in light which no man can approach unto; whom no man hath seen, nor can see. Whatsoever doth make manifest, is light*, Eph. v. 13. Yet divine light is a covering of God, Psalm civ. 1, 2. that no creature can see through; John i. 18. *No man hath seen God at any time; the only begotten Son, which is in the bosom of the Father, he hath declared him.* This truth stands on three foundations. 1. The greatness of God, and of his glory. 2. The shortness of mens reach as creatures. And, 3. The corruption of their minds as sinners: Eph. iv. 18. *Having the understanding darkened, being alienated from the life of God, through the ignorance that is in them, because of the blindness of their heart.* A dreadful, but true picture of that dungeon that all men by nature are born in, and must live and die in, and go through it, and from it, into outer darkness. In what way God did, and doth manifest himself and his glory unto the holy angels, and how they behold him, is quite hid from us. Though our Lord tells us, that *in heaven they do always behold the face of my Father which is in heaven*, Matth. xviii. 20.; yet what this is, we know no more than we do that in Rev. xxii. 4. of the triumphant church that *shall see his face.* To come a little lower, and to

speak

speak of the first man who was made a little lower than the angels: This also is beyond our understanding how God did manifest himself unto him, and how he beheld God's glory: though we are sure that both were. But when sin came in, then plainly the minds of all men are so defiled and darkened, that there is a necessity that they must be all taught of God that do know the Lord; and blessed be his name, that he hath promised this in the new covenant, and fulfils it to *the heirs of promise*, as they are called in Heb. vi. 17. John vi. 45. Jer. xxxi. 32, 33, 34. Yet, when the saving knowledge of God and faith are given, such is the weakness of this eye, that, on any special appearance of the glory of God, fear and amazement seizeth on their hearts. Whence that saying, so usual in old times, Judges xiii. 22. *We shall surely die, because we have seen God*; though God appeared in mercy to Manoah and his wife, and with a promise of a son to them, and a judge and saviour to Israel. Jacob had wrestled and prevailed with the angel, and was blessed by him: yet he saith with thankfulness and wonder, *I have seen God face to face, and my life is preserved*, Gen. xxxii. 30. What made Isaiah to say, on his seeing of God's glory, *Wo is me, I am undone*, chap. vi. 5.? Did God threaten him, did God smite him? No; but, *Mine eyes have seen the King, the Lord of hosts.* " I have seen his glory, and " his spotless holiness hath been proclaimed in my " ears. Thereby I see, that my own uncleanness, " and the uncleanness of others I dwell amongst, doth " greatly endanger me."

3. Notwithstanding all this depth of God's glory, and darkness in all mens minds by nature, since the fall of Adam; yet all men, in all ages, have been seeking out, and studying, and making to themselves, some representations of God. They know that there is a God; they quickly come to know that this God is out of their sight; and, on a little deeper thinking, they know that this invisible God is also beyond the

reach of their minds and thoughts. Is there a curious student of God's works of creation, that findeth not something in the smallest of his creatures, that our understanding cannot find out? What must we think of the Former of all things? *Can any find out God to perfection?* Job xi. 7. A conviction of this depth in God, and darkness in man, seemeth to have been declared in the inscription on the altar at Athens, Acts xvii. 23. This Paul takes for his text, (if I may so say), and makes an excellent sermon upon it. The conviction that is in mens hearts, of the depth of God, and of the darkness in themselves, hath bred a desire in all men to know somewhat more of God than they do, that they may please, and serve, and worship him, and obtain his favour. And this darkness and desire have brought forth two great plagues on the world, that are like to last as long as the world lasts, and as long as sinners live in it; two representations of God devised by men.

1st, The first way of mens studying to represent God unto themselves, is the more fine way of the better sort of the Heathens, and their philosophers. And that was, by framing thoughts, ideas, and contemplations of God, from the light of nature, and exercise of their reason. This way the apostle takes notice of, as a poor way, and unprofitable, Rom. i. 20. That philosopher spoke like a divine, who, when he was asked by his prince, What God was? desired a day's time to think on it. When that was granted, and done, he asked two days time to think on the question. After the two days, he asked four days. And when the king wondered at his delays, he gave this true and ingenuous answer: " The more I think " of God, the less can I tell what he is." And this will be the sure effect of all that, without the light of God's word and Spirit, do busy themselves to frame representations of God himself in their minds. The heathens have indeed spoke and wrote many good thoughts of some of the divine attributes, which may

be

be read with profit; and some do read them with wonder, how they came by such thoughts; and many have thought, that some of these philosophers might have seen some part of the Old Testament scriptures. Paul quotes one of them at Athens, Acts xvii. 28. whom he calls *one of their own poets;* and another in Tit. i. 12. whom he calls *a prophet of their own:* yet what he quotes of this last, is a complete Greek verse of poesy; and the other but a half-verse. But their philosophers taught and wrote, both in prose or verse. Yet though we who have the light of God's word, may make good use of their sparks of nature's light; we must not thence think, that they by their wisdom did know God savingly; contrary to 1 Cor. i. 21. *The world by wisdom knew not God.* An ungrounded charity to the salvation of the Heathen, that never knew God in Christ, is a reflection on the gospel of Christ. And if men will coin a new gospel, and a way of saving sinners, by Jesus Christ, as only preached to the Heathen, by sun, moon, and stars, contrary to the word of God, John. xiv. 6. and xvii. 3. Eph. ii. 12. Acts iv. 11, 12. do you know and remember, that it is false coin. And mens coining of another way to God but by his Son Jesus Christ, revealed in and by the gospel, is treason against the Majesty of heaven; and though it may deceive men on earth, it will never pass as current in heaven.

2dly, The other way of mens representing God unto themselves, is by images and outward representions of God. An old abomination. It is like it was not before the deluge: for it is not named; but only violence, and lusts, and general corruption in manners, are given as the procuring causes of God's destroying the world by water. Besides, the world was but lately created, and the glory of the Creator stared every man in the face; and that Mathusalem, who died a little before the flood, had lived some hundreds of years, while the first man, Adam, lived.

Besides

Besides, Enoch's prophecy, cited by Jude, ver. 14, 15. makes no mention of idolatry. But however it was before the flood, idolatry came quickly into the world afterwards, and is like to continue, till it be purged by fire. Now, what is idolatry? and whence is it that the world is so *mad upon idols*, Jer. l. 38.? Idolatry is the worshipping of the true God by and under any image or representation of God, devised by mens heads, or framed by mens hands. The first command of the moral law forbids the having and worshipping of any, but the true God. The second command forbids the making of any resemblance or image of God, and worshipping of God by it. Divine worship is *that glory that God will not give to another, neither his praise to graven images*, Isa xlii 8.; and that because he is a jealous God. Worship is God's throne in the world of angels and men; and he will admit of no rival or partner in it. The idolaters pretend that they only honour God, and give no divine glory to the image: but the Lord calls worshipping him by an image, *a worshipping of the creature more than the Creator*, Rom. i. 25. Now, how comes in idolatry into the world? And what keeps it up in it, since all men by their reason think, as Paul saith, all *ought to think, that the Godhead is not like unto gold, or silver, or stone graven by art or man's device?* Acts xvii. 29. The true cause of this sin's rise and reign in the world, is this. *"* men by nature know there is a God that made the world, and that they ought to worship him; but who he is, and what is pleasing worship to this God, they know not. They know, that if there be a God, he must not be like any creature in heaven or earth. The distance betwixt God and creatures, is, in its greatness, known only to him that can comprehend his own glorious majesty, and the emptiness of nothing creatures. And therefore we see how he speaks in Isa. xl. 17. *All nations before him are as nothing*, (that is, pretty low; but he yet lays them lower), *and they are counted to him*

him less than nothing, and vanity. To whom then will you liken God? ver. 18. But though God only can comprehend the greatness of this distance betwixt God and creatures; yet all men do apprehend, that it is, and must be great. Then, when reason tells them, that this God that made all things in time, is eternal; that he is immense and unsearchable in all perfections; that he is a Spirit; every one of these names of God do stun and puzzle the man's understanding; so that all must say, as one did, Job xxxvii. 23. *Touching the Almighty, we cannot find him out.* So that, in this confusion and darkness, they must (as they did, John iv. 22.) *worship they know not what;* and because *they know not God, so as to glorify him as God,* &c. *they change the glory of the uncorruptible God, into an image made like unto a corruptible man,* &c. Rom. i. 21, 22, 23. Man in his ignorance and sinfulness, first *thinks that God is such an one as himself,* Psal. l. 22.; and then thinks any representation of God may serve. And indeed the meanest creeping thing is an image too good for such a god. A god altogether like a sinner, is no other than *the god of this world,* the devil, 2 Cor. iv. 4. See the first gross idolatry among Israel in the wilderness, Exod. xxxii. They had heard the fiery law proclaimed dreadfully, but about forty days before; and idolatry specially prohibited and threatened in that law: yet they had hardly the dread of that voice out of their ears, before their hearts are turned aside, their hands busied in making an idol, and they on their knees worshipping it. In ver. 1. they say, *Up, and make us gods to go before us.* What a poor God is he that is of man's making? All Israel could not make one fly or gnat; yet they are for God-making. When they had their golden calf, they said, ver 4. *These be thy gods, O Israel, which brought you out of the land of Egypt.* Did they not know, that, a few weeks before, they had brought that gold out of the land of Egypt, of which they had now made their

idol?

idol? Did they not know, that this idol could no more go one step before, nor with them, nor after them, than a stone? And doubtless they meant to carry it, if Moses had not made them to destroy it, and drink it, ver. 20. But they had brought up their idolatrous hearts out of the land of Egypt, Ezek. xxiii. 3, 8, 19.; and they thought this a fit representation of the true God: and therefore *proclamation is made of a feast to-morrow, to the Lord, to Jehovah,* Exod. xxxii. 5. As long as God is not known by his word and Spirit, no man is secured from falling into idolatry. Let us look into the Antichristian state; and there any Christian may see, that the whole of their worship, from the beginning to the end, is a mere mass of idolatry, and wicked representations of God. Their hearts, their houses, their streets, and highways, their temples, are all filled with idols: many false gods, as angels and saints; many wicked representations even of the divine persons, Father, Son, and Holy Ghost. Justly may it be called, as old Babylon was, *a land of graven images,* Jer. l. 38. The old Pagan, and the new Antichristian Rome, equally full of idols; only with difference in names. Heathen names laid aside, and Christian names taken up in their rooms: but the idols the same, and the idolatry the same; with the addition of a god made of bread, to be first made, then worshipped, and then eat. An abomination enough to make the natural conscience of a cannibal to keck at.

To conclude this head, about worshipping of God by images, I would say only, that it is a sin as plainly forbid in God's word as any sin whatsoever; as fearfully punished as any sin: that it is a sin that both riseth from unworthy thoughts of God, and increaseth these unworthy thoughts. It stupifies men, and takes away their reason: Isa. xliv. 20. He (*the* idolater) *feedeth of ashes: a deceived heart hath turned him aside, that he cannot deliver his own soul, nor say, Is there not a lye in my right hand? But they that make*

make them, are like unto them; so is every one that trusteth in them, Psal. cxv. 8. The idol, and the idolater, are much alike. The idol is void of all natural life and sense, and the idolater is as void of all spiritual life and sense. Hath that man the soul and spirit of a man in him; hath he any sense of the majesty of the true and living God, who can call a log of wood, or a bit of bread, a god, and worship it? I have said the more of idolatry, because it is the sin most dishonourable to God, most destructive to the souls of men, and a dreadful stumbling block to the Jews and Turks, who do justly abhor idols, for as blind and sottish as otherwise they be. Nor can any man wonder that they stumble at the name of Christianity, when they see the greatest part of such as profess that name, as much given to idolatry, as ever the Heathen were, either before or since Christ came into the world. This sin is also a disgrace to mankind, and a shameful defacing of that image of God in which he was first made; when a man so *debaseth himself even unto hell,* (Isa. lvii. 9.), as to worship what either his own or other mens hands have made. Yet this sin of idolatry is a demonstration, that the light of nature, and the notion of God, (notwithstanding all the weakness, darkness, and corruption mixed with it in fallen man), is deeply and strongly rooted in mens hearts, that they will rather take up with any thing for a God, yea, make a God to themselves, rather than have none. It is no rare thing, to see an idolatrous prince, who is as proud as Lucifer, and who saith in his heart as he did, Isa. xiv. 12, 13, 14.; and who hath pride and ambition enough to desire to be lord of the whole earth: yet such a wretch as this, who is not worthy to live among his fellow-mortals, will humble himself, and kneel before a proud priest, confess his sins to him, and ask, and receive pardon from him, as from a God, and worship the work of the meanest of his subjects hands. This was the proud boast in the last age, of a confessor to a great king,

"When I have my king on his knees before me, and "my god (meaning the confecrated wafer) in my "hands, what can I not do?" From fuch gods, fuch kings, and fuch priefts, may the only true God deliver us, and all the nations on earth. But as long as the fpirit of Demetrius prevaileth, Diana will not want a rich temple, and many worfhippers: Acts xix. 25. *Ye know that by this craft we have our wealth.* For if falfe gods were not rich gods, and rich-making gods, they quickly would have neither priefts, nor temples, nor worfhippers. And quickly may it be, is the hearty prayer of every true Chriftian.

And this leads me to the point in hand, That the Lord Jefus Chrift, God-man, and our Mediator, is the only true reprefentative of God unto the church. God only makes himfelf favingly known to men in his Son Jefus Chrift. Men that would know God favingly, worfhip God acceptably, and enjoy God forever, they muft feek and get all in and by Jefus Chrift.

In handling of this, I would fpeak to two things. 1. The fitnefs of Chrift to be God's reprefentative to his church, 2. The glory of Chrift in being fo.

Firft, As to Chrift's fitnefs to reprefent God unto men: It appears in three things.

1. In the divine dignity of his perfon. He is God's eternal Son, and God equal with the Father. I know that this rock, the church of Chrift is built upon, is boldly ftruck at in thefe laft and worft days. But we fhould know as well, that *the gates of hell fhall not prevail againft it*, Matth. xvi. 18. I would only fay now, that that man or woman that owns the authority of the New Teftament, (though Chrift's Godhead fhines very brightly in the Old Teftament), and fhall read but three firft chapters, John i. Col. i. and Heb. i. and can fay, that Chrift is a mere man and creature, is under a judicial blindnefs. All that worfhip Chrift, and call on his name in prayer, and deny

deny him to be true God, are guilty of idolatry. A mere creature image and representation of God used in worship, is an idol. But the eternal Son of God, who is in his person *the image of God*, and *the character of the Father's person*, is fit unspeakably to declare God unto men, John i. 8. He alone doth it, and none else can.

2. The Son's assuming man's nature unto his own divine person, makes him fit to represent God to men, John i. 1.----18. His being God-man, made him fit to represent God to men, and to represent men to God. God is only to be savingly known by men, as he is a God in Christ; and sinners are only accepted of God, as they are in Christ. His human nature is a creature; but the Son of God that assumed and dwelleth personally in this nature, is a divine person. It is not his nature as man, but his divine person dwelling in that nature, that doth make him the only right representative and image of the invisible God unto his church.

3. Christ's being installed in the office of Mediator, makes him fit to represent God unto men. He is the *one Mediator between God and men, the man Christ Jesus*, 1 Tim. ii. 5. Such as, on this account, talk of Christ's being a God by office, know neither God, nor Christ, nor his office. Our Lord Jesus Christ is God in office; and to be worshipped by his people, as clothed with it. In this office, as Prophet, he represents and revealeth the mind and will of God, to be known and believed by the church; which is commanded by the Father to *hear him*, Matth. xvii. 5. As King, *all judgment is committed to the Son: that all men should honour the Son, even as they honour the Father. And he that honoureth not the Son, honoureth not the Father which hath sent him*, John v. 22, 23. And as Priest, as all in that office are *taken from among men, and ordained for men in things pertaining to God, that they might both offer gifts and sacrifices for sins*, Heb. v. 1.; so *the Son was consecrated* for this office

office *by an oath*, Heb. vii. 28.: and as Prieſt, he *muſt have ſomewhat elſe to offer*, Heb. viii. 3.; which offering was himſelf, and this he hath offered, Heb. ix. 26. and x. 5.----10. And after this offering, *he entered in*, as Prieſt, *into the holy place; even into heaven itſelf, now to appear in the preſence of God for us*, Heb. ix. 12. 24. And there he remains, and *liveth for ever to make interceſſion for us*, Heb. vii. 25. until *he ſhall appear the ſecond time, without ſin, unto ſalvation*, Heb. ix. 28. Now, in this office Chriſt repreſents his church unto God; and in his prophetical and kingly office, he repreſents God unto his church. Both equally needful for our ſalvation, and both only performed by Jeſus Chriſt as Mediator; who only can repreſent God unto us, that we may ſavingly know God; and repreſent us ſo to God, that we may be graciouſly received by him. *Wherefore, holy brethren, partakers of the heavenly calling, conſider the Apoſtle and High Prieſt of our profeſſion, Chriſt Jeſus*, Heb. iii. 1. Conſider how fit he is to do all God's buſineſs with us, and all our buſineſs with God, for our ſalvation, and his Father's and his own glory. He is clothed with a moſt honourable office of Mediator, (the honour and work of which office no mere creature could bear and diſpatch), furniſhed with all fulneſs for its diſcharge and management. This office he diſcharged when on earth, in our nature as man; and in the ſame nature, is doing what remains to be done in that office, in heaven. And this high officer, this man Jeſus Chriſt, is *God over all, bleſſed for ever*, Rom. ix. 5. So that his fitneſs for making a true and ſaving repreſentation of God to his people, is evident; but ſo great and glorious, that we cannot fully apprehend it by faith. We have in our Lord Jeſus Chriſt, a Mediator between God and men, to take away the breach that ſin had made between them, and to make an everlaſting friendſhip; a Mediator ſo furniſhed for his office, that any may truſt him in it. We have this Mediator

in

in our own nature, *a partaker of flesh and blood*, as we be, Heb. ii. 14, 17.; *in all things made like unto his brethren*, that he might be the fitter for us, and that we might be the more familiar with him. And this Mediator by his office, this real and true man by the taking of our nature, is God, *the only begotten of the Father.* Can any make a doubt of this truth we are upon, That the Lord Jesus Christ, God-man, Mediator, is the true, real, and only representative of God to his church?

So much for this first head.

Secondly, What is Christ's glory, in being God's representative to his church? Herein he is exceedingly exalted. How greatly is it expressed, Eph. i. 20,----23. and in Phil. ii. 6,----11.? and how hard to think suitably of them? I shall only touch at three particulars in it.

1. It is glory to Jesus Christ, that all the saving discoveries of God are made to men in and by him: 2 Cor. iv. 6. *The light of the knowledge of the glory of God shineth to men, in the face of Jesus Christ.* Till a man know Jesus Christ, he knows not God; nay, he hath not a God: Eph. ii. 12. They that are without Christ, are *without God in the world:* " Ye were " Atheists," (so is the Greek word); though the Ephesians, to whom he writes, had been great idolaters, and had gods and goddesses more than were worth having, Acts xix.

2. Great is Christ's glory in this, that all the worship that is given to God, if right, and as it is commanded, is given to God in and by Jesus Christ. *No coming to the Father, but by him,* John xiv. 6. If *we believe in God*, we must *also believe on him,* John xiv. 1. *Thro' him we believe on God,* 1 Peter i. 21. If *we believe on him, we believe not on him* (only, or alone), *but on him that sent him. And he that seeth him, seeth him that sent him,* John xii. 44, 45. If we pray, we must do it *in Christ's name,* John xiv. 13, 14. and chap. xvi. 23, 24. Yea, *whatsoever we do, whether in word or deed,*

deed, *must all be done in the name of our Lord Jesus Christ, giving thanks unto God and the Father by him,* Col. iii. 17. All our gospel-sacrifices are to be offered to God by him, Heb. xiii. 15. Now, consider how great a person this must be, as the apostle argues about his type, Melchisedec, in Heb. vii. 1,---4. And he is there exalting that unknown man's priesthood above the Levitical, in this, that Abraham, Levi's great-grandfather, gave the tenth of the spoils to him. How much greater is Jesus Christ, of whom Melchisedec was but a type and shadow, to whom we must not only give a tenth, but all, of that worship and service we pay and owe to God?

3. All the mercy, favour, and bounty of God to men, comes to us in and by Jesus Christ. No *spiritual blessings in heavenly things* doth God *bless us with,* but *in Jesus Christ,* Eph. i. 3.

APPLICATION. All the use of this doctrine I shall at this time make, is in one warning; which I wish may be as well taken, as it is needful, both to me to give it, and to you to take it. And it is this, That the secret moth and poison in many people's religion is, that it is not Christianity. *God out of Christ is a consuming fire;* God not worshipped in Christ, is an idol; all hopes of acceptance out of Christ, are vain dreams; a heaven out of Christ, is little better than the Turks paradise. How sad is it; how visible is it, and common that many men and women do pray every day, and hear every day, and would fain know God rightly, and worship him acceptably; and, if we might believe their words and profession, they know a great deal of God, and serve him not a little; when, in the mean time, Jesus Christ, as the only glass in and by which the true God and his glory is to be known and adored, is not minded by them? They have no sense, no experience of it, no conviction of the necessity of Christ's representing an invisible, incomprehensible God, unto them; they make no essays
to

to know God in and by this only right way. Hence is it, that there is so much of that that bears the name of *religion*, that not only men may carry to hell with them, but that pusheth them into hell. Hence is it, that so many have a form of godliness, who are fatal strangers to its power. Is it not sad, to see and hear men, who bear the name of Christians, playing the philosophers about God's nature and attributes, while in the mean time they are utter, yea contented strangers, unto this only true representation of God unto men, in his Son Jesus Christ? All I shall say now, is to glance at one scripture, in 2 Cor. iv. 3, 4, 6. *If our gospel be hid, it is hid to them that are lost*, I cannot deny, would the apostle say, but that for all the plainness and closeness of our preaching, of which in ver. 2. yet our gospel is hid; but it is so to a lost company. But how comes it, that under such preaching as Paul's, the gospel is hid from any that hear it? This he answers, ver. 4. wherein he names two causes concurring, one sad effect flowing from these causes, and destruction consequent on the effect. The causes are, unbelief in their hearts, and Satan's working with it, and securing of it. The sinner is blind by nature, his blindness grows by the abused light of the gospel, and the devil spreads a thick vail over their blind eyes, that let gospel-light shine by an apostle, no ray, no beam shall dart in upon them. Now what is the effect of this double-blinding? What doth Satan design in his pains on unbelievers? What is he afraid of, and studies to prevent? It is, *lest the light of the glorious gospel of Christ, who is the image of God, should shine unto them.* As if the apostle had said, the devil in his diligence to keep sinners in the dark, thinks and knows, that if ever one beam of the glory of Christ in the gospel, comes in to sinners hearts, they are lost to him, and saved to Jesus Christ. O that sinners knew this, as well as the devil doth? But why hath not this busy devil the same power on all? How come any to have

their

their eyes opened to see? To this he answers in ver. 6. *For God who commanded the light to shine out of darkness, hath shined in our hearts, to give the light of the knowledge of the glory of God, in the face of Jesus Christ.* Observe, that the apostle in speaking of the causes of the perdition of unbelievers, names their own blindness and unbelief, and Satan's activity; but as to the salvation of believers, he ascribes it solely unto the grace of God, and its power and freedom; without which Satan would prevail on all, as he doth on many. But, for as blind as unbelievers are, and for as diligent and powerful as the devil is, God that commanded light in the first creation, did so to us, and this light so commanded, gave us the *knowledge of the glory of God, in the face of Jesus Christ*, by which we are saved. There are many glorious truths, that shine with some beams of light into the minds of natural men, so as that they are convinced of them, fall in love with them, and make profession of them; but never is a sinner throughly changed and converted to God, nor rescued from Satan and the power of darkness, till this light, this knowledge, this glory of God in the face of Christ, be given by this great Commander and Creator. Paul himself, while an unbeliever, had the light of the knowledge of the glory of God, in the works of creation and providence, as a man of sense and reason; he had the knowledge of the glory of God in the law, as a zealous Jew; but the knowledge of the glory of God in the face of Jesus Christ, he never had, till *it pleased God to call him by his grace and to reveal his Son in him*, Gal. i. 15, 16. And let me tell you, that unless you have seen more of the glory of God in the face of Jesus Christ, and in God's way of saving sinners by him, than ever you saw of his glory in his works of creation and providence (in both which, not a little of his glory shineth) the Lord hath not yet dealt with you, as he doth with them he saveth. The right saving knowledge of God centers in this one person, Jesus Christ.

See

See how the apostle prayeth, Col. ii. 2, 3. *That their hearts might be comforted, being knit together in love, and unto all riches of the full assurance of understanding, to the acknowledgment of the mystery of God, and of the Father, and of Christ; in whom are hid all the treasures of wisdom and knowledge.* So that all who would be enriched with true wisdom, and the saving knowledge of God, must by faith dig in Christ, and find them.

SERMON X.

John xvii. 24.

Father, I will that they also whom thou hast given me, be with me where I am; that they may behold my glory which thou hast given me: for thou lovedst me before the foundation of the world.

THIS great subject, the glory of our Lord Jesus Christ, which he hath received of his Father, is that which his people see somewhat of here by faith, Heb. ii. 9. and are called to the hope of full beholding of it hereafter, when this prayer of our Lord shall be fully answered. It is so deep a theme, that it is not easy to enter upon it, but impossible to declare the thing plentifully as it is. All I mean to speak on it, I shall confine to two heads; the glory of Christ, as representing God unto us; and his glory, as representing us to God. In the first, he represents God unto us, to our saving knowing of God: in the other, he represents us to God, unto our saving acceptance with God. I began to speak of the former last day, and did proceed to it by these three

three steps. 1. That the true knowledge of God is simply needful for man's happiness, both in this and the next life. 2. That God in himself is incomprehensible, unbeholdible, unknowable, unless he is pleased to make himself some way known to men. 3. That yet men in all ages have been still framing representations of God in their own minds. A little of nature's light remains, and of the ruins of that estate God made man at first in; but so defiled and mixed with the darkness brought on men by the fall, that natural light and sinful darkness, mixed together, are but like the chaos in the beginning of the creation, Gen. i. 2. So that we may apply that to this case of mens inquiring after God, in Eccl. vii. 29. *Lo, this only have I found, that God hath made man upright: but they have sought out many inventions.* A man can think of nothing, but in and by that thought there is some idea or representation of it made in his mind. When we think of our own souls, (by which we do think), how dark is our idea of them? But when we begin to think of creatures higher and nobler than ourselves, as angels are, what a dark idea do we frame of them? When we say they are spirits, what know we what a spirit is? When we say a spirit is an intelligent being, free of matter; how far is this from planting a just representation in our minds of those noble creatures? If we raise our thoughts above all creatures, unto the perfect Former of all things, the great JEHOVAH; every thought of him, every name and perfection of his, swallows us up; as Job xxxvii. 19. *Teach us what we shall say unto him; for we cannot order our speech* (or our thoughts) *to him by reason of darkness.* Our own light in us, is but darkness; and the infiniteness of his light and glory, is as darkness to us. *Shall it be told him that I speak? If a man speak, surely he shall be swallowed up,* ver. 20. If a man know, either who he is that speaketh, what he either speaks or thinks, or who he is that is spoke or thought of. The world hath been striving, either

by

by their wisdom to know God, 1 Cor. i. 21. or in their folly to represent an invisible God to their bodily senses. And this last hath filled so great a part of the earth with idols; an old abomination, which, it may be, will continue till this earth be purged by the last fire. And these things led me to the only relief in this dismal state of mankind, as to the right and saving knowledge of God; that the Lord Jesus Christ, the Son of God, clothed with man's nature, and with the office of Mediator between God and men, is the only true representative of God to men. That he is such, and of his glory in being so, I have spoke somewhat; and shall enter upon the use we should make of him, as the representative of God unto his church, after I have given you a little account of the gradual rising of this light in and unto the church.

When our first parents had sinned, and were ashamed of themselves, and afraid of God, and ignorantly thought to hide themselves from him, he calls them to his bar, arraigns them for their sin; and when they had no reason to expect any thing but present judgment and execution, instead of that, the Lord, in a threatening against the serpent, brings forth the first promise of salvation by Jesus Christ, called there *the seed of the woman;* who, though he should suffer by the serpent, should yet *bruise his head,* Gen. iii. 15. In the faith of this, and it may be of other explanations of it not recorded, the believing fathers before the flood lived and died. And Abel and Enoch are noted, Heb. xi. 4, 5. the one a martyr, the other translated to heaven. And Noah, before, in, and after the flood, ver. 7. is called *an heir of the righteousness which is by faith:* which none but a believer is. No righteousness is by faith, but that that hath both the Lord our righteousness in it, the light of God's word to discover him and it, and a promise of the covenant to warrant faith's apprehending of it. If we go on to the Patriarch Abraham, we find the light growing more bright, especially if we

read

read Gen. xii. 14, 15, 17. &c. with Paul's comments on them, in Rom. iv. in Gal. iii. and iv. and in Heb. xi. 8.----20. and what our Lord said of Abraham in John viii. 39, 40. 56, 58 Who can read these, and not be persuaded, that Abraham knew the Son of God, and God in him, and justification and salvation by him? Let us next take a view of the church-state which the God of Israel brought his people into; first, in a more transient manner in the wilderness, and thereafter fixed them in it in Canaan. In this state, we find that the tabernacle and temple, their ordinances, priests, and sacrifices, and all their ceremonies, were all but types and shadows of Jesus Christ, Heb. ix. and x. There were many things in that dispersation that had some appearance and semblance of idolatry; but there was none in it, for two reasons. 1. Because they were all of God's own appointment. 2. Because they were instituted on purpose to prefigure the Messiah to come. If therefore any of Israel had devised of his own head a worship of this sort, then that man had been as guilty of transgressing the second command, *Thou shalt not make unto thyself any likeness*, &c. as if he had served Baalim. And because they were all types and shadows of Christ, and of the good things to come by him; therefore if any church or person, now after the substance is come, and the shadows are gone, should attempt to bring Christians under the Levitical dispensation of the Old Testament church, they justly might be called *Antichristians, and deniers that Christ is come in the flesh*, 1 John iv. 3. Come we to the prophets, David in the Psalms, Isaiah, and all the prophets, we find a fair dawning of the knowledge of the glory of God in the face of Jesus Christ, wrought in their hearts by the Spirit of God, and shining in their ministry to the church. This is so plain, that it need not be insisted on; and so full, that it would be too great a digression to insist on it as it deserves. We find Stephen, Acts vii. and Paul, Acts xiii. preaching Christ by

SERM. X.   *the Lord's Prayer.*   167

by such a narration; warrant enough for this small account. Let us now go forward to Christ's coming into the world. The angels proclaim him, a *born Saviour, Christ the Lord,* Luke ii. 11. Old dying Simeon calls him, when a babe in arms, *God's salvation,* and *the light of the Gentiles,* and *the glory of Israel,* ver. 30, 31, 32. Yea, Elisabeth calls him, when in the womb, *My Lord,* Luke i. 43. What a great anointing of the Holy Ghost was on this good woman, and how strong was her faith in Christ? When he is to be made manifest to Israel, John Baptist proclaims him to be *the Lamb of God, that taketh away the sin of the world;* to be *the baptizer with the Holy Ghost;* to be *the Son of God;* and that *all grace is received out of his fulness,* John i. 15.----34. When he is baptized, what a glorious testimony is given from heaven to him, Matth. iii. 17? When he lived on the earth, and went about doing good, all that knew him, paid him divine worship in faith, and love, and prayer, and obedience; and were never checked for it; as Peter did Cornelius, Acts x. 26.; and the angel, John the divine, twice, Rev. xix. 10. and xxii. 9. Yea, when he was dying, one saw him to be God, and dealt with him by faith for eternal life: the rarest faith in all the scripture. When dead, and supposed by Mary Magdalene to be still so, she called him, *My Lord,* John xx. 13. Thomas calls him when risen, *My Lord and my God,* John xx. 28. Yea, when he had *led them out as far as to Bethany, and had lift up his hands and blessed them; and while he blessed them, he was parted from them, and was carried up into heaven;* (a blessed parting; and there will be shortly as blessed a meeting again); *they worshipped him, and returned to Jerusalem, with great joy,* Luke xxiv. 50, 51, 52, 53. Strange joy! when, at the tidings of Christ's leaving them, *sorrow had filled their hearts,* John xvi. 6. But, now their Lord had done all his work on earth, and was received up into glory, they worshipped him joyfully still; knowing, that

though

though now no more could they worship him as they did, when he was with them, with the help of that bodily presence of Christ with them, and with that sight they had of him by the eyes of their bodies terminated on his visible appearance; yet by faith, and with joy from that faith, they worshipped him still. But when Christ was not only ascended into heaven, but had sent down the promise of the Father, his Holy Spirit, upon the infant Christian church, Acts ii. *the light of the knowledge of the glory of God in the face of Jesus Christ,* shone out as the sun in its strength. All believers, all preachers, all ordinances, were filled with Christ's glory. In this gospel-temple, did *every one,* every thing, *speak of his glory;* as the word is, Psal. xxix. 9. All divine worship was given to him, and to God by him; all grace dispensed by him. And thus it will be until his coming again. While God hath a church on earth, it is *gathered together in Christ's name;* built on Christ as the rock and foundation, 1 Cor. iii. 10, 11.; *grows up in him,* and on him, Eph. ii. 20, 21, 22. 1 Pet. ii. 4, 5.; worships him, and the Father in him and by him; is fed and nourished by his Spirit, and the influence thereof, until that blessed state it is to be brought to at the last *appearance of the great God, and our Saviour Jesus Christ,* Tit. ii. 13.

I would finish this narrative with two singular texts, amongst many, to the same purpose; one in the Old Testament, and another in the New Testament. That in the Old Testament is in Numb. xii. 8.; that in the New Testament is in Col. ii, 9.

The first in Numb. xii. 8. I would labour to explain. What the matter was that occasioned the strife betwixt Moses and Aaron and Miriam, we know but little; whether Moses did right or wrong about the Ethiopian woman whom he married, ver. 1. Yet one would think, that Aaron the high priest, and his elder brother, and Miriam his sister, and a prophetess, might have reproved him for what they thought was
amiss,

amiſs, without ſo ſevere a rebuke from the Lord. But their ſin lay in reflecting on the high ſtation God had put him in. And their ſin was ſomething akin to that of Korah and his company againſt both Moſes and Aaron: Numb. xvi. 3. *You take too much upon you.* To this ſtrife between Moſes and his brother and ſiſter, the Lord puts an end by very extraordinary words. I will read them, becauſe one part of them belongs evidently to our preſent purpoſe: Numb. xii. 6. *Hear now my words: If there be a prophet among you,* (as there were ſeventy ſet apart in the preceeding chapter), *I the Lord will make myſelf known to him in a viſion, and will ſpeak unto him in a dream.* (And theſe were the uſual ways and means of God's darting in prophetical light into the minds of his prophets; either when awake, by viſions; or when aſleep, by dreams; and both were attended, doubtleſs, with ſuch ſignatures of God's intereſt therein, as did ſatisfy and ſecure their faith). ver. 7. *But my ſervant Moſes is not ſo, who is faithful in all my houſe.* "(I have ſet him above thoſe "ways and ordinances"). ver. 8. *With him will I ſpeak mouth to mouth,* (the ſame with *face to face,* Exod. xxxiii. 11. *as a man ſpeaketh unto his friend;* and in Deut. xxxiv. 10. So Moſes ſaith of God's way of giving the law: Deut. v. 4. *The Lord talked with you face to face in the mount, out of the midſt of the fire), even apparently, and not in dark ſpeeches,* (as Pſalm. lxxviii 2. *I will utter dark ſayings of old); and the ſimilitude of the Lord ſhall he behold,* (as much beyond the other, as *ſeeing* is beyond *hearing* darkly of a perſon or thing): *Wherefore then were ye not afraid to ſpeak againſt my ſervant Moſes?* Now what was this *ſimilitude of the Lord* that Moſes did behold, and was ſo dignified by reaſon of this ſingular priviledge? You know he tells them, Deut. iv. 15, 16. *Take ye therefore good heed unto yourſelves, (for ye ſaw no manner of ſimilitude on the day that the Lord ſpake unto you in Horeb, out of the midſt of the fire), leſt you corrupt yourſelves,*

selves, &c. It is like, if there had been any seen that day, that they might rather incline to make the resemblance of that in their idol, than of the Egyptian ox or calf. There are divers opinions about this *similitude of the Lord that Moses did behold*. But that I like best, and think it nearest the truth in so dark and deep a matter, is what you have in the annotations of Mr Pool, a learned and godly divine, on this place: "That the Son of God appeared to Moses in an hu-"man shape: which he took up for a time, that he "might give Moses a foretaste of his future incarna-"tion." And many grave divines think, that most of the appearances of God to Abraham, and to the patriachs and prophets, were made by the Son of God in a human shape, foretelling his being made flesh in the fulness of time. Man was made *in the image of God, after his likeness*, Gen. i. 26. If this sense be not approved, that it was so done, because God had purposed, that one of the blessed three, even his eternal Son, the natural and essential image of the Father, should in time be sent in the likeness of man; yet this is certain, that the first man was made *in the image of God;* and, by his fall, got on him and his posterity the image of the devil: and to recover us from this woful likeness, and to bring us to a better likeness to God than Adam was made in and lost, God's Son takes to him *the likeness of sinful flesh*, Rom. viii. 3. yet without sin, that in and by that likeness men might come to know God savingly, and be made like unto God.

The other scripture is in Col. ii. 9. *For in him* (Jesus Christ) *dwelleth all the fulness of the Godhead bodily*. A remarkable text, and so is the context. What dwells in Jesus Christ? The Godhead, the fulness of the Godhead, and all the fulness of the Godhead. How dwelleth it in him? Bodily, really, substantially, not typically, as in the temple and sanctuary. *The fulness of the Godhead* did not only thus dwell in Christ when he was on earth, but it dwelleth in him still, and for ever.

ever. Where then can a man find God, but in this man Jesus Christ, *in whom dwelleth all the fulness of the Godhead*, really, substantially, and eternally? The context hath two things in it. 1. A warning against seduction, ver. 8. 18, 19. Their and our danger lay in two things, that then were, and to this day are, the chief springs of apostasy from Christ, and *the simplicity that is in him*, as 2 Cor. xi. 3. The one is adhering to the Old Testament ordinances and ceremonies, antiquated by Christ, the end and substance of them all. The other is, man's reason, wisdom, and philosophy; which never could, nor can, find out God, so as to direct men to know God savingly, and to worship God acceptably, 1 Cor. i. 21. And therefore, by its poor principles, and *beggarly elements*, (as Gal. iv. 9.), this wisdom of man rebels against the saving wisdom of God in his Son Jesus Christ; and doth but *puff up men by their fleshly mind*, Col. ii. 18. And from those two cursed springs, all the heresies, apostasies, and the grand Antichristian defection, have evidently flowed.

2. In the context we have the privileges of Christians by Christ, that should endear him to them, and engage them to that stedfastness in the faith which he had exhorted them to in ver. 5, 6, 7. Those privileges are many and great. The Christian is *complete in him*, ver. 10. and needs not hunt after any good out of him. All is to be found in Christ, and in him only. He is *circumcised in him*, that is, sanctified, ver. 11. He is *buried with Christ, and risen again*, ver. 12.; made to die to sin, and to live to God. He is *quickned with Christ*, ver. 13. and *forgiven*. All the Christian's enemies conquered, the law cancelled, and the devil over-come, and triumphed over by Christ, at and by his lowest, ver 14, 15.

Now, to come to the application of this doctrine so oft named, That the Lord Jesus Christ, God-man, Mediator, is the only true representative of God unto the church: There are three exhortations I would give from it. 1. Study God in Christ. 2. Content yourselves with this knowledge of God in Christ. 3. Use and improve the knowledge of God you have in and by Jesus Christ.

Exhort. 1. Study God in Christ. You must know God, if ye be saved. You cannot know him, but as he reveals himself; he reveals himself no other way but in Christ, so as to be savingly known. There are four books (if I may so call them) that many use in their studying to know God; but they are, and will be but poor scholars, if they have not better, and fitter, and plainer books. 1. Some will study an absolute God; God as in himself. An absolute God is a pit, and an abyss, that all that go near it, fall into it, and will be destroyed. It was a bold word of blessed Luther, " Let hypocrites and unbelievers do as they please, " I will have nothing to do with an absolute God." God as in his Son, God as in covenant with us in his Son, God as clothed with grace and mercy, shining in his promises in Christ, is the God we must study to know; and when by his grace we attain it, we may glory humbly in it: Jer. ix. 24 *Let him that glorieth, glory in this, that he understandeth and knoweth me, that I am the Lord, which exercise loving-kindness, judgment, and righteousness in the earth: for in these things I delight, saith the Lord.* 2. Some study God in his works. And much of his glory shineth therein, and we ought to observe it. But what is all the fruit of this alone! Only to *render men inexcusable,* Rom. i 20. This light of the knowledge of the glory of God, is both dim and cold light. It hath no heat nor power in it. Never did a man come by the saving knowledge of God by the study of the book of creation and providence, though a true Christian may both study and profit much by it, when he *hath known God, or rather is known of God,* Gal. iv. 9. 3. Some study to know God in his holy law. And in it is a glorious discovery of God. But it is of a holy, just, sin-hating, sin-forbidding, sin-threatening God. Here he is seen as a terrible judge. No man ever did, or can know God savingly, in bare law-light. Only God can be savingly known in that representation of him wherein he is manifested as a saving God; and that is, only in his Son Jesus Christ. 4. Some study to know God in and by his ordinances. Precious appointments of God, much to be valued and used by us; and their profit great, when blessed by their appointer, and when used by us in the right manner. But we must know, that as the virtue of all the Old Testament ordinances lay in their relation to, and shadowing forth the Messiah then to come; so all the virtue of New Testament ordinances lieth in their relation to, and shewing forth of Christ come. If therefore a man now shall study to know God savingly in and by the greater light of the gospel-appointments, without regard to Christ's interest in them, that man will as surely perish in ignorance of God, as a carnal Jew, uncircumcised in heart; as Jer. ix. 26. Rom. ii. 20, 29. Phil. iii. 3.

But, above all these, if you would know God savingly, study to know him in and by that only saving representation he hath made of himself in his Son.

1. For here it is you have the only true, and new place to find God in. Job in his distress said, *O that I knew where I might find him! that I might come even to his seat,* or *throne!* Job. xxiii. 3. He is only to be found in Christ. God dwelleth in Christ, Col. ii. 9. There, and there only, you must seek him, and find him, and know him savingly; and *acquaint yourselves with him, and be at peace,* Job xxii. 21. There is no creature, no part of the work of God's hands, that is so nearly related to God, as the nature of the man Christ, assumed by the divine person of *the Word, the only begotten of the Father.* This is *the true tabernacle which the Lord pitched, and not man,* Heb. viii. 2. This is *the new and living way, which he hath consecrated for us through the vail, that is to*

say, his flesh, Heb. x. 20. And this is the only *way to the holiest,* ver. 19. The devil, Christ's great enemy, hath done much to darken and disgrace this way to the world: on the one hand, by the gross idolatry of Antichrist, wherein a vain show is made, by images of Christ, and of his flesh, and sufferings in it; all obscuring and perverting of Christ as the ordinance of God for our salvation. On the other hand, when men by their reason see the vanity of this Popish pageant and puppet-shew, into which Antichrist hath turned the true gospel-representation of Christ, Satan hath brought in a mystical and metaphysical gospel, on the pretence of greater spirituality; wherein the flesh of Christ, and his saving performances in that flesh, are either hid, or turned into allegories, and mysteries, and notions, that have no room but in vain minds that hatch them, and are quite unprofitable to them, that harbour and hug them. But let Christians beware of both, as of ways of perdition; and by faith fix on the flesh of our Lord and Saviour Jesus Christ, which was given by him *for the life of the world,* John vi. 51. In this tabernacle of his body we by faith see God the Son personally dwelling, and by the same faith see the Father dwelling in the Son. And thus only do we savingly know God.

2. In Christ only we have the new names and relations of God, in and by which God only can be savingly known. When God sent Moses to Israel, and to Pharaoh, to bring Israel out of Egypt, Moses saith to the Lord, Exod. iii. 13. *If they shall say to me, What is his name? what shall I say unto them?* (And what a deep answer is given to this bold question, ver. 14?) So may we, What is that name and relation of God that he only can be savingly known by? It is easily answered, God can only be savingly known in and by that saving name by which he makes himself known; and that is his name in Christ. The Lord said to Israel in Exod. xxiii. 21. *Beware of him, and*

and obey his voice, provoke him not: for he will not pardon your transgressions: for my name is in him. And this awful word about Christ, the angel of the covenant, that he will not pardon refusers of him, is but the same we have in Heb. xii. 25. But all the saving names and relations of God unto us, are all in and from his names in Christ, and relations to Christ. He is Christ's God and Father, and so ours, John xx. 17. But more of those anon.

So much for the first exhortation, Study God in Christ.

Exhort. 2. Learn to be content with the knowledge of God in Christ. Seek no more knowledge of God, seek no other knowledge of God, save in Christ. Ask not Philip's question; or if you do, take Christ's answer to it, and seek no other, John xiv. 7, 8, 9. Christ had told them, that *they knew his Father, and had seen him,* Philip, not understanding this, *saith unto him, Shew us the Father, and it sufficeth us.* " Thou " hast told us much of thy Father, of his love to us, " and of his mercy in sending thee to save us; Lord, " give us but one sight of the Father, and we will " ask no more." To this Christ answers, *Have I been so long time with you,* (and three or four years was not long time, but that one day of being with Christ was a vast mercy), *and yet hast thou not known me Philip?* He saith not, " Have I been so long time " with you, and hast thou not yet known the Father?" (as he told the unbelieving Jews, John viii. 19. *Ye neither know me, nor my Father;* and John xvi. 3. *They have neither known the Father nor me.*); but, *Hast thou not known me?* " You do know the Father, " because you know me; though you do not know so " distinctly that you do know him." Therefore Christ adds, *He that seeth me, hath seen the Father;* as John xii. 45. *He that seeth me, seeth him that sent me.* " But thou Philip hast seen me, both with thy bodily " eye, and with the eye of faith," (as this same Philip saith to Nathanael, John i. 45. *We have found him*

him of whom Moses in the law, and the prophets did write. "He hath been long promised by God, long looked for by Israel; now he is come, and we have found him; *Come and see.*") : *How sayest thou then, Shew us the Father? Believest thou not, that I am in the Father, and the Father in me?* "If thou truly believest in me, this thou must believe, and dost believe." And to this way of believing he exhorts him, ver. 11. It is no easy thing to hold a strait rein on an inquisitive mind, and to confine all our knowledge of God's glory unto that that shineth in the face and person of Jesus Christ. There is enough there to busy us happily in time, and to eternity; and no good can be got in transgressing this landmark. If men go but one step in studying God out of Christ, they wander immediately, and they do wander dangerously; as every man may feel in himself, and see it visibly in many others.

Exhort. 3. Use and improve this representation of God in Christ. It is our greatest privilege to have it; and our greatest care and diligence should be used in the improvement of it; and our greatest profit comes to us by that improvement. This I would insist upon in these particulars.

1. Improve this representation of God in Christ for fixing and determining your spirits, in all your thoughts of God. There must be thoughts of God. His people are called *thinkers on his name*, Mal iii. 16. On the contrary, of the wicked it is said, Psal. x. 4. *God is not in all his thoughts.* There are two thoughts about God in Christ, that I am afraid some deceive themselves by. 1. Some think that they do know God in Christ, when they know that Christ is God. This is indeed absolutely needful to salvation. But it is not all. A notional assent unto this truth, that shineth so brightly in every page of the New Testament, may be in an ungodly man. The devil knows, and believes it, Mark v. 7.; and he only puts a wicked *if* upon it, in his tempting of Christ, Matth. iv.

iv. 3. 2. Some think they know God in Christ, when they know that Christ only can reveal God unto men, Matth. xi. 27. and John i. 18. This is indeed a proper work for Christ only; but that pertains to his prophetic office. But we must go further; not only to believe that Jesus Christ is true God, and the only true and effectual teacher of the knowledge of God; but that all the right knowledge we have, or can have of God, is of God as he is in Jesus Christ. What Paul resolved on in his office, (and it may be that he meant more than his way in his office of apostleship), you must take up in all your religion: 1 Cor. ii. 2. *I determined not to know any thing among you, save Jesus Christ, and him crucified.* And if we had more ministers of Paul's spirit in their preaching, we should see more of Christianity in the people's religion. But when some ministers preach, as if they had taken up the reverse of Paul's determination, even to know, and to make known any thing, every thing, save Christ, and him crucified; is it any wonder, if many of their hearers may say, as they did about the Holy Ghost, and his dispensation, Acts xix. 2. *We have not so much as heard whether there be any Jesus Christ, and that crucified?* And such may justly say also of the Spirit, *We have not so much as heard whether there be any Holy Ghost*: for the Spirit is received only by believers on Christ, John vii. 39.; and *by the hearing of faith, and not by the works of the law*, Gal. iii. 2.

2. Improve this representation of God in Christ, in your dealing with him for eternal life. Whoever would be saved, must have some heart-dealings with God about it, and for it. You know it is *the gift of God, through Jesus Christ our Lord*, Rom. vi. 23. Any way, every way of dealing with God for salvation, will not succeed. There is one special, and the only right way; and that is with God in Christ. Can you deal with God as the Creator of the world, and as a Lawgiver? Unless God had revealed himself in

Christ,

Christ, no sinner durst lift up his face before God's throne, to beg eternal life, or to expect it.

3. Improve this representation of God in Christ, in all your worshipping of God. The word is *the word of Christ*, Col. iii. 16. We pray; but how? We must *pray in Christ's name, and ask, whatever we ask of the Father, in Christ's name,* John xiv. 13, 14. and xvi. 23, 24. The God that the apostle prayed to, is *the God and Father of our Lord Jesus Christ, of whom the whole family in heaven and earth is named,* Eph. iii. 14, 15.; and to him he gives glory by Christ Jesus, ver 20, 21. O that men did know, that to worship God out of Christ, is to *worship they know not what!* as Christ saith in John iv. 22. *But we know what we worship: for salvation is of the Jews.* Out of them the Messias cometh, and salvation by him; and in him God is savingly known, and knowingly worshipped.

4. Let all Christians improve this doctrine in their spiritual exercise, and in the actings of the graces of the Spirit. All those graces are from God in Christ, and dispensed and enlivened by the Spirit of grace. And they are (if you take the expression rightly) as so many distinct members and powers of the new man, whereby it acts on its original. I would name several of them, and shew of what use this representation of God in Christ is in their acting.

1*st*, Faith. We *by Christ believe in God, who raised him up from the dead, and gave him glory,* 1 Pet. i. 21. Faith is justly called the fundamental, radical grace in the new creature; because it is that grace whereby he is built on Christ the foundation, and taketh root in Christ, in whom is all the Christian's life, sap, and fatness. There are two acts of faith I would speak of; an act of faith for peace, and an act of faith for supply.

(1.) Faith acts for peace. There is a sad quarrel betwixt God and us by sin, which must be taken away, or no peace can be. God hath provided the way;

way; Chrift hath made the way, yea, is become the way; the gofpel reveals it, and faith improves and ufeth it. I fhall give you four names of God in Chrift, which you will know and ufe, if you ever know what believing is. 1. The name of God is *love to finners,* John iii. 16. 1 John iv. 8, 9, 10. 16. It is impoffible that a finner can act any dependance on God for falvation, unlefs there be fome manifeftation of his name, as love. Whenever any beam of this love darts in upon a poor finner, the man begins to live and hope immediately. I mean not, that every one fhould believe this propofition, That God loves me; but only, that God hath a wonderful great love to fave finners, which he hath proved in giving his own Son to be a Saviour; that this love runs out to men in and by Jefus Chrift; and all that would have it for themfelves, fhould ftrive to get near to this fun, that when its light and heat is feen and felt, they may be faved. 2. Another name of God that faith acts on, is God *with his redeeming blood.* Stumble not at the phrafe; it is that of the Holy Ghoft, Acts xx. 28. When the apoftle is counting the privileges of Chriftians under the New Teftament, fee how he rifeth, Heb. xii. 22, 23, 24. *Ye are come unto mount Sion, and unto the city of the living God, the heavenly Jerufalem, and to an innumerable company of angels;* (all beyond what the Old Teftament church was brought to); *to the general affembly and church of the firft-born, which are written in heaven, and to God the Judge of all, and to the spirits of juft men made perfect.* But is it not terrible to be brought to *God the Judge of all?* No; for ye are come *to Jefus the Mediator of the new covenant, and to the blood of fprinkling, that fpeaketh better things than that of Abel.* As if the apoftle had faid, "Fear " not to *come to God the Judge of all,* when ye fee " *Jefus the Mediator of the new covenant,* and his " blood that fealed and confirmed that covenant, fo " near to God. God the Judge is your friend, and " will

"will absolve you; and *the blood of the covenant* (as
"it is called, Heb. xiii. 20.) will speak better things
"for you, and speak louder for your salvation, than
"the guilt of sin, and the thunders of the law, can
"speak against you." And never had a sinner been
saved, if the voice of Christ's blood had been outcried
by any voice from heaven, or earth, or hell. 3 Another name of God in Christ, is, he is *a God that justifies the ungodly*, Rom. iv. 5. Papists, and others, in
their pretended zeal for holiness and good works, do
either desire that this name of God were not in the
Bible, or the true sense of it were taken out of the
church. It is this plainly: That as no man needs the
blessing of justification, but a sinner and an ungodly
man; so whenever God gives this blessing, he gives it
freely to a man that is ungodly till he get it. And
when a sinner pleads for it, he doth plead as guilty
and ungodly. He begs it of God as an alms of free
grace; the Lord gives it as such; and he that gets it,
holds it, and praiseth for it, as such an alms of mere
grace. *God be merciful to me the sinner*, said the justified publican; Let the unjustified Pharisee boast of
his fastings, prayers, and good works, Luke xviii. 9.
14. 4. *The way by which peace with God is brought
about in and by Jesus Christ*, is a name of God in Christ
that faith hath much to do with. When God proclaimed his name to Moses, Exod. xxxiv. 5, 6, 7. (Moses had earnestly desired to see the Lord's glory,
God promiseth it graciously, chap. xxxiii. 18, 9):
Let us read this glorious proclamation: *And the Lord
passed by before him, and proclaimed, The Lord, the
Lord God, merciful and gracious, long-suffering, and
abundant in goodness and truth, keeping mercy for thousands (of generations*, as Exod. xx. 6. and Psal. cv. 8),
*forgiving iniquity, and transgression, and sin, and that
will by no means clear the guilty; visiting the iniquity
of the fathers upon the children, and upon the childrens
children, unto the third and to the fourth generation:*
Here was much of the glory of God's grace discovered;
and

and Moses made good use of it, ver. 8, 9. But yet how dark and dreadful was this name! how hard to understand it! Here is both grace in pardoning sin, and justice in visiting for sin. By this name we cannot tell when, and whom God will pardon; and when, and whom he will not clear; for all are guilty. By this name we cannot tell how God can do both; how he can pardon, and yet not clear the guilty; how he can pardon without reflecting on his justice; or how he can punish iniquity, and not reflect on his grace and mercy. In chap. xxxiii. 9. the Lord saith, *I will make all my goodness* (or *beauty* and *glory*) *pass before thee*. Yet was it short of New Testament light: for the bright gospel-name of God in Christ resolves sweetly this riddle, Rom. iii. 24, 25, 26. In Christ only *mercy and truth are met together, righteousness and peace have kissed each other*, as Psal. lxxxv. 10. And by this meeting and kiss, we are saved; and when we see it by faith, we are comforted. By these, God's glorious names of justice and mercy kiss one another, and do kiss and save the believer; and the believer by faith kisseth the Son of God, as Psal. ii. 12.; and then the Father, as a reconciled God, in him. I would speak somewhat of this from two scriptures, both deep in themselves, and yet full of light and comfort to believers. One in 2 Cor. v. 19, 20, 21. In this place, the apostle tells us what his gospel was, as committed to him, and preached by him. It was this good news, That *God was in Christ reconciling the world unto himself*, (But *the world lieth in wickedness*, 1 John v. 19. and God is holy, and a hater of wickedness; how then can such a God as he is, be reconciled to such a world as this is?), *not imputing their trespasses unto them*. God out of Christ judgeth and condemneth the sinful world for their trespasses; and this is the glory of his justice. But God in Christ does not impute their trespasses unto them; and this is the glory of his grace. But how can this be? The world is guilty; trespasses they have committed;

mitted; sin is not a transient act, no more to be heard after it is committed; but as it is in us, it flows from a depraved sinful nature, and contracts a permanent guilt, binding us over unto eternal vengeance, and is only removeable and dissolved by pardoning grace. The nature of God, and his law, requireth that this high crime of sin be either avenged on us, or satisfied for by us, or by another for us. The just revenge of sin, is the eternal ruin of the sinner; and satisfaction to justice for sin, is eternally beyond the power of the sinner, or of any creature whatsoever. How then can God be just, and not impute sin to the sinner? It is answered in ver. 21. *For he hath made him to be sin for us, who knew no sin; that we might be made the righteousness of God in him.* The sinless Son of God in man's nature, is by God made sin for us, that the sinful sons and daughters of men may be made the righteousness of God in him. How can this be; that one that is sinless is made sin, and that such as are true and real sinners are made righteous, yea, made the righteousness of God in him that was made sin; and they are made thus righteous, by his being thus made sin? Is not this to depress Christ too low, and to exalt believers too high? No; it depresseth Christ no lower than his Father did lay him for our salvation, and exalteth believers no higher than saving grace designed them. How is he made sin? By the bearing of, and being a propitiation for sin. Sin was imputed to him: not his own: for he had none, and could not have been our Saviour if he had had any; Heb. vii. 26. *For such an High Priest became us, who is holy, harmless, undefiled, separate from sinners, and made higher than the heavens.* But the iniquity of all his flock was laid on him, Isa. liii. 5.; for this was he bruised by law and justice, and by these stripes are we healed, Isa. liii. 5. Christ was sinless in himself, and only made sin for us. We are sinners in ourselves, and far from, and void of all righteousness in ourselves; yet by grace are made the righteousness of God in him;

not,

not, nor never in ourselves. The sanctified believer is made truly holy in himself, by Christ's holiness imparted to him by the Spirit of Christ. The glorified are made perfectly holy. But neither of them are made sanctification or righteousness for themselves, or for others. The glory of this is Christ's crown and property, 1 Cor. i. 30. and the blessing of it is the glory and salvation of his people. Another scripture, among many to this purpose, is in Gal. iii. 13, 14. *Christ hath redeemed us from the curse of the law*, (a great mercy; but how?), *being made a curse for us;* (How proves he it?): *for it is written, Cursed is every one that hangeth on a tree;*---(taken from Deut. xxi. 23.) For he that is hanged, (i. e. on a tree, as ver. 22.), *is accursed of God*, or *the curse of God;* Hanging to death on a tree, was named in the law an accursed death, (though it probably be one of the easiest ways of putting malefactors to death, as it is generally used in Christian kingdoms), on the account of one Jesus Christ, the Messiah, who was to die this way) :---*that the blessing of Abraham might come on the Gentiles through Jesus Christ.* What is the blessing of Abraham? It is that that comes to men by faith in Christ: Gal. iii. 9. *So then they which be of faith, are blessed with faithful* (or *believing*) *Abraham*. Both are blessed with the same blessing, and by the same Blesser, and in the same way of believing in Christ. These two scriptures (as Christ himself was) have been a stone of stumbling, and a rock of offence, and as signs to be spoke against. But can any say or think, that the inspired writer of them did not highly honour his Lord and Master, Jesus Christ, or that he did not wisely consult the edification of the church, in his using these words? No; no mere man excelled him in both. Zeal for Christ's glory, and love to sinners salvation, did eat him up. If we rank these words amongst *some of the things that are hard to be understood, which they that are unlearned and unstable wrest, as they do also the other scriptures, unto their destruction,* 2 Peter iii. 16.; yet surely they are most needful to

be

be understood, are capable of a very good meaning, and are made very plain unto many. Sin against God, and the curse of God for sin, are the worst things in this and the other world. Sin, and the curse for it, are inseparable. If sin be committed, it is imputed, and the curse follows in course of law. If the curse fall on a man, sin did precede it, and deserve it. Yea, when our Saviour bore our sin by imputation, the curse must follow that charge. But observe the dialect of the Holy Ghost in these two scriptures, and see what provision is made for the honour of Christ in this way of speaking, as well as for our peace and salvation in what is spoken. 1. Christ is said to be *made sin*. Thus no sinner was, or can be. When angels fell, they were made sinners, but not made sin. So of Adam, when he sinned, he became a sinner, and a sin and death-conveying head to himself, and to all his natural posterity; but he did not become sin, tho' he came nearer it than ever any other sinner did or can. When we sin, (and, alas! when do we not sin?), we were sinners by nature, before we commit actual sin; but by sinning we only become greater sinners, and are not made sin. *Jeroboam did sin, and made Israel to sin*, 1 Kings xiv. 16. The idols he set up, *became a sin*, 1 Kings xii. 30. But neither he, nor they were made sin. So Christ is said to be *made a curse*. And this is not to be said properly of any, but Christ. A sinner unpardoned hath the curse lying on him, and he is under it, as Gal. iii. 10; but he is not made a curse. 2. Christ is said to be *made sin by God*. All sinners are made such by Satan and themselves. God makes no sinners; but to save them, he makes his Son to be sin. So Christ was made a curse, and that by God too. He that laid sin on him, laid the curse also. 3. Christ is *made sin and a curse for others*. So it is in both places, *for us*. A proper sinner hath both his own sin charged on him, and God's curse laid on him, for himself. He hath none to blame but himself, Hosea xiii. 9. The sin is committed by him-

himself, charged on himself, and punishment lights on himself. All quite contrary to God's way in dealing with his Son. All the charge on him was for others. 4. Christ's sinlessness and blessedness in himself is expressed in 2 Cor. v. 21. and hinted in Gal. iii. 13, 14. He knew no sin, yet is made sin. He was the great blessing of his church, yet is made a curse for it. Lastly, Observe the fruit, design, and effect of this marvellous way of God's making of Christ. He is made sin, that we might be made righteousness. That imputed righteousness in which believers stand before God, is the fruit of Christ's being made sin for them. Our blessing we have, springs out of Christ's being made a curse for us.

So much for the grace of faith, and its acting for peace with God. Whenever you are in good earnest in dealing with God for his favour, and reconciliation with him, one or more of these names of God in Christ, *God as love, God with his redeeming blood, God that justifies the ungodly, God making his Son to be sin and curse for his people;* I say, some of these names of God must either be your anchor-ground, or you will perish in the sea and storm of your sin, and of God's wrath and curse. I know, that while men are secure, (as the most are), and know not what God, nor sin, nor conscience are, they may either deride them, or wantonly talk *pro* and *con* of these sacred things of God: but I can assure you of this, that if ever (and woe to you, if you never felt) the terrors of God, and the power of his law, break in upon your awakened consciences; if you ever think in earnest of death and judgment, you must have your recourse unto God in Christ, or perish eternally. No refuge but in him, Heb. vi. 18, 19.; no hope but from him, and on him.

2. There is an act and exercise of faith for supply. When a sinner is made by grace a believer, and hath peace with God, he is yet in a wanting condition. He may be poor and needy, not only in his own eyes,

eyes, but really, on whom the Lord thinketh favourably, Pfal. xl. 17. Every believer can tell fomething, none can tell all he wants. How are they fupplied? Phil. iv. 19. *My God fhall fupply all your need, according to his riches in glory, by Jefus Chrift.* It hath *pleafed the Father, that in him fhould all fulnefs dwell,* Col. i. 19. And how pleafing fhould it be to his people, that it is lodged in fo fure a hand? And how pleafant ought it to be to them, to come, and afk, and receive, till their joy be full? John xiv. 13, 14. and xvi. 23, 24. We all know, by natural light, that God is the fountain of all our fupplies, *from whom cometh every good gift, and every perfect gift,* James i. 17. But gofpel-light tells us by whom he giveth, and on what ground; even out of Chrift's fulnefs, and according to his promifes in Chrift.

So much for the grace of faith.

2*dly,* Another grace that this reprefentation of God in and by Chrift directs us in the acting and exercife of, is, *repentance unto life,* as it is called in Acts xi. 18. There is a faving repentance, as well as there is a faving faith. Both are given to them whom God faveth. No impenitent perfon is faved, nor unbeliever. Two things only I would note about repentance. 1. Never man did truly repent, but a believer in Chrift. 2. Never did a man truly repent, but for his fins againft God in Chrift. If you know nothing more of repentance but what you feel in the twinges of your confcience, by the light and heat of God's holy law, you are not yet come to gofpel-repentance. Poor and confufed are the notions that moft finners have. They think, that all their fins are againft God, and all their relief is in Jefus Chrift; but they do not know, and lay to heart, that all their fins are againft God in Chrift, and that all their relief againft fin is likewife in God in Chrift. Men *fin againft Chrift,* 1 Cor. viii. 12.; they are *forgiven by Chrift,* Col. iiii. 13. He is *exalted with the right hand of God, to be a Prince and a Saviour, for to give repentance to Ifrael, and forgivenefs* *ness of sins*, Acts v. 31. If, in the exercise of your repentance, you forget that you have pierced Christ by your sins, you are not acted by the promised Spirit of grace, Zech. xii. 10. And all expectations of pardon that are not only grounded on Christ and his mediation, are not only vain, but sinful.

3dly, I might speak of the grace of love, that precious and everlasting grace. Love must act on God in Christ. It is sad to see and hear people busying their heads with speculations about the excellencies and perfections of the divine nature, and imagining by the force of their reasoning on these things, to blow up a fire of love to God. But let men know, that till God be known to us as love, no love that is true, will ever kindle in our hearts. Now, God as love is only discovered as he is in Christ: 1 John iv. 8,---19. *We love him, because he first loved us.*

4thly, All holy obedience is to be performed unto God in Christ: Col. iii. 17,---24. *And whatsoever ye do, in word or deed, do all in the name of the Lord Jesus, giving thanks to God and the Father by him.* Yea, relative duties are urged by most spiritual motives and patterns; husbands love to their wives, by Christ's love to his church; wives subjection to their own husbands, by the church's subjection to Christ, who is its Head and Saviour, Eph. v. 20,---33. Even Christian servants obedience to, and serving of their masters, is required and sweetened by this, that therein *they serve the Lord Christ.* It is not unlike, that, in those times, Christian servants might be slaves and servants of infidels, and of such as served the devil; yet, saith he, " in your lawful service of such masters, ye serve Christ, " though they do not know him." Surely, the spiritual tincture of true worship is lost, when Christ is forgotten in it; and the savour of Christian obedience is perished, when it is not done as to the Lord.

5thly, Patience under affliction is a grace that every saint hath need of, as Heb. x. 36.; and must use in all his race heaven-ward, Heb. xii. 1. *Let us run with pati-*

patience the race that is set before us. There is not a step in our journey wherein patience is needless. Running and patience seem inconsistent; but he that runs without patience, makes but fools haste. Now, this needful and useful grace can only be exercised by faith in God through Christ. If God afflict us as our Creator, as our Judge, as our Lawgiver, reason and morality may afford not a few arguments to patience and submission to his will: but true Christian patience will never be found, unless the love of the afflicter be in some measure seen by the afflicted. Our blessed Lord gave us an example to follow, John xviii. 11. *The cup which my Father hath given me, shall I not drink it?* If men or devils only had given it, (and they had no little hand in it), the matter had been otherwise. *He was oppressed, and he was afflicted, yet he opened not his mouth,* Isa. liii. 7. Christ's cup was more bitter, his sufferings greater, than ever any of his people tasted and felt. His patience was invincible, and that because his faith was perfect, Isa. l. 6,---9. David saith, Psal. xxxix. 9. *I was dumb, I opened not my mouth, because thou didst it.* When God is seen as an enemy, affliction will rather work fretting than patience. Therefore when the apostle is directing Christians how to bear God's afflicting hand rightly, without fainting, or despising it; his main argument is, that in all of them the Lord dealeth with them as a father with his children, Heb. xii. 5,---11. And surely no man can have the comfort of this relation to God, of a child to his heavenly Father, that by faith takes not up the high foundation of this relation, that God is the God and Father of our Lord Jesus Christ.

6*thly, lastly,* The hope of glory ariseth from, and acts on God, as God in Christ. This grace is a great mercy; and that all that have it know. It should be tenderly cherished. But this is a great fault in many Christians, that they do not seek it so diligently as they ought, when they want it; nor act it so carefully, when they have any of it: and sorely do they

smart

smart for this, in *walking mourning without the sun*, so many days, as Job xxx. 28. See the exhortation in Rom. xii. 12. *Rejoicing in hope, patient in tribulation, continuing instant in prayer;* and all this is to be done in *serving the Lord*, ver. 11. You all readily think, that murmuring under afflictions, and restraining prayer before God, are ungodly practices; and yet you do think it no fault (but a great misery you will own it to be) to neglect the leading duty, to *rejoice in hope*, and *in the hope of the glory of God*, Rom. v. 2. This hope is in Christ; yea, *he is our hope*, 1 Tim. i. 1. *Christ in you* is *the hope of glory*, Col. i. 27. The hope of glory grows on no root but Jesus Christ. He is *eternal life*, 1 John i. 1, 2. He that knows him, knows eternal life. *He that hath Christ, hath eternal life*, 1 John v. 11, 12, 13.; and he that hath Christ *dwelling in his heart by faith*, Eph. iii. 17. *hath eternal life abiding in him*, which the apostle denieth of a murderer, 1 John iii. 15.

And thus I would conclude this truth, of the glory of Christ as he is the representative of God to his church, and of the good use we should make thereof. I have insisted longer upon it than I designed. But the importance of the subject may excuse it. But when all is said, we need to begin again, that we may inculcate this truth deeply into the heart and consciences of Christians. Assure yourselves, that God out of Christ is an idol whom all the world worshippeth, (as Demetrius said of Diana, Acts xix 27), except the few that can say, as 1 John v. 20, 21. *And we know that the Son of God is come, and hath given us an understanding that we may know him that is true: and we are in him that is true, even in his Son Jesus Christ: this is the true God, and eternal life. Little children, keep yourselves from idols. Amen.* All representations of God, save what is made to you in his Son, are idols. And as you love his glory, and your own eternal well, watch, and ward, and keep yourselves from all, or any of them.

John xvii. 24.

Father, I will that they also whom thou hast given me, be with me where I am; that they may behold my glory which thou hast given me: for thou lovedst me before the foundation of the world.

YOU have heard at some length of the glory of Christ, as he is the representer of God unto his church; and the rather I insisted on it, because it is a point of divine truth of the main importance to be believed, and of the main influence and direction in the whole of Christianity. There are many poor souls that are ruined with irreligion; and not a few are ruined in and by their religion, such as it is. Some know not that there is a God, or live as if they thought there was none, or wished that there was none. And some say, they know and believe that there is a God, and they make some fashion of worshipping and serving him; but they know not who he is, and what his right name is. It is only God in Christ who can be only known, and savingly known, by men. It is only a saving name of God that can be savingly known by men. And this name of God is only proclaimed in his everlasting gospel; and the knowing of this name can only be attained by Christ's declaring it, John xvii. 6, 26. 1 Cor. xii. 3. by the Holy Ghost. All contemplations of God out of Christ are but vain imaginations, and can never bring a man to the saving knowledge of God: and all worshipping of God out of Christ, is but will-worship, and provocation.

Secondly, It now follows to speak of another beam and branch of Christ's glory; and that is, in Christ's representing his church and people unto God. It is one part of his glory, that he doth so represent God unto his church, that all the saving knowledge of God is only in him and by him. Another part of his glory (if the word *part* were proper in speaking of his infinite glory; but ye know what I mean, and none can mistake but the wilful) is, in his representing his church so unto God, that all the acceptance we have with God, all the saving mercy we receive from God, and all the favourable views God hath of us, are from our being seen as in Christ, and as we are represented by Christ unto him. God out of Christ is a maze, a labyrinth to men, yea, a dreadful enemy: and men out of Christ are an abomination in his eyes.

My work on this second head of Christ's glory, shall be in three things. 1. I would shew you wherein Christ represents his people unto God. 2. What is Christ's fitness for making this representation. 3. What is his glory in making of it.

First, Wherein doth Christ represent his church unto God? By his church I mean a select company of Adam's seed (not excluding our first parents themselves) appointed to eternal life by Jesus Christ. This is his body, whereof he is Head and Saviour, Eph. v. 23. All the favourable appearances they make in God's sight, are all as they are represented unto God by Jesus Christ. This I would instruct in a few of the main and principal.

1. May I begin with the first, the deepest of all, election, that sacred eternal purpose of God's grace concerning his church? This grace is in Jesus Christ: Eph. i. 3, 4, 5. *Blessed be the God and Father of our Lord Jesus Christ, who hath blessed us with all spiritual blessings in heavenly places* (or *things*) *in Christ; according as he hath chosen us in him before the foundation of the world, that we should be holy, and without blame before him in love: having predestinated us unto the adoption of children by Jesus Christ to himself.* It is but little that we do, or can know of God: little of his works, little of his word; but least of all of his
thoughts

thoughts and purposes. But when men think of these thoughts of God's heart, and judge of them according to their own, no wonder that they widely mistake: *For his thoughts are not our thoughts, neither are our ways his ways, saith the Lord,* Isa. lv. 8, 9.; but as far above them are his ways and his thoughts, as the heavens are above the earth. How far is a purposing, decreeing God, above the reach of the most discerning of creatures! Yet vain man that would be wise, and quickly dreams that he is so, (and thereby bewrays his folly), will venture to pry into, judge, and reason of the unsearchable counsels of God; when they that have most of the Spirit of God say, as in Rom. xi. 33, 34. *O the depth of the riches, both of the wisdom and knowledge of God! how unsearchable are his judgments, and his ways past finding out! For who hath known the mind of the Lord, or who hath been his counsellor?* We cannot be his counsellers; but we may, and must be his scholars, and learn, and adore, and believe what he revealeth. And in the scripture named, we have much to learn about his purposes. As, 1. That all spiritual blessings in Christ Jesus flow from election-grace. 2. That this election grace is eternal. 3. That this election-grace passed upon distinct persons, *us* and *we*. 4. That the means, and way, and the end, are all included in this decree and purpose: *That we should be holy, and without blame before him in love;* and the end is, *the adoption of children,* ver. 5. the heavenly inheritance, ver. 11. And, 5. That which pertains to my present purpose, is, that this election-grace, thus expressed, thus qualified and distinguished, is in Jesus Christ, ver. 4. *by Jesus Christ,* ver. 5. *This purpose and grace was given us in Christ Jesus before the world began,* 2 Tim. i. 9. Now, what is Christ's interest in election-grace? It is not to be thought, that Christ purchased the love of election, as he did all the fruits of it; but only that election-love passed first on Christ the head, and then on his body the church: (though I own, that the

the words *first* and *second* are very improperly applied to the counsels of God, which are but one act in the divine mind; but we must think as a child, and reason and understand as a child, while we are as a child, 1 Cor. xiii. 11.). Christ was chosen head to the church, and the church chosen to be his body. He is *chosen of God*, 1 Pet. ii. 14.: and his church is *a chosen generation*, ver. 9.; and chosen in him, not without regard to him. Election determines all the persons; election determines all the blessings these persons are to be blessed with; and election determines the way in and by which all these blessings are to be given to all these persons: and that way is in and by Jesus Christ.

2. Christ represents his church unto God in redemption. This redemption is *in Christ Jesus*, Rom. iii. 24.; it is *in him we have it*, Eph. i. 7. There is a Redeemer; the Lord Jesus Christ, the Son of God. There is a price of the redemption; himself, his life, his blood. There are redeemed ones; a great multitude *out of every kindred, and tongue, and people and nation*, Rev. v. 9. In speaking of the redemption in and by Jesus Christ, I would consider it four ways.

1*st*, This redemption is to be considered as required and demanded by the Father from the Son. The work of redeeming was laid on the Son, and the price of redemption fixed upon: Even that the Son of God should, in the fulness of time, take on him man's nature; (but as *the childrens nature*, Heb. ii. 14. as *the seed of Abraham*, ver. 16.): that in that nature he should stand in their room and stead, and suffer what his people deserved by their sins; and purchase blessings for them, which they could never procure to themselves, and without which they must perish. This price of redemption was required of Christ, John x. 18.; and required in honour to God's holy justice, in love and mercy to his chosen, and in a design of glory to his Son. A price of redemption for a sinner was never required by God of a sinner. He knoweth well,

well, that they have nothing to pay. Yea, the damned in hell are not sent thither to pay, but to be punished. Your proverb, That a prison pays no debts, is true of God's dreadful prison, hell, and of the miserable prisoners there. The Lord save you from it, and instruct you in the only way to escape it. You are great debtors to God; you can never pay the first, much less the last farthing of it. He doth not require payment of you; but all he craveth of you, is, that you would humbly own your debt, and your inablity to pay, and betake yourselves unto the surety's payment. It was no improper saying concerning the gospel, used by a minister in preaching to an ignorant people: " The gospel (he said) is nothing but good " news, that a rich man is come into the country to " pay poor folks debts." On this errand the Father sent him: and for this end we should believe on him.

2dly, Consider Christ's redemption as paid by Jesus Christ, and so wrought out by him. All the price demanded, he paid fully. The debt was perfectly paid, in full measure, heaped up, and running over. For when the righteousness of God is paid for the redemption of sinners, and of their transgressions, (as in Heb. ix. 15.), we quickly see where the advantage lieth: for the demerit of sin is mainly heightened by the dignity of the party offended; and the merit of righteousness, by the dignity of the party that performs it. On this, as on other accounts, *grace doth much more abound than sin,* Rom. v. 20, 21.; and *this grace doth reign, where sin had reigned.* Since sin came into the world, and grace appeared in the first gospel-promise, Gen. iii. 15. there never was a sinner redeemed and saved, never was any propitiation made for sin, but what our Lord Jesus Christ the Redeemer did, and made, by his dying at Jerusalem. The virtue of it, according to the covenant, was effectual to believers, before and after his death, Acts xv. 11.; and will still be till his second coming, Heb. ix. 28.

3dly,

3*dly*, Confider redemption as accepted by God. Though a price be demanded, and paid as demanded: yet the redemption is not a concluded bargain, unless it be accepted. But the price of the church's redemption was accepted with the highest good-will: Eph. v. 2. Chrift *loved us, and gave himself for us, an offering and a facrifice to God for a fweet-fmelling favour.* The facrifice was offered to God, but offered for us. The favour of this facrifice afcends upwards, and giveth fatisfaction to divine juftice; and it defcends downwards to the hearts and confciences of believers, for their peace and falvation, Heb. ix. 14. *It pleafed the Lord to bruife him, he hath put him to grief,* Ifa. liii. 10. And both this way and means, and the fruits and effects thereof, are the pleafure of Jehovah, which profpers in the hand of our dying Lord Jefus; as in that verfe, *The Father loved his Son, for laying down his life for his fheep,* John x. 17, 18. And this *commandment he received of his Father.* Our Lord had this commandment in his heart, and came to do it, and delighted in doing it, Pfal. xl. 6, 7, 8. with Heb. x. 5.----10. The divine acceptance of the price of his church's redemption, is demonftrated two ways especially. 1. In the glory that the Lord Redeemer was admitted unto, Phil. ii. 6.----11. Eph. i. 20.----23. Heb. i. 3. ii. 9. and xii. 2. and in many places. Only confider his own words to his difciples, and to his Father. To the difciples, in John xvi. 10. *He (the Holy Spirit whom I will fend from my Father) fhall convince the world of righteoufnefs, becaufe I go to my Father, and ye fee me no more.* The conviction is deep, and fo is the reafon and ground of it. Chrift going to leave them, and their feeing him no more, as before and now, was their main grief. They could not think that any good fhould accrue to them by this fad parting, much lefs fo great bleffings as Chrift told them of, and which quickly after they knew and owned: Acts ii, 33. *Being by the right hand of God exalted, and having received of the Father the promife* *of the Holy Ghoſt, he hath ſhed forth this, which ye now ſee and hear.* And as he ſpoke this, and words to the ſame purpoſe, in the fulfilling of this promiſe, three thouſand ſinners, and bloody ones too, are convinced of ſin, righteouſneſs, and of judgment, and made believers. Chriſt's words to his Father are in John xvii. 4. *I have glorified thee on earth; I have finiſhed the work which thou gaveſt me to do* (in it). If Chriſt came back again into the world, (ſave to judge it; and that will be in the clouds), men might think, that he had not done all he firſt came for. But he did all, as it was foretold in Dan. ix. 24. *He finiſhed the tranſgreſſion, and made an end of ſins*, (as Heb. ix. 26. *He put away ſin by the ſacrifice of himſelf), and made reconciliation for iniquity, and brought in everlaſting righteouſneſs, and ſealed up the viſion and prophecy, and anointed the moſt holy.* 2. As Chriſt's glory in heaven, on his paying the price of redemption, is a demonſtration of its acceptance with God; ſo all the grace and glory on earth, and in heaven, in time, and to eternity, which is poured forth abundantly on men, (all which flows from the virtue of this price), is another demonſtration of God's acceptance of this required and paid moſt precious price. Of which anon.

4*thly*, Conſider redemption in Chriſt as it is applied to the redeemed. As the price was demanded by the Father, as it was paid by the Son, as this payment was accepted of the Father; all thoſe concern the redeemed nearly: but all is only about them, and for them. But application is to them, on them, and in them. And all the application of Chriſt's redemption, depends on, and flows from the deſign of the Father and Son in this great work of redemption. I would conſider redemption as applied to perſons, and to bleſſings, and their order. 1. As to perſons. Chriſt's redemption is applied to all, and none but them, for whom it was paid. *He ſhall juſtify many:* (whom! how many! and how! and why!): *for he ſhall bear their*

their iniquities, Isa. liii. 11. Universal election is rather nonsense, and a contradiction in its terms, than an error: for if there be an election of grace, (as there is, as sure as there is a sovereign *God of all grace*, as he is called, 1 Pet. v. 10), some are chosen, and not all: and therefore some are passed by. Universal salvation is a gross and damnable error, that few or none dare own. But universal redemption hath many advocates and patrons. Whoever defend it so as to exclude the special, particular redemption of the elect of God, they do fight against the tenor of the gospel. Christ died for distinct known persons for his sheep whom he knew, John x. 14. 27. He died for them, in love to them: and doubtless he knew well whom he loved. His blood, the price of redemption, is *the blood of the everlasting covenant*, Heb. xiii. 20. which did confirm this covenant, Heb. ix. 15, 16. And was not this price paid according to the terms of this covenant? And did not this covenant fix both the price, and who should pay it; and the purchase, and who should enjoy it? This you all may be sure of, that however men, by their wit and learning, may dispute and talk about Christ's death, and its extent, in his and his Father's designs in it; yet this precious gospel-truth, of redemption by Jesus Christ, is never rightly known, rightly believed, nor rightly used, till a particular, lost and sold sinner put in by faith for a share and interest in it. Thus Paul, Gal. ii. 20. The Son of God *loved me, and gave himself for me.* How could Paul know this? When Christ died, and redeemed his church, Paul was an ungodly wretch, a very hypocrite; and after Christ had died, and rose again, and ascended up into glory, Paul hated the very name of Christ, and persecuted to death all that called on his name. But after *God, that had separated him from his mother's womb, had called him by his grace, and revealed his Son in him,* Gal i. 15, 16. then, and not till then, he knew that Christ died for him, and that in love to him; and ever after he lived by the faith of it. 2. This redemption by Christ is applied as to blessings also, and that in a wise order. Faith is first, and a fruit of Christ's redemption: John xii. 32. *And I, if I be* (or *when I am*) *lifted up from the earth, will draw all men unto me;* i. e. "All whom I am lifted up for, them will I draw unto me." It is no wonder, that some men do not look on faith as the purchase of Christ's redemption, that dream of a kind of saving faith that Christ the Redeemer is not the object of. But we know, that unto us *it is given on the behalf of Christ, to believe on him,* Phil. i. 29.; and that such as have true faith, *have obtained this precious grace, through the righteousness of our God and Saviour Jesus Christ,* (for so it should be read, according to the original), 2 Pet. i. 1. And he is *the author and finisher of our faith,* Heb. xii. 2. And this leads me to speak of the blessings of Christ's redemption, that the redeemed get by the virtue of it, and by Christ's representing them unto God.

(1.) They are represented by Christ unto God for their justification; and obtain it, when, and as, and because, represented to God in him, and by him. This justification of a sinner by faith in Christ Jesus, is, ever was, and ever will be, the darkest riddle, and the greatest stumbling-block, to all the unbelieving world. And it is always so as to gospel-truth; that the nearer relation a gospel-truth hath unto the person and undertaking of the wonderful Saviour, (as he is called, Isa. ix. 6.), the less a natural man seeth, and the more ready is he to stumble at it, and to mistake it. It is but a vain attempt of them, (how good soever their design be, and how learned and wise soever they be that manage it), who study to accommodate the gospel-doctrine of justification by faith in Jesus Christ, unto the gust, liking, and understandings of unbelievers. Such will never, nor can know, and like it, 1 Cor. ii. 14. It is (as all the things of the Spirit of God are) dark, and foolishness to them.

And

And they that know least of Christ, and of faith in him, and of justification by faith, are most bold and daring to reproach all, and to speak evil of things they know not. None need to wonder at what a poor wretch said and wrote, (though he bore no small name in the world), " That of all the writers of the new " testament, Paul was the darkest and most obscure " author." It was however plainly (though wickedly) said; and it is the true meaning of all unbelievers, and the fruit of their unbelief; and remains in all men *till faith come,* as Gal. iii. 23, 25. This attempt of making justification by faith in Christ palatable to a natural man, is not only vain and ineffectual; but it hath no small influence on manifold corruptions of this truth, and of mens bringing in of another gospel, (Gal. i. 6.), that a natural man may sooner know, and better like. When natural men hear of the doctrine of justification, (by which they understand, that a sinner is counted and accepted as righteous before God, and is pardoned all his sins, and adjudged to eternal life), they all immediately and naturally think, that this blessing can only come to men, by one, or other, or both those ways, which are both false ways: 1. Either that God will abate somewhat of the strictness of his law: or, 2. That he will some way enable a sinner to do something, and to bring something to God, in order to his acceptance with God: Either that God will bring down his law to a sinner, or bring up the sinner to obey it. As to the first, That God will abate of the strictness of his law, and demand less; it is a vain and false notion. But it is natural and constant in unrenewed men. Christ's great enemies, the scribes and Pharisees, that were wholly for righteousness by works, to support this Babel, did necessarily explain God's holy law in such a manner as was no hard thing to fulfil it; and all their successors are driven to the same shift. Our Lord, (who *came not to destroy, but to fulfil the law,* Matth. v. 17.), to overthrow their rotten foundation, tells all, in ver. 20. *Ex-*

cept

cept your righteousness shall exceed the righteousness of the scribes and Pharisees, ye shall in no case enter into the kingdom of heaven. This our Lord proveth, by a true interpretation of the law in its perfection, and spirituality, and vast extent; so as that no sinner can fulfil it, and get righteousness and life by it. And thus always God's law ought to be preached to men; as so holy and perfect a law, that no sinner can fulfil it; and as so strong and dreadful, that no sinner can escape its reach, nor endure its sentence; that they may look out for relief in Christ alone. 2. The other thought of a natural man is, That a sinner must do some good, and be made holy, that he may be justified and pardoned. And though the poor sinner is all naught, hath nothing, and can do nothing that is good; yet the legal spirit in himself, and the legal teachers whom he loveth to hear, do use him more severely than the Egyptian taskmasters did the children of Israel. For Israel had earth to make Pharoah's bricks of, and, with much pains, might gather stubble in the land of Egypt instead of straw. But a sinner under the law is in a worse condition: for there is neither earth nor straw in all God's world for a sinner to make one brick, one good work, of; and yet they are called upon daily to do a great many; and are severely beaten when they do not fulfil their tasks. Many are ready to say, Doth not God command sinners in his word to repent, believe, and to do well? Yes, surely he doth. The old and new testament is full of such commands; and ministers may surely, and must teach men what God commands. But they should teach men those things as God means and intends; and that is declared in his word. They should teach them as God will have them to teach, and all men to learn; that is, that those things are God's will, and our duty; but those things are God's will, and our duty; but that power and will to obey is not in men, but must be wrought by grace in them: Phil. ii. 13. *For it is God which worketh in you, both to will and to do of his*

his good pleasure. John xv. 4, 5. *For without me ye can do nothing.* If so it be said of believers, and of true branches in the true vine, what must be said of sinners, in and of themselves? Those commands are not given to make sinners proud, and to think what they can do; but to tell them God's mind, and what is their duty to do; that by the hearing of God's holy will, and feeling of their own utter inability to do any good, they may be humbled, and betake themselves to Christ by faith, on whom all our help is laid. But a replier against God may yet say, Where is justice in commanding what he knows we cannot do, and then in punishing for not doing? Many things have been said to answer such a cavil. I shall name but three. 1. All were once in Adam able to do God's will. This ability is lost by the first sin. If man by his sin have lost his power to do God's work, God hath not lost his authority and power to command man's duty, nor his right to punish man's sin. 2. All men naturally think that they can do something that is good, and a great deal too. The Lord therefore justly tries them, and lets them try what they can do. 3. This natural inability in sinners to do any good is what they love; and so is doubly sinful, as well as miserable. His *cannot*, is inseparable from his *will not*. He is a captive to the devil at his will, 2 Tim. ii. 26. And the captive loves his jailor, and his chains, and his drudgery; and neither longs for liberty, nor welcomes the news of a Redeemer; yea, striveth against him, till Christ subdue him by his grace, 2 Cor. x. 4, 5. So that either of those notions are false, that God will abate of the strictness of his law, or will enable a sinner to do any thing pleasing to God before he be justified. Besides, if either of those were, they would quite alter and invert that mystery of justification by Christ that is revealed to us so plainly in the scriptures. It is not the justification of a good and holy man, but of a sinner; yea of a sinner under the law, guilty of manifold breaches of this law, for which he is accused, arraigned, curfed, and condemned by it, and his mouth ftopped; having no defence and no excufe to make; and no fhift or way of efcape left him, but what the gofpel reveals, Rom. iii. 9.----31. It is about the juftification of a man in this fad condition that the gofpel fpeaks, and tells us thefe good tidings.

1. That a perfect righteoufnefs, anfwering fully all the commands and the demands of the law, hath been wrought out by the Lord Jefus Chrift. He was made under the fame law his people are under whom thus he redeems, Gal. iv. 4, 5. If we had been under one law, and Chrift made under another, it would not, nor could it have been fit and profitable for us. You hear by fome of the mediatorial law, proper to Chrift only. It is true, never had any but Chrift a command from God to redeem loft finners; and it is as true, that this was in the fame command, that he *fhould be made of a woman, and made under the law, that he might redeem them that were under the law.* So that the work of Chrift to redeem, and his being thus made for that work, are equally peculiar to Chrift. For as the work and glory of redeeming the church is his only; fo his being *made of a woman,* and *made under the law,* can be faid of none, but of Chrift as man; no more than it can be faid of any but Chrift, that he is God's own Son, fent, Rom. viii. 3. Adam the firft man was created by God; the firft woman built and made of the man, Gen. ii. Of this blood all nations do fpring in an ordinary way; and fo all mankind are begotten by a man, and born of a woman. But the Son of God took man's nature of a woman only; and fo, whereas all befides are born of a woman, he alone was *made of a woman.* So we all are born under the law, and under its curfe, by Adam's firft fin. Chrift only was *made under the law.* This law demands perfect obedience to all its commands and demands, and layeth on the finner God the lawgiver's wrath and curfe for the leaft difobedience. Chrift anfwered the law in both. As the

eternal

eternal Son of God, he was above the law; and as sinless man, the law had nothing to say against him. But when he took on him man's nature, and therein took on him the law-place of his people, and they so sinful; obedience was justly craved of him, and the debt of his people's sins justly exacted on him. And both he chearfully and fully did perform and endure. And thus are we saved.

2. That this righteousness wrought out by Christ, was wrought out for others, and not for himself. He wove and made this coat, for the covering and clothing of his naked people. The gospel is full of this, in telling us both the errand his Father sent him on, and the work and business he did when he came. He needed no such garment for himself; but wove it out of his own blood and bowels, for his people, whom he loved, and who he well knew needed it greatly.

3. That this righteousness, thus wrought out by Jesus Christ, is freely and fully tendered and offered to all that hear the gospel: all of it (for it is not divided nor divisible) unto every man and woman; (for gospel-offers have no exceptions). Thus Peter made the offer to every one of them that heard him, Acts ii. 38. He excepts not the very murderers of Christ, nor the mockers at him on the cross, when Christ was working out this righteousness. So his *beloved brother Paul* (as he calls him, 2 Pet. iii. 15.) preached, Acts xiii. 38, 39. *Be it known unto you therefore, men and brethren, that through this man* (alas! this man is little known by most men) *is preached unto you the forgiveness of sins; and by him all that believe, are justified from all things, from which ye could not be justified by the law of Moses.* Do you then believe on him, and be justified by him; left that word be fulfilled on you, *Behold, ye despisers, and wonder, and perish,* ver. 41. And no longer than the next Sabbath-day was it in fulfilling, ver. 46, 47, 48. And if the company were never so great nor so bad, a gospel-minister may make this large offer, as Christ himself did,

John vii. 37. *In the last day, that great day of the feast,* (when the great convocation of the people was), *Jesus stood and cried,* (that he might be seen and heard by all), *saying, If any man thirst, let him come unto me, and drink.* And this coming to him, and drinking, is believing on Christ, ver. 38, 39. When he is in heaven, and sending a letter by John his messenger, to a sorry church, and in a sad case, he saith so to them, Rev. iii. 20. *Behold, I stand at the door and knock: If any man hear my voice, and open the door, I will come in to him, and will sup with him, and he with me.* To name no more of the large offers of Christ in the gospel, I will conclude with the last in the Bible, Rev. xxii. 17. *And let him that is athirst, come: and whosoever will, let him take the water of life freely.*

4. That this large offer made of Christ in the gospel, is the ordinary and appointed means of working faith in Christ. Thus, Rom. x. 17. *Faith cometh by hearing, and hearing by the word of God;* and Rom. i. 16, 17. *I am not ashamed of the gospel of Christ;* (and never did an honest preacher make a poorer life in worldly things, of the gospel, than Paul did): *for it is the power of God unto salvation to every one that believeth; to the Jew first, and also to the Greek. For therein is the righteousness of God revealed from faith to faith: as it is written, The just shall live by faith.* I need not insist on so plain a truth.

5. That this righteousness of Christ is upon all that believe. It is offered to all to be embraced by faith; and it is given and conferred upon all that believe, upon their believing. Whenever the hand of the Lord is upon the hearts of hearers of the gospel, and draws them forth to betake themselves to this righteousness of Christ, to embrace it, and to trust all their acceptance with God upon it alone, they are justified by it: Rom. iii. 22, 23. *The righteousness of God, which is by faith of Jesus Christ, is unto all, and upon all that believe; for there is no difference: for all have*

have sinned and come short of the glory of God. A blessed saying, and an odd-like reason to confirm it. Are all sinners alike? and are all believers alike? No, surely, Are not some sinners greater sinners than others? and some believers better believers, and greater saints, than others? Yes, surely. But in this matter of Christ's righteousness there is no difference. All sinners are alike in this, that they are in a condemned state alike, and alike past all relief, save in and by Christ and his righteousness: and all believers in Christ are alike in that saved state they are in, by Christ's righteousness being on them. All sinners are alike needy; and all believers are alike partakers of this righteousness of God.

6. Lastly, That upon this righteousness of Christ's being on a believer in him, these three things follow: That the believer is justified; God justified in justifying of him; and the justified man's mouth is stopped as to all glorying, save in the Lord. The believer is justified, counted and reputed a righteous man, thro' the righteousness imputed to him. On the account of this same imputed righteousness of Christ, all his sins are forgiven and blotted out, and he is *passed from death to life, and shall not come into condemnation,* John v. 24. Rom. viii. 1, 33, 34. He is reconciled to God, and dealt with as a friend of God. God is also justified in his passing this sentence of justification on the believer. In all things, and above all, we should be tender of God's glory. There are specially three acts of God's righteous judgment that are censured much by the ungodly, and that Christians should be careful to justify God in. One is, his just judgment on the first Adam and his posterity. How full are most mens hearts, and some mens mouths, and too many pens, with censures of this awful, but just sentence? The other is, the Lord's way of dealing with the second Adam, Jesus Christ. He was not spared, but put to sore sufferings. Any may see amazing mercy; but who behold, and glorify God's righteousness and justice,

justice, in the death of Christ? And the third is this I am upon, the justice of God in justifying a believer. And the cause of mens censures and mistakes about all the three, is much the same, and the censures are usually in the same sort of persons. The true cause of these challenges of God's *judgments,* which *are a great depth,* Psal. xxxvi. 6. is, mens ignorance of the justice, majesty, and greatness of God. Unto such arguers against God, the words of Elihu to Job may properly be applied, Job xxxiii. 12, 13. *Behold, in this thou art not just: I will answer thee, that God is greater than man. Why dost thou strive against him? for he giveth not account of any of his matters.* In these three instances we may easily see how this ignorance of these worketh. In the first act of justice in God, we find one man's one act of disobedience conveying guilt, condemnation and death, to all his natural offspring. In the second instance, we find all the sins of many sinners charged and laid on a sinless person, and justice dealing with him as with a criminal. In the third, we find the righteousness of Christ, which he wrought out in making a propitiation for sin, imputed to the justifying of a believer: and in this God is justified: Rom. iii. 26. *To declare at this time his righteousness; that he might be just, and the justifier of him that believeth in Jesus.* Lastly, In this justification, the justified man's mouth is stopped as to all glorying, but only in the Lord. For as vast a blessing as it is, there is no place left for glorying. Therefore, in the next verse, the 27th, he saith, *Where is boasting then? It is excluded. By what law? of works? Nay; but by the law of faith.* The law, when it condemns, stops the sinner's mouth from replying, to justify himself, Rom. iii. 19.; and the gospel, when it absolves, stops the believer's mouth from glorying in himself, when justified. But doth not the law of works exclude boasting sufficiently? That law that commands more than the man can do, doth it not shut out boasting? Can any man say, that he hath fulfilled

fulfilled that law? No, surely. No man that in any measure knows the holiness of that law, and knows himself, his heart and doings, will say so. But besides that many are so blind and ignorant, both of God's law and of themselves, that they are ready to boast without any cause; all men that seek justification by the law, and by doing, they do design boasting, though they never reach it. Though they cannot reach glorying before God, yet would they fain be at it. But the justified believer, as he never reacheth it when he is justified, so he never designs it when he seeks justification. The righteousness in which he is justified, is wholly wrought out by another; and one so great, that none that know him will adventure to put in for a share in his crown; *the Lord our righteousness*, Jer. xxiii. 6. Yet the blessing of it is given to his church, and she is called by her husband's name, Jer. xxxiii. 16. The revealing of this righteousness is from the Lord, by his word and Spirit; without which no man could ever find it out. The faith by which he layeth hold on it, is the work of God; and neither grew up in his heart, nor was acquired by his own industry, nor conveyed by the power of any creature. The imputing of this righteousness unto his justification, is God's act of free grace, Rom. iii. 24.; nothing in the man moving God to impute it; and nothing in God but his grace in Christ Jesus. The sinner, when he seeks it by faith, looks on nothing but this grace; and when he hath got it, and knows it, owns heartily, that this spiritual blessing (as all others are, Eph. i. 3.----7.) is *to the praise of the glory of his grace, wherein he hath made us accepted in the beloved.* It cannot be denied, but a man may be proud of his justification, and of his faith. But in that case I am bold to say, that one of these things are: Either that it is a false justification, and a false faith, that this man boasts of, (and these are too common amongst professors); or that true justification is out of his sight, and his faith out of exercise, when

any

any boasting riseth in the heart of a real believer. For let but a believer set himself before God the Judge of all; let him read God's law, and his own heart and conscience; and see what he hath to boast of: nay, he will see, that he hath all reason for fear and shame, when he stands before this tribunal. Let him next by faith see Jesus Christ at this same judgment seat, charged with this man's sins, and discharging that debt, and buying all grace and glory for him by the price of his precious blood; and, lastly, let him, by the same faith, behold God justifying him freely, and fully, and only, on the account of this satisfaction given by Christ: and then, and thus, let this man see and own, that as there is no room left for boasting, so he will find no inclination in his heart unto it. It is the character of a true Christian in Phil. iii. 3. *For we are the circumcision* (true Jews, as Rom. ii. 28, 29.) *which worship God in the Spirit, and rejoice* (or *glory*) *in Christ Jesus, and have no confidence in the flesh.* So that, whereas righteousness by the law is both sought by men in pride; and when they dream that they shall either reach it, or that they have got it, (and such dreams are not rare, though groundless), pride and boasting increaseth so much, that not only are their hearts puffed up within, not only do they glory before men, as Christ tells us of such hypocrites in Mat. vi but they dare boast before God, as the Pharisee did, Luke xviii. 11.: so, on the other hand, the justifying righteousness of God, wrought out by Christ, and applied to the believer on Christ, was appointed of God, brought in by Christ, revealed in the gospel, and given to the believer, for the highest glory of the free giver, and the deepest humbling of the happy, but unworthy receivers. And thus is that prophecy and promise fulfilled in Isa. xlv. 24, 25. *Surely, shall one say, In the Lord have I righteousness and strength. In the Lord shall all the seed of Israel be justified, and shall glory.*

What then is God's justifying a believer in Jesus Christ

Christ? It is nothing else, but God's gracious looking on a man, judging of him, and dealing with him, as in Christ, and as represented by Christ to God, for justification of life. There is a similitude commonly used, taken from Jacob's getting his father Isaac's blessing, in his brother Esau's raiment, Gen. xxvii. All similitudes, even in scripture, taken from mens ways, to express God's ways, want some grains to make them pass current; and this especially: for old Isaac was deceived in bestowing his blessing, Heb. xi. 20. *By faith Isaac blessed Jacob and Esau, concerning things to come.* Though Isaac did so by faith; yet the blessings he gave his sons, were not only greatly different, but he was also at first deceived in the persons whom he did bless. Yet though Jacob supplanted his brother of the birthright, Gen. xxv. 30.----34. and Gen. xxvii. of the blessing, by his mother's cunning, and his own lying; yet neither of these did hinder Isaac's faith, nor the lighting of the blessing on Jacob, according to the election of grace, and the oracle that declared it, when they both were in the womb, Gen. xxv. 23. But though Jacob deceived his father in the way wherein he sought the blessing; yet, in giving of his blessing by faith to Joseph's sons, Ephraim and Manasseh, Heb. ix. 21. he guided both his hands wittingly, and his words wisely, and gave the blessing, by the spirit of prophecy, Gen. xlviii. 14.----20. But *the Lord* always *knoweth who are his,* 2 Tim. ii. 19. He always knows whom he blesseth, and what blessing he gives. All our acceptance with, and justification before God, comes by the representation Christ makes of us to God. He was charged at the bar of justice for our sins; he answered this charge by a perfect satisfaction, and thus was *justified in the Spirit,* 1 Tim. iii. 16.; and when this satisfaction is put to our account, we are *justified by his blood,* Rom. v. 9.

So much for the first blessing of justification.

(2.) Christ represents his church unto God for their

their sanctification. Election in Christ is an eternal purpose in God's heart and counsel about his people. Redemption by Christ, is a divine bargain for them and their salvation betwixt the Father and the Son. Justification is a gracious sentence of God in Christ, on them that are represented by him for acceptance. By this act and sentence the state of their persons is favourably changed. But sanctification is a divine work on them, that changeth their heart and nature. The Spirit of sanctification is a precious gift of divine love; and is only given to them that are in Christ, and because they are in him: Gal. iv. 6. *And because ye are sons, God hath sent forth the Spirit of his Son into your hearts, crying, Abba, Father.* All the anointings of the Holy Ghost that believers receive, are but some drops that fall down from the head of our High Priest, unto the skirts of his garments, Psal. cxxxiii. 2, 2. He *received the Spirit without measure*, John iii. 34. that to his people, even *to every one of them, grace may be given, according to the measure of the gift of Christ*, Eph. iv. 7.; not according to the measure that Christ got, but the measure that Christ giveth. And all of them receive it. Rom. viii. ix. *If any man have not the Spirit of Christ, he is none of his.* Let him not *name the name of Christ* (as his Lord and Master), *that departeth not from iniquity*, 2 Tim. ii. 19. All whose iniquities Christ did bear for their expiation, in due time Christ *blesseth them, in turning every one of them away from their iniquities*, Acts iii. 26. This blessing of sanctification is of pure grace: for as there is nothing of worth in a man, or regarded by God in justifying; so there is nothing of goodness, or of fit matter, for God to work upon in his sanctifying. God's word is as clear about this, as about the other. The account that we have so largely of the natural state of all men without Christ, is sufficient to show the absolute necessity all stand in of God's grace to save them, and to declare both the freedom and power of that grace in all its applications to men.

Grace

Grace is the spring of salvation, and of all its parts; Christ is the root of all; and eternal life and glory is the ripe fruit of all that grace of God, that *reigns through righteousness unto eternal life, by Jesus Christ our Lord,* Rom. v. 21. See but these texts, and read them, and conclude this truth, 1 Cor. vi. 11. Eph. ii. 1.----7. and Tit. iii. 3.----7. In all which places justification and sanctification are joined, (as they are certainly and constantly in all that partake of them); unworthiness in the receivers overcome, and passed over, by the grace of the giver; and the interest of Jesus Christ, in God's giving, and in his people's receiving of both these blessings, is plainly told us.

(3.) All the communion, and fellowship, and familiarity with God, that a believer receiveth, and is admitted unto, is all by Jesus Christ, and by his representing him to God, Rom. v. 1, 2. 1 John i. 3. John xiv. 23. Blessed be God there is a great deal of it; and more might be attained, if we were painful and diligent. This is so great a mercy, that *come and see, come and taste,* is the best counsel can be given, Psal. xxxiv. 8. And such as taste it, know its worth better than the apostle can tell them; and that it all comes by the grace of God in Jesus Christ. He is not only the only Mediator of reconciliation and of intercession, but of fellowship with God: Eph. ii. 18. *For through him we both* (Jews or Gentiles, if believers) *have an access by one Spirit unto the Father.*

(4.) Lastly, The crown of glory, and admission to heaven, is granted to believers upon the account of the righteousness of Christ on the believer: Rom. vi. 22, 23. *But now being made free from sin,* (from the condemning and commanding power of sin, in justification and sanctification, of which the apostle had been speaking in the 5th and 6th chapters), *and become servants to God, ye have your fruit unto holiness, and the end everlasting life. For the wages of sin is death: but the gift of God is eternal life, through Jesus Christ our Lord.* Sanctification *by faith in Christ,* Acts

xxvi. 18. is a precious gift of God. The perfecting of it by faith on the promises, is a blessed design and exercise through the whole life of a Christian, 2 Cor. vii. 1. It is most pursued after, but never attained by the best, till they attain *the prize of the high calling of God in Jesus Christ*, Phil. iii. 13, 14. But when this prize is attained by them, and bestowed on them, it is not given them because they are holy, (though none but the sanctified inherit it, Acts xxvi. 18.), but because they are in Christ, members of his body; and because he is made all things for them for their salvation, 1 Cor. i. 30.; and because they are represented by him, and presented unto God, for this last, greatest, and everlasting acceptance. *Behold, I, and the children which God hath given me*, Heb. ii. 13. The righteousness of Christ is the eternal robe of the glorified, and their most glorious one; and the cause of their perfection in holiness, and of its eternal duration. The glory and whiteness of their robes, is in their being *washed, and made white in the blood of the Lamb*, Rev. vii. 14. If Christians be but careful to give God's grace in Christ its true use and praise, while they are on earth; no doubt but all that get to heaven, will sing the song of the Lamb with everlasting joy, *To him that loved us, and washed us from our sins in his own blood, and hath made us kings and priests unto God and his Father, to him be glory and dominion for ever, Amen*. Rev. i. 5, 6. and v. 9, 10. And though some true Christians may possibly (either by the snare of dark or unsound doctrine, or by a mistaken zeal for inherent personal holiness) have less exercise by faith on Christ's righteousness than some others, and though some may advance by grace farther in sanctification than others, (and it is a very valuable attainment); yet all of them, when they come to die, and to knock at heaven's gate for entrance into their Master's joy, do mind far otherwise the blood that bought the inheritance, than any thing wrought in them to make them meet for it, Col. i. 12.

or than any pains they have been at in walking and running their race towards it.

So much for the first thing, Wherein doth Christ represent his church unto God?

Secondly, What is Christ's fitness for making this representation of the church unto God?

1. In the constitution of his person. He is a rare, singular person; God-man, God's Son made man. And because he is God-man in one person, he is a person only fit, and highly fit, to represent God unto man, and man unto God. He is fit to represent God unto man; for in Christ we see God in a man, in our nature. And he is fit to represent man unto God; for God seeth our nature in his Son. We see God in him, and God seeth us in him. We can never see and take up God rightly and by faith, but as he is in his Son Jesus Christ; nor can God ever graciously look on a sinner but in his Son.

2. Christ is fit for making this representation of his church to God, by his office of Mediator. None is fit for this office but Christ; none is put in it but he, 1 Tim. ii. 5.; and none but God-man can discharge it. The greatness of the work that is to be done in this office, and the greatness of the glory that follows on its discharge, are far too high for a mere creature. Such as deny that Christ is true God, or deny that he is true man, or deny that he is God-man in one person, (and from the apostles days to ours, the enemy hath been sowing such tares in God's field), do deny a fit Mediator betwixt God and men, and thereby strike at the rock the church is built upon. Now, the office of a mediator is to deal with two parties: Gal. iii. 20. *Now a mediator is not a mediator of one;* but he is betwixt two. The high priest under the law, was in his office a type of Christ in his priesthood. Aaron and his successors did, as high priests and typical mediators, represent all Israel (then God's only church) unto God, especially in the solemn day of atonement, Lev. xvi.; when the high priest offered

the sacrifice, after confessing of, and a typical imputing of Israel's sin to the innocent creature to be sacrificed, and went with its blood into the holiest of all, (a piece of earth likest heaven of any thing or place made with hands), there to make atonement. This high priest was also to *bear their names* (whom he represented) *before the Lord upon his two shoulders for a memorial*, Exod. xxviii. 12. and ver. 29. *And Aaron shall bear the names of the children of Israel in the breast-plate of judgment, upon his heart, when he goeth in unto the holy place, for a memorial before the Lord continually.* Aaron bare but the general names of the tribes of Israel: but Christ our High Priest hath a larger heart and breast plate; and bears upon it all the particular names of his people, and represents them all unto God, both in his offering of himself as a sacrifice for them, in his entering in with his own blood into the true holiest of all, and in his appearing in heaven in the presence of God for them, Heb. ix. 12.----24. And, by the way, I may say, that the epistle to the Hebrews is a key to all the Old Testament, and especially to the book of Leviticus, and the Old Testament worship.

Thirdly, What is the glory of Christ in making this representation of his church unto God? We easily conceive, that there is much glory in his representing God unto his church; but his glory in representing them unto God, is not so easily seen by us. But it is surely a great glory. So the apostle saith, Heb. v. 5, 6. *Christ glorified not himself to be made an High Priest; but he that said unto him* as in Psal ii. 7. and Psal. cx. 4. He glorified him, and made him an High Priest. But what glory was there in this, when he was to be the sacrifice himself who was made the priest; and to make this sacrifice in all the lowest and most humbling circumstances, smitten of God, despised of men, and abased even unto death and the curse; wherein was the glory of this? At first view, nothing appears

appears but shame and dishonour. A few things shall conclude this matter at this time.

1. Consider whom he did, and doth represent unto God for acceptance. They are all sinners. The vilest thing is sin; the basest creature is a sinner: yea, sinners are not properly creatures of God's making, but are vile things of the devil's and of their own making; the only shameful things in God's world. And sin had never been permitted to enter into the world, if God had not resolved in himself to gather in a rent of glory to his justice, in punishing it in many; and to his mercy, in pardoning it in others. And this glory to pardoning grace comes by the redemption in Christ Jesus, Eph. i. 7. Many of these pardoned sinners are of the worse sort of sinners, 1 Cor. vi. 9, 10, 11.; and all of them think themselves such, 1 Tim. i. 15, 16.; and they therein do not think amiss. And they are a great many, as will appear in the day of their last *gathering together to Christ*, as it is called, 2 Thess. ii. 1.; though not so many as the lost. Thence we read of a lost world, and of a saved world, in the word. When a sinner hath his eyes opened to see himself, he lothes himself; and thinks that he is enough to pollute, and defile, and burden the whole creation of God: he abhors himself, and thinks every one, especially the godly, should abhor him too: but mainly he judgeth himself most justly lothsome to God. Must it not be a great and glorious thing in that person, that can, and doth represent such vile creatures unto a gracious acceptance with God?

2. Consider to whom they are represented for acceptance; even to an holy and just God; a God that hates all iniquity where-ever he seeth it, Hab. i. 13.; and seeth it where-ever it is; and punisheth it where-ever it is not covered and pardoned. All discoveries of God's glorious holiness, and of our own sinful vileness, render this representation for acceptance the more needful to be got, and the more hard

to

to be believed, (as all exercised Christian, know), and the more glorious to Christ when it is obtained.

3. Lastly, Consider what a glorious acceptance this representation by Christ doth procure. They for whom it is made, are accepted, Eph. i. 6.; are beloved; are received into all familiarity with God; and, in that love, adjudged unto all blessings in heavenly things in Christ Jesus.

APPLICATION. I shall at this time only add one word of application; and it is this. I have been speaking to you of Christ's glory in representing his church unto God; I would only ask your consciences this one question, How do you think to appear before God? You all know, or profess you know, that there is a God, (as certainly there is; and, I may say, more surely than that there is any thing else; for God only is the necessary, all creatures are but contingent beings, Rev. iv. 11.); you know, that this God doth always see you; that as he thinks of you, so is your state in his sight; that God will at last judge you, and proclaim to you, and all the world, his thoughts and judgment of you; you daily worship and serve him: But how do you now appear before him? is a question few ask. Many never think of this till it be too late. By what means and ways shall I make such an appearance before God, as to be graciously accepted with him? This seems to be on their hearts in Micah vi. 6. though they did not know the right way. And so is it at this day with many sinners. I would warn you of some of those false ways in which men think to appear before God.

1. Some think to appear before God in the same poor state that their father Adam left them in. They own, that they are not so good as he was, nor so good as they ought to be; but they think, that since men are so impoverished by Adam's fall, God will now accept a man with a little, if it be his all. But such deluded people do not know, that as Adam left them

them nothing at all that is pleasing to God; so he hath left them in a state of sin, wrath, and condemnation, in which all his posterity are born, and live in, and perish at last in, unless they are delivered from it by Jesus Christ.

2. Some think to appear before God in the best dress they can make for themselves, by their good meanings and purposes, their good duties and works. They labour hard and long to amend their ways, to adorn their duties, and themselves by them; and thus think to present themselves to God's acceptance. This garment of our own righteousness is beautiful in their own sight; for self-love naturally makes men to prize their self-doings. It is a garment beautiful also in the sight of men; and of them they have their reward, as Christ told such men, Matth. vi. 2. 5. 16. And this dress is the more praised when it is in fashion. Hypocrites praise hypocrites: and the church is full of them. So, from their own valuing, and others praising of them, they, in their ignorance, think that God will be as well pleased with them. But, alas! this is no better than that sad state Paul speaks of, Rom. x. 3. *For they being ignorant of God's righteousness, and going about to establish their own righteousness, have not submitted themselves unto the righteousness of God.*

3. Some think to appear before God for acceptance with their sufferings. If they can do but little, they think they suffer much. This is a strange vanity. Of these sufferings, some are voluntary, sinfully imposed on men by themselves. That people speak strangely, Micah vi. 6, 7. *Wherewith shall I come before the Lord, and bow myself before the high God? shall I come before him with burnt offerings, with calves of a year old?* (and these were commanded in the law); *will the Lord be pleased with thousands of rams, or with ten thousands of rivers of oil?* (those were more than ever God commanded, or than they could bring); *shall I give my first-born for my transgression.*

gression, *the fruit of my body for the sin of my soul?* A strictly forbidden abomination. When you read of this practice that some were left unto, to offer their children in sacrifice, think not that they hated their children: nay, they loved them as well as you do yours; but they loved their souls better, and feared God's anger more; and they thought, that what was dearest to them, and what they were lothest to part with, God would most accept of. (What a conviction may this give to many Christians, who find it so hard to submit to the Lord's taking away their children, either by a natural or violent death; when a blind idolater is so mad upon his idols, that he will voluntarily make a sacrifice of his children unto their false gods, or *devils,* as they are called, Psal. cvi. 37.?). So natural is it unto men, in their ignorance of God, to think, that what they do impose upon themselves, especially if it be troublesome to their flesh, is pleasing unto, yea meritorious before God. From this spring do all the voluntary self-scourgings, *&c.* amongst Papists proceed; which have no better example in God's word than that of Baal's prophets in 1 Kings xviii. 28.; and have no better acceptance with God than they had. But what will not a sinner do; what shift will he not betake himself unto, who seeth his sins, feels or fears God's wrath for them, and is ignorant of the only city of refuge, Jesus Christ? Many mock at the folly both of Pagans and Papists, in their ways of seeking pardon and peace, who, if they were as much awakened in their conscience, and as ignorant of Christ as they, would either betake themselves to the same poor shifts, or to others as vain. Again, Some sufferings are commanded; as James iv. 9 *Be afflicted, and mourn, and weep: let your laughter be turned to mourning, and your joy to heaviness.* There is a time to mourn, and there are calls to it; and we should discern both, and set about this duty. There are many merry and jovial professors, that never mind mourning for themselves or o-
thers,

others, but when God makes them by his rods; and it is well if they do so then. But now, when a man, with much pains, hath laboured with his heart, and hath afflicted it with grief and sorrow; and when this storm within breaks out in tears, and he pours them out before the Lord, as they did, Judg. ii. 4, 5. and may call his bed, (as David did his, Psal. vi. 6.), or chamber, or closet, a *Bochim*; how easily doth a man grow proud and vain, and think within himself, "Now I have offered an acceptable sacrifice to God?" It is true, that *the sacrifices of God are a broken spirit: A broken and a contrite heart, O God, thou wilt not despise*, Psal. li. 17. But we must always remember these three things about all our spiritual sacrifices. 1. That as they must be all of his requiring, so they must be of his providing. We have nothing to offer to God that he will accept, till he give it to us, and till he first work it in us. David's broken heart was first given to him. Dreadful sins first lay quiet in his hard heart, till God broke it. 2. That a broken heart is always a humble heart. It begins to grow whole again (and quickly it will, unless the breaker of it keep it broken) when it begins to be proud. Such as have a good opinion of their own hearts, know not what a broken heart means. He that hath a broken heart, is broken with his vile heart; as the Lord speaks of his grief at mens whole hearts, Ezek. vi. 9. 3. That all our spiritual sacifices, and a broken heart, must be offered to God for acceptance on the right altar, and by the right High Priest, Jesus Christ. As he, in dealing with God for our redemption, was both altar, and priest, and sacrifice; so, in all our dealings with God by him, we must be furnished with our sacrifice out of his store; we must offer up all to God by him as our Priest, Heb. xiii. 15.; for they are only *acceptable to God by Jesus Christ*, 1 Pet. ii. 5. And we must have and use Christ as our altar to *sanctify our gifts*, Matth. xxiii. 19. It is grievous to hear what sad ground there is to fear, that some professors think more oft, and think more highly, of their own tears, than of the redeeming blood of the Son of God. Lastly, There are afflictions of God's inflicting and laying on; always laid on justly and righteously. No man should complain of them, or of God, when under them. All believers should neither despise nor faint under them, Heb. xii. 6, 7. But no man must think of appearing before God with acceptance, merely because he is afflicted. God afflicts his children in love; and he loves them not the less that they are afflicted. But affliction itself, and our own cross, must not rob Christ's cross of its glory, of making peace with God for sinners, Col. i. 20. I should not mention this, but that you know, that there are some so ignorant as to say when greatly afflicted, "I am now enduring the "punishment of my sins;" yea, when dying, they think that the very agony of death is a punishment of, yea an expiation for all the sins of their life. So grossly ignorant are many that live in a land of light. It is true, that all the miseries of this life, yea death itself, to an unbeliever, are the punishment of sin; they are but a small and short part of that punishment. But, alas! where is the payment of sin, and the satisfaction that God demands, and will only accept? Nothing a sinner can do or suffer, can ever amount to that.

I would conclude this exercise with these two words.

1. All that adventure to appear before God as they are in and of themselves, are ignorant both of God and of themselves. They neither know how holy and just he is, nor how vile they are. If they did, they would never venture stubble fully dry before this consuming fire.

2. All that dare not adventure on Jesus Christ, and on his representing them to God for acceptance, know neither the Father nor the Son. This is the
glorious

glorious contrivance in his eternal counsels, and is delivered to us in his word, as *the record of God*, 1 John v. 10, 11. extracted out of these counsels, that a great number of sinners, vile and unworthy in themselves, shall be accepted in that beloved, and shall be beloved for his sake, and in him. How hard a thing do believers themselves find it to believe this firmly and constantly, what a glorious representation Jesus Christ can make of such vile creatures as we be in ourselves, when he clothes us with his righteousness? It is no easy thing for a true Christian, when he is digging into the dunghill of his own heart, and lothing himself for all his abominations; at the same time to believe, that he stands accepted before the throne of God, as found and seen in Christ, clothed with Christ's garment of a spotless righteousness, that no fault can be found with, even at the highest tribunal, nor any condemnation can come from thence to the happy man that wears it. *There is no condemnation to them that are in Christ Jesus;* because *it is God that justifieth* all that believe on him, Rom. viii. 1. 33, 34.

SERMON XII.

John xvii. 24.

Father, I will that they also whom thou haſt given me, be with me where I am; that they may behold my glory which thou haſt given me: for thou lovedſt me before the foundation of the world.

I Am yet on the third thing in the matter of our Lord's prayer in this verſe. The firſt was, the deſcription of them he prays for: *Thoſe whom thou haſt given me.* The ſecond is, the bleſſing he prays for to them: *That they may be with me where I am.* The third is, the end for which Chriſt prays for this bleſſing to them. What ſhall they get by being with Chriſt where he is? What ſhall they do, and how ſhall they be employed? *That they may behold my glory which thou haſt given me.* That will find them work enough, and bliſs enough, to eternity. On this I propoſed two things to be handled. 1. The glory of Chriſt. And, 2. The beholding of his glory.

On the firſt of theſe, the glory of Chriſt, I have ſpoke a little on two heads. 1. Chriſt's glory as he repreſents God to men. 2. As Chriſt repreſents men to God. There are two moſt important queſtions that riſe in the mind of every ſerious man; and he is a ſinful and miſerable perſon that never found them in his own heart, and knows not how to anſwer them rightly. 1. How may a ſinful man ſo take up God, as to know him truly and ſavingly? And, 2. What way may God look upon a ſinful man graciouſly? Both anſwered one way. It is only in his Son Jeſus Chriſt. If we look on God out of Chriſt, we are confounded; if God look on us out of Chriſt, we are deſtroyed.

destroyed. We are not able to behold the glory of God, but in the face of Christ; and we are not able to avoid his wrath, unless we be found in Christ, and accepted of God in him.

Wherein Christ represents his church to God, how fit he is to make this representation, and what Christ's glory is in making of it, I spoke of last day. This representation that Christ makes of his church unto God, is for their acceptance with God; and that acceptance never fails, where this representation is made. It is acceptance with that God that knoweth all things, and judgeth rightly of all things and persons. How then can a just God accept a man that in himself is a sinner, and therein do justly? A hard question, that only is answered in the gospel. It is, because Christ represents a sinner to God for acceptance; and this acceptance must be, where this representation is made by Christ. 1. Because Christ covers all that is sinful and lothsome in the man, by his righteousness. And, 2. By the same righteousness, not only covereth his nakedness and deformity, but puts a beauty upon the man; though it is not in him, but in Christ, yet is on him by grace; as Ezek. xvi. 14. *Thy beauty was perfect through my comeliness which I had put upon thee, saith the Lord.* By this imputed righteousness of Christ put upon a believer in Christ, his own sin is covered, and the believer stands clothed, and so is beautiful in God's sight, in this gifted righteousness, and is justly justified by God the Judge of all. See Psal. xxxii. 1, 2. with Paul's comment on it, in Rom. iv. 6, 7, 8. *Even as David also describeth the blessedness of the man unto whom God imputeth righteousness, without works, saying, Blessed are they whose iniquities are forgiven, whose sins are covered. Blessed is the man to whom the Lord will not impute sin.* A few remarks on these two scriptures, shall be all I shall say on the doctrinal part, and then proceed in application. The first thing I remark, is this: That the apostle names only those

words

words of the Psalmist that belong to his present purpose. He is handling the doctrine of the justification of a sinner. This blessed doctrine he had taught in the preceeding chapter, with so clear a light, that all the darkness of hell will never be able to put out, or quench, in the church of Christ. This blessing, he teacheth, comes by the free grace of God, in and by the redemption made by Christ; and is given by God, and possessed by men, by faith in Christ's redeeming blood, without any interest of the works of the law therein. Christ indeed dealt with the law, and fulfilled all the righteousness thereof, for our justification: but we have nothing to do with the law, in our dealing with God for our justification; but to come with its condemning sentence in our guilty conscience, that we may lay hold of Christ's righteousness; which, as it fulfilled the law, when wrought out by Christ; so it sprinkles our consciences, when applied to us by his Spirit and grace, and when it is applied unto by us by faith. And those two applications are inseparable, and both the fruits of the saving grace of God. This doctrine Paul confirms by two instances, in two eminent saints, in this fourth chapter; Abraham before the law, ver. 1.----5. and afterwards in this chapter; and David under the law, ver. 6, 7, 8. Whatever difference there was in the dispensations they were under, (and there was a great one); yet there was none in the way of their justification before God. Both were by God's grace, without the works of the law, without work, without hire, without any glorying before God. Now, David had said in Psal. xxxii. 2. *Blessed is the man* also, *in whose spirit there is no guile.* But this pertaining to the blessing of sanctification, though inseparable from that of justification, (which is the apostle's distinct theme in this context), is therefore wisely omitted by the apostle. A second thing I remark, in comparing these two scriptures, is this: That whereas David lays the blessedness on the *pardoned man, the man whose sins are covered, the man to whom the Lord imputeth not iniquity;* Paul tells us, that herein David *defcribeth the bleffednefs of the man unto whom God imputeth righteoufnefs without works,* when he faid fo. David faith nothing of the imputing of righteoufnefs, but only of the *not imputing of* fin. Paul teacheth, that the *not imputing of fin,* is the fame with *the imputing of righteoufnefs, and that without works* alfo. A few things will ferve to clear this. 1. Every man's ftate before God, is as God judgeth and reckons of him. His account and reckoning of a man is always right and true; and it is always decifive and determining; for it is the higheft Judge's fentence. Thus is it now, thus will it always be. This judgment of this fupreme Judge concerning them, is always about fin, or righteoufnefs. His condemning fentence is for fin; his approving fentence is for righteoufnefs. *To clear the guilty,* and *to condemn the righteous, are both an abomination to the Lord,* in an earthly judge, Prov. xvii. 15. And who, without blafphemy, can charge the Judge of all the earth with it! Gen. xviii. 25. Every man therefore, even now, is in God's fight under a fentence, either of condemnation, becaufe of fin; or of approbation, becaufe of righteoufnefs; that is, in the dialect of the Holy Ghoft, hath either *fin imputed to him for condemnation, or righteoufnefs imputed to him for the juftification of life,* as Paul calls it, Rom. v. 18. 3. Sin and righteoufnefs are contraries, and expel one another, and cannot confift together. Guilty, or not guilty, every one is, and muft be in the eye of God, and at the bar of God's law and judgment. If guilty, then not righteous, and therefore condemned; if not guilty, then righteous, and therefore abfolved and acquitted. This alternative, *finful,* or *lawful,* reacheth to all our thoughts and actions; and thus are they judged by God, as contrary or confonant to the law, the rule. And alfo *guilty,* or *not guilty,* or *righteous,* reacheth to the ftate of all perfons before God; and thus are we all judged and accounted

accounted of by the Lord, as we are under sin, or under righteousness. 4. Now when man is fallen, and there is nothing but sin in man, and no righteousness can be found in him, God hath provided a righteousness without him, in and by which he may only, and may surely, and may justly, be justified before God. Of which we have been speaking. This is that righteousness of Christ, in which all believers on him stand accepted before God. It is imputed to them, and therefore their sin is not imputed to them; and thus are they judged and absolved at God's throne of grace in Christ Jesus. So that, to conclude this, unless all that we are, all that we have done, be covered by this righteousness; unless there be a reckoning of this righteousness of Christ to us by God; sin, our own sin, will be imputed to us for condemnation. It is only this righteousness that is justly precious in the judgment of God, and makes sinful man accepted with him.

Inference 1. Behold here the wonderful grace of our Lord Jesus Christ, in thus representing his church and people to God. The apostle saith, 2 Cor. viii. 9. *For ye know the grace of our Lord Jesus Christ, that though he was rich, yet for your sakes he became poor, that ye through his poverty might be rich.* He supposeth, that all true Christians doth know Christ's grace: and justly; for God knows, and all men may judge them unworthy of that name, that do not know it. Christ's grace is a lovely theme to hear of, and to think on, by all that have tasted of it, and live by it. This grace shineth brightly in his representing his people to God for acceptance. It was a great condescendence of his grace, to take the office of a representer of his church. He knew his own divine dignity; he knew the vileness and unworthiness of them whom he was to represent: yet neither of them hindred his chearful undertaking of this office. And as it was condescending grace in him to undertake it;

(so

so was it costly grace to him to go through with it, and discharge it. Blessed Jesus laid out all his estate (to speak so) to redeem the lawful captives of justice. Before they can be represented to God for acceptance, he must die, and shed his blood; and in his garments dyed with his own blood must he present himself as a perfected Mediator unto God, and in the same garments present his church to God for acceptance. This matter of our acceptance with God is not brought about by the prayers of Christ on earth, nor by his intercession in heaven: though we are apt to think, that such prayers of such a supplicant might do any thing. Yea, any thing but this: *Without shedding of blood, there is no remission*, Heb. ix. 22. And no blood but Christ's goes for an atonement, Rom. v. 9, 10. He had no sin of his own. But when he was charged with the sins of his people, he must shed his blood as a sacrifice for propitiation. When Christ stands thus charged at the bar of justice, he was not spared, but was dealt with as strictly as another sinner. When law and justice takes a sinner by the throat, it saith to him, *Pay me that thou owest*; as Matth. xviii. 28. in the parable there. And this charge is still on all that are out of Christ; though they are now deaf, and do not hear it. This charge is on all the prisoners in hell, " Pay your debts to " God, or no getting out of prison." But this charge was only on Christ, " Pay what thou owest as surety " for a multitude of beggars and debtors. They have " nothing to pay; thou art rich, and able to pay. " Thou hast undertaken to pay; and therefore full " payment must be made ere thou enter into glory, " and thy people be presented to God with accep- " tance." And this charge Christ obeyed and answered, by which his church is saved. So great was his obedience to his Father's commandment, so great was his zeal for his own and his Father's glory, and so great was his love to his church, that he gave himself for it, Eph. v. 25, 26, 27. Now, as it is all

Christians duty to behold this grace of our Lord Jesus Christ, and it is their great advantage so to do; so the best find it no easy thing to believe it with application to themselves, so as to say, as in Gal. ii. 20. *Christ loved me, and gave himself for me.* For when they see a little of themselves, (and but a little is seen, and all bad), and a little of his glory, (and it is but a little of that that believers can see, with such bad eyes as the best have, and in so dark and distant a place as this is where we are); then they find it hard to believe, that Christ will clothe their filthy nakedness with that garment of salvation wove out of his own blood and bowels; and in it present them to God's favour and love, and to all the precious fruits of it. But for as hard as it is, all the true worshippers in the New Testament temple are bound to believe, that their great High Priest set over the house of God, doth represent them unto God for acceptance, far more really, (for that was but typically), and much more successfully, than Aaron did Israel in the solemn day of atonement. But it is as truly, as commonly, said, That such as think believing easy, know not what believing is.

Inference 2. Here we may see the excellent way of our acceptance with God. We are accepted in his Son Jesus Christ. The salvation we get upon our acceptance with God, and the blessed way in which this acceptance cometh, are equally to be beheld with wonder, and praise, and faith. This excellent way is the only way of a sinner's acceptance with God. There was another way; but that was of the acceptance, not of a sinner, but of a sinless man, with God. But that is gone. In commending this only way now, I would have you consider, that there have been two ways of man's acceptance with God, of God's making. One way was, that in the first Adam; that is past. The other is in the second Adam; this stands, and will remain for ever. There is also another way, of man's making, that is neither in the

first,

first, nor second Adam. This is a dream that the greatest part of mankind dream to hell in. They dream of it as long as they live; and when they die, and go to hell, they awake, and behold it was a dream: for neither the mourning of the law, nor the piping of the gospel, awakens them out of it, Matth. xi. 17. And this way is by a sinful man's own doing, and pleasing God. Of each of those a little.

1. The first way of man's acceptance was fixed in the first Adam, and in God's covenant with him. Obedience was required, and death threatened for disobedience. But God graciously furnished him with endowments sufficient for his work. The Lord by this way, did therein signify, that mankind should stand accepted with him as represented by his covenant-head. So in Rom. v. 14. the first Adam is called *the figure* (or *type*) *of him that was to come;* that is, Christ. The apostle is, from ver. 12. to the end of the chapter, shewing vast unlikeness, yea, contrariety betwixt these two heads of mankind: in what each did; obedience and disobedience: in what they brought in; the first man brings in by his disobedience sin, condemnation, and death; the second man brings in by his obedience, righteousness, justification, and eternal life: all as contrary as light and darkness, heaven and hell. How, and wherein is Adam then said to be the figure, the type of Jesus Christ? Is it not in this, that as the two were true men, and so they were single persons; yet they both were federal, covenant-heads, and representatives of a great many; Adam of all his natural offspring; Christ of all his spiritual offspring, given to him of the Father? And as the first Adam stood accepted with God in the righteousness of his obedience; so did his posterity stand on the same account. And if he had continued in his obedience, all his posterity had been accepted in him: but because he became by his fall a sinner, the first Adam became thereby a destroyer, and brought in sin and

death on all his posterity, by the justice of the curse of the broken covenant; and hath the guilt of sin imputed, and the depraved nature which by his sin he contracted, propagated unto all his posterity. So that the best of saints is *conceived and born in sin*, Psal. li. 5.; and all are *by nature children of disobedience, and of wrath*, Eph. ii. 3. So this way is quite unpassable. A covenant betwixt a holy God, and a dead defiled sinner, was never intended by God: and it is dishonourable to God's holiness, and wisdom, and justice, to imagine any such covenant.

2 The other way of God's making, is, for the acceptance of sinful men by his Son Jesus Christ, and God's covenant with him for his redeemed offspring. If our Father Adam had stood as God had placed him, there had been nothing required of us, or needed by us, in order to the instating us in the favour and friendship of God; whatever had been needful for our continuing in it. His obedience, if continued, would have entailed and conveyed that to us in our several generations. So now in Christ, the second Adam, the favour of God was bought for us by him, (for it was lost by the first Adam); it stands in him, and is conveyed to us through him, when *the law of the Spirit of life in Christ Jesus, doth make us free from the law of sin and death*, Rom. viii. 2. Those are all the ways of God's making. But,

3. There is a way of man's making and devising, (as fallen man is full of foolish inventions); and it is this, to obtain God's favour by their own doings and obedience. The Lord never put any to this, though many think that he hath put all men to it. There never were but two sinless men in the world; Adam and Christ. The obedience God required of Adam was not to instate him, and bring him into God's favour and friendship; (for that he was created in): but it only was to continue him in it, and to convey the same friendship with God unto all his posterity. But how to regain God's favour when lost by sin, what

what way to make up the breach when made, Adam did not, could not know it, till God revealed it after his fall. So Chrift's work and bufinefs in the world, was not to obtain God's friendfhip for himfelf; for he from eternity was the Son of his Father's love, and his Father's everlafting delight. As man, when conceived in the womb of the virgin, he was *that holy thing that was to be born of her*, Luke i. 35.; and while he lived in the world, he *always did thofe things that pleafed his Father*, John viii. 29. As to his office of Mediator, he was inftalled in it moft honourably, and glorified by it, Heb. v. 5. His difcharge of it was *the pleafure of Jehovah*, Ifa. liii. 10. He made it *his meat to do the will of him that fent him, and to finifh his work*, John iv. 34.; *was ftraitened, pained, till his baptifm, in his own blood, was accomplifhed*, Luke xii. 50.; *defired with defire to eat his laft paffover*, Luke xxii. 15. After that, he appointed his fupper for a memorial of his death, and for an ordinance-feal of that new teftament which he was the next day to confirm and ratify by his blood. And when all this is done, he opens his heart in love to his difciples about his death, and the good they fhould get by it in his abfence; with a firm promife of their happy meeting again, in a better place and ftate than he either found or left them in, in John xiv. 15, 16. And laft of all, he opens his heart to his Father, John xvii. 4. *I have glorified thee on the earth: I have finifhed the work which thou gaveft me to do.* When all things ftood thus betwixt Chrift and his Father; what need then was there of all the heavy fufferings which he was put to, and which he muft endure, as he often told them before? That neceffity he was under of fuffering, was from this, That *he came to give his life a ranfom for many* Matt. xx. 28.; and *was verily fore-ordained before the foundation of the world, to redeem his people with the price of his precious and fpotlefs blood*, 1 Peter i. 19, 20.

But this invention of man's heart, in feeking God's favour

favour and acceptance by their own works and doings, is not only not appointed by God, and never successful to any man, (for *that no man is justified by the law in the sight of God, it is evident*, Gal. iii. 11.; but no evidence is convincing to a blind and proud legalist); but also this way is a perverting of both the ways of God's appointment. If they will be for God's old way with Adam in innocence, then they must be sinless, and in God's friendship, as he was; they must have all the abilities Adam had for obedience, to maintain that friendship. But though sinful man be proud and vain, yet none have the forehead to pretend to innocent standing Adam's covenant-state and ability. As for the only way of regaining God's favour by Jesus Christ, this new and wicked way overthrows it: *For if righteousness come by the law, then Christ is dead in vain;* and Paul should *frustrate the grace of God*, if he sought to *live by the law*, Gal. ii. 19,---21. But the unbelieving world runs after this invention: for they are too poor to answer the exact perfect holiness of God's true law, and too proud to submit themselves to the righteousness of God. They do as the cunning knave did, Luke xvi. 3, 4 they cannot dig with old Adam, and to beg of the second Adam, they are ashamed; and therefore strive to live by tricks and cheating. But God is not mocked. And thus multitudes perish, not only in the Heathen and Antichristian world, but in that that is called Christian: For this damnable error is natural, and is in the heart of every one that is an unbeliever, profess what he will in words and principles.

But the only gospel way of sinners acceptance with God, by the representation that Christ makes of them unto God, hath these things to commend it above God's first way with Adam and his seed in the first covenant.

1. In that it is a most glorious way of acceptance, far higher and better than what Adam had while he stood, or than his posterity would have had if he had stood.

stood. For, on this supposition of Adam's standing, sin had indeed been kept out; but the acceptance continued to Adam and his posterity, had had no better and nobler foundation than that of the obedience and righteousness of a creature, a mere man. But now believers in Christ stand accepted of God, in the obedience and righteousness of Christ, who is *God over all, blessed for ever:* so that every one of them may say, as Isa. xlv. 24. *In the Lord have I righteousness and strength.* I own that this way stops all glorying in ourselves; but it is fitted for raising, and keeping up eternal glorying in the Lord, 1 Cor. i. 29,—31. It is not the least, but the greatest, rather, of the honour of the crown of glory in heaven, that the crown itself, and the kingdom, and the heirs of it, were all bought with the blood of the Lamb; and that their title to it now, and their possessing of it to eternity, hath no other, nor lower foundation, than the righteousness of God, the righteousness of a man, who is *the Lord our righteousness,* Jer. xxiii. 6. And thus God's *Israel shall be saved in the Lord with an everlasting salvation.* Isa. xlv. 17.

2. This way is a more safe way and sure than Adam's way, or God's old way with Adam. The uncertainty of that way was seen in the event quickly. The stock of mankind was all in his hand: he was furnished with sufficient grace to keep him standing, (his case is enough to make us hate the popish distinction, and sense, of sufficient and efficacious grace, with reference to fallen man); but he was but a mere man, and was left to the freedom of his own perfect will, (enough to disgrace the false name of free will in a sinner, a slave to his will and lusts, and a *captive to the devil at his will,* 2 Tim. ii. 26). But it pleased God (and against that no man should reply) not to give him establishing, preserving grace. It seemed fit unto God, that establishing grace should only be dispensed in and by Jesus Christ, who was to restore fallen man, and to be the head of *a new and better cove-*

covenant, *of which Christ is Mediator, which was established on better promises*, Heb. viii. 6. Establishing grace was given to the standing angels. Christ is their head, Col. ii. 10.; and they are called *elect angels*. 1 Tim. v. 21. Now, if it had been asked Adam, or an angel, concerning him, How long shall Adam stand in God's favour? the only answer could have been, As long as he is obedient to his maker and covenant-party. Ask again, How long shall Christ the Mediator stand in God's favour? It is answered, For ever: and it is impossible it should be otherwise. But if it again be asked, How long shall a believer in Christ, whom Christ hath represented to God for acceptance, how long shall he stand accepted? this hath several answers, but only one good one. And that is, A believer stands always accepted with God, as long as Christ is accepted with God as the representer. As long as the believer is represented by Christ, so long continueth his state of acceptance with God. Adam, in his first state, had all grace but establishing grace, in his good state. The elect angels had it, and thereby stood, and do *always behold the face of Christ's Father which is in heaven*, Matth. xviii. 10. They need no other grace, but establishing grace to keep them well, when they were well. But Adam fallen, and all his offspring, need restoring grace to make them well, and more grace to make them better, and preserving grace to keep them unto the heavenly kingdom. All this grace is out of Christ's fulness, and secures the happy state of all that are in him.

3. By this way of our acceptance with God in Christ, a greater blessedness cometh unto men than could have come by Adam if he had stood. The first mention of eternal life, is made after his fall, Gen. iii. 22. It is indeed a deep and dark text; but that I named it for, is, That in it, *living for ever*, is first named, which afterwards is so frequently promised in
Christ

Christ to his church. To this that plainly relates, Rev. ii. 7. *To him that overcometh will I give to eat of the tree of life, which is in the midst of the paradise of God.* We need not trouble our heads about the extent of the blessings in the first covenant of God with Adam, and mankind in him. The Spirit of God speaks very little thereof: and that wisely; for why should he reveal blessings which no man was to partake of? But what is plainly revealed, is, that this covenant was utterly broke by Adam's sin; and by that breach, guilt, and wrath, and death, came in upon the world; for which the only relief is by Jesus Christ. The first dawning of which our first parents saw in that first gospel, Gen. iii. 15. and expressed their faith of it in that worship which was appointed them, Gen iv.; and they did recover the favour of God by this new way and covenant, which they had lost by their sin under the first. There was doubtless somewhat singular in that communion with God, which our parents, and Abel, and who else of mankind were then born, had, that is called *the face of the Lord*, Gen. iv. 14. and *the presence of the Lord*, ver. 16. that the reprobate Cain counted it his misery and punishment to be banished from: for he thought, that when he was cast out of God's presence, he was also cast out of God's protection; and then was afraid, lest every man or beast might prove his executioner: and therefore God gave him a pass and a protection; which it is like was all he sought, or got. But now in Christ Jesus, and on the account of his righteousness, not only all the curse of the first broken covenant is removed, but greater blessings are conveyed to us, and bestowed on us, and a better paradise provided for us, than that which Adam sinned in, and was driven from. He sinned in it almost as soon as he was put in it; and was driven out of it as soon as he had sinned: and both of them concern and affect all us his posterity, as much as they did him. Sinners we are in and by his sin, and cast out of God's favour in and by his being cast out; and there is no relief for us but in Jesus Christ. But this relief is with vast advantage, Rom. v. 12,---21.

Examine then your hearts, how they stand affected towards this new and living way to the holiest of all by Jesus Christ. It is a good rule for one to judge his own state by; even by his true, fixed, and approved thoughts of Jesus Christ, as the only way to God's favour and friendship, 1 Cor. v. 23, 24. 1 Pet. ii. 7. How blind must that man be, who hath hopes of heaven, and hath no hearty favour and relish of God's only way to heaven? If men mind heaven, and seek it, and hope for it in ways of their own devising, they are never a whit the nearer to it, nor the surer of it. That you may not be deceived now, and disappointed wofully at last, I would shew you some thoughts of mens hearts, that are common, sinful, and dangerous; that ye may beware of them.

1. Some say within themselves, and it may be to God too, "O that God would accept of me of his "great mercy, and look graciously on me!" And is not this a good wish? Is it not a frequent prayer of saints in the word? and is it not to be still used by all? Yes: all this is true. But it is only good when it is well meant: in many it is ill meant; and therefore is a faulty wish. All the mercy of God flows to men only in and by Jesus Christ. If Christ be forgot in your prayers, you can never put up one good one, nor get a good answer. The mercy of God without Christ, is a dream that the greatest part of the world dream to hell in; and all the while think they are in the right road to heaven. How oft have you heard, that there is no God to be savingly known, and rightly worshipped, but in Christ? and that there is no saving mercy to be found from God, but in Jesus Christ?

2. Some say, and think they say better, "O that "God would make me perfectly holy, that I may be "accepted of him!" Is not this a brave desire and
prayer?

prayer? True holiness is indeed an excellent blessing; a main part of the image of God in standing Adam, utterly lost and defaced in fallen man, renewed again by Jesus Christ in regeneration, and perfected in heaven. The study of holiness is an excellent study, and a study for all our days. We should be still perfecting of it. 2 Cor. vii. 1. but cannot in this life be perfect in it, Phil. iii. 12. Perfect holiness is an excellent aim and design, and is in the heart and eye of every one that is truly holy. Diligence, and continuance in it, and to grow in holiness, is a saint's best exercise; and success therein his choicest mercy. The holiest man on earth is surely the happiest man on earth: and the perfection of holiness in heaven, is a necessary constituent of the happiness of heaven. A patron of sin, a despiser of holiness, and he that desires but a little of it, hath not the Spirit of God. But for all this, there may lurk some evil thing in this wish for perfect holiness. To search it out, I would name a few things to you. 1. There is no true holiness but what is from Christ, who is *made of God unto us sanctification,* 1 Cor. i. 30. None are sanctified but *by faith in him,* Acts xxvi. 18. It is Christ's image in them. All the moral virtues of the Heathen, for all their splendid lustre, had not any bit of true holiness in them. And so is it as to the morality that is so prized and praised by many. 2. As all that are truly holy, would fain be perfectly holy, (for no man is void of this desire, but such as would sin more, and love sin); so no man is truly holy, but he hath a mean and low esteem of his own holiness; and the most happy proficient in holiness, is surely the humblest saint. 3. Whenever holiness is sought to recommend us to God's acceptance, without faith in Christ, there is no holiness in that desire, nor will it ever be granted. For in this case the language of the heart is, "O that I were so holy, that I might not need Jesus Christ!" What an ungodly wish is this? I hope you all abhor the thought of it.

3. It is also common with many to say, "O that God would accept of me, and my good works and duties, for Christ's sake!" Many poor creatures take pains to do all they can in obeying God's will; and when they find it is but little they do, and that also full of sinful mixture and imperfection, then they bring in Christ to help them out. But this is to abase, and to affront Christ: for Christ was never appointed to help men under the first covenant of works; but only to bring them out of it; and then save them by the new and better covenant, wherein the Mediator doth all the redeeming work for them by himself alone; and by his Spirit given them, works in them what is pleasing in his sight. But this carnal wish of having our works accepted for Christ's sake, saith, 1. That the man thinks he can do something (and that is no small thing in this vain man's eyes) without Christ; contrary to the well-known word of his, John xv. 5. *Without me ye can do nothing*, spoken to, and of them that were in him: and much more may it be said of them that are not in him. Yet there is hardly to be found a natural man, who thinks not but that he can do somewhat that pleaseth God, and may further his acceptance with God: but because it is not so much and so good as it should be, he would have help from Christ to make it better, and more effectual with God. But the bottom of all this is self. 2. Christ's righteousness was not wrought out by him, and tendered to men in the gospel, as a clout, or patch, or ornament, to be put upon any one part of the shameful nakedness and deformity of a sinner, but as a perfect and entire garment for covering all. So that they that have it all on them, have none of it; and he that received it not at all, and doth not trust alone to Christ's righteousness, as to the only screen from the holy justice of God, and the only ornament of beauty in God's sight, is still stout-hearted, and far from righteousness. 3. The

The acceptance of our service and obedience to God, is indeed a precious thing, and much desired by all sincere Christians; but the way it is got, is little known by many that seem earnest for it. The Lord's way is this: First, by Christ, and union with him, the believer's person is accepted of God; and then through Christ the fruits of his faith (as all true good works are) become accepted also. So in the beginning of the world, Gen. iv. 4, 5. when the two brothers offered their sacrifices, and both to the Lord, to the same true God, and the offerings in themselves lawful, and afterwards by the written law were required; yet it is said, that *the Lord had respect to Abel, and to his offering; but unto Cain and to his offering he had not respect.* Wherein lay the difference between their offerings? Heb. xi. 4. *By faith Abel offered unto God a more acceptable sacrifice than Cain; by which he obtained witness that he was righteous; God testifying of his gifts: and by it, he being dead, yet speaketh,* or *is spoken of.* And from distinguishing grace, as Abel was received and accepted: so Cain was enraged, and turned a murderer of his brother, 1 John iii. 12.; which made Luther say, that Cain hath been murdering Abel in all ages, to this day; that is, the zealots for the righteousness of works, do still hate and persecute *the heirs of the righteousness which is by faith,* as Noah is called in Heb. xi. 7.

But the only right breathing of the heart of one that truly knoweth and believeth this truth, That Christ is the only representer of his people unto God for acceptance, is that of Paul, in Phil. iii. 8, 9, 10. and it is in three things. 1. That he *might win* or *gain* Christ, ver. 8. Then he counts he is rich enough, and despiseth all losses, for this gain. 2. That he *might be found in Christ,* ver. 9. As if he had said, " I know the day is coming, when God the judge of " all will find out every man, and me also. My de- " sign and desire is, that *I may be found in Christ;* " and then I am sure I shall be found in peace."

But

But how would he be found in Christ? *Not having mine own righteousness, which is of the law,* (I am afraid and ashamed of appearing before God in it); *but that which is through the faith of Christ, the righteousness which is of God by faith;* that righteousness which is of God's providing and accepting, that which is of Christ's working out, and which is applied and put on by faith. It is this righteousness the apostle desires to be found in, in order to his acceptance with God; and so will every person do that hath that spirit that Paul taught this doctrine by. 3. *That I may know Christ,* ver. 10. " If I win Christ, I am rich " towards God; if I be found in him, I am safe; if " I know him, I am wise to salvation." Blessed is that man or woman that feeleth in his or her heart, somewhat of that deep humility, strong faith, and warm love, which wrought in Paul's heart, when he, by the Holy Ghost, wrote these words. Then they would be plainly and easily understood. But when men know and feel nothing of themselves, and of their own unrighteousness, nor of Christ, and of his righteousness, and no Christian should wonder at such mens blundering about, and mistaking of such evangelical expressions of faith in Jesus Christ, which shine as day to an exercised believer; while the unbeliever, though a master in Israel, can see no light in them, but *gropes, as if he had no eyes, and stumbles at noon-day, as in the night;* as it is said in Isa. lix. 10.

So much for the two inferences from this doctrine.

I would now further apply this truth in two exhortations; one to unbelievers, and another to believers.

Exhort. 1. Unto unbelievers. Who are they? By unbelievers, we mean such as never had any business with Christ, to obtain by him acceptance with God for themselves. He is an unbeliever, call him by what name you will, that never employed Christ for representing him unto God for acceptance. Of such there are many sorts; passing what hath been said of some, that seek the acceptance of their works, not of their

their persons. Some beg communications of grace and mercy from God, and use not God's way of giving all, in and by Jesus Christ. Some beg the pardon of their sins, and the washing away of their defilements; but do not ask this, How shall a sinful man stand so beautiful in God's eyes, as that God may look on him, and not be angry; may look on him, and love him? That sort of pardon that many seek, is never given; and if given, would not answer the end. A mere pardon of sin, (if it were possible), without a garment of righteousness upon a man, might deliver him from wrath and hell; but would not make him lovely in God's eyes, nor intitle him to eternal life: for it is *grace that reigns to eternal life through righteousness;* and that *grace,* that *reign of grace,* that *righteousness,* and that *eternal life,* are all by *Jesus Christ our Lord,* Rom. v. 21. But true gospel-forgiveness, and the imputing of Christ's righteousness, are inseparable and indivisible.

Of those unbelievers are specially three sorts. 1. The secure, sleepy unbelievers; such as have no heart concern about this matter; and never think in earnest how they shall stand accepted of God: nor of Christ's concern in procuring it, nor of their own concern in obtaining it by him. Such men are much like to that great man, though a blind Pagan, in Acts xxv. 19. *They had certain questions against him of their own superstition, and of one Jesus, which was dead, whom Paul affirmed to be alive.* Little did that poor Roman know, that he must perish for ever, if he knew not this Jesus, and the virtue of his death, and the power of his resurrection. As indifferent and careless are many sinners this day, that when they hear of Christ, and of the necessity of his righteousness to sinners for their acceptance with God, they are ready to say, That they are certain hard questions about things and persons that they have no concern with. Whether Jesus was dead or alive, whether the Jews or Paul was in the right; all was alike to Festus. So to many now, Whether a sinner can weave and work for himself a garment to stand accepted with God in? or, Whether he must have one made for him, and given to him by Jesus Christ, or perish for ever? are counted but questions for ministers and scholars, and such as they have different and contrary opinions about. And the careless unbeliever troubleth not his head about them; and that only because his heart never felt the weight of sin, and the vast concern of eternal salvation. All such are gross unbelievers. They may sometimes ask what ministers, what Christians think of them; but never this, " What doth God think of me? How shall I stand " accepted before him?" Assure yourselves, that all other cares, concerns and inquiries about yourselves, are mere trifles in regard of this; and that all such persons are but triflers in religion, pretend and profess what they will, who mind not salvation in the first place, as the one thing needful, Matth. vi. 33. and Luke x. 42.

2. There are awakened and roused unbelievers, like many of John Baptist's hearers, whom he wondered at: Matth. iii. 7. *O generation of vipers, who hath warned you to flee from the wrath to come?* Such men come to know, and feel, from the light and power of God's word, 1. That their eternal state and lot stands in God's judging; that so it will and must fare with them to eternity, as they are accepted or not accepted with God. 2. That man comes to know, that as yet there is nothing in him to procure this so necessary acceptance with God; yea, he seeth, that this God, in whose hands is his eternal lot, is many ways provoked to wrath against him for all his sins. In this condition, the native shift that all men take, is a new course of obeying, and doing the best they can, not knowing Jesus Christ. They take the first water, and next at hand, to wash away the filth that is upon them; but, alas! their filth increaseth by this washing; their soul-disease grows upon them

by

by this washing; their soul-disease grows upon them by false means of cure. There is no physician for sick souls, but Jesus Christ; no balm for a wounded conscience, but his blood; no washing from sin, but in it; none recover of the mortal disease of sin, but his patients.

3. There are desponding, despairing unbelievers. And there are of them at all times, and in greater numbers than many are aware of. This sad frame riseth thus. 1. By clearer discoveries of the holiness and purity of God, and of the righteousness of his holy law. 2. By further discoveries of their own vileness and sinfulness; when they see sin within them, sin without, sin round about them; and that they are under sin, Rom. iii. 9.----19.; as a man may be said to be full of the sea, when he is cast into the midst, and lieth at the bottom of it. 3. A discovery of utter impotence to do any thing to help himself out of this woful plight. He hath tried many ways, and all ineffectual. Thus when a sinner seeth a holy God threatening ruin, feels conscience condemning him as deserving ruin, and all refuge failing him; in this case despair is natural, and would be the result of all sound awakenings, if the Lord's mercy in Christ do not interpose, and discover itself in this extremity. It is no sin for the damned in hell, but their great misery, to despair of ever getting out; but it is their sin to blaspheme God. But for a sinner out of hell so despair, is a grievous sin, but too frequent: Ezek. xxxiii. 10. *If our sins and our transgressions be upon us, and we pine away in them; how should we then live?* " If we be so guilty, and God be so exact upon us by his judgments, must we not perish?" Nay, saith the Lord, Turn to a gracious God, and live. Unto such despairing unbelievers I have nothing else to say, but what Paul and Silas said to one in this case, Acts xvi. 31. *Believe on the Lord Jesus Christ, and thou shalt be saved.* And to back this exhortation to

such, I would recommend four things to be considered by them.

1st, Consider how greatly Jesus Christ is accepted with God and his Father. You may think, that this is remote from your concern; but it lieth nearer than you are aware of at first view. He is highly accepted and beloved of God, not only as his own Son, but as our Saviour: Isa. xlii. 1. *Behold my servant whom I uphold, mine elect in whom my soul delighteth.* It would be a great encouragement to faith on Christ, to think what a great favourite in heaven Christ is; how graciously, yea infinitely, he is beloved of his Father. His person, his office of Mediator, his performances, his actions, his sufferings in that office, are all of sweet-smelling savour before God. Unbelief hath in its root, low, mean, and sorry thoughts of all these. Say then, " How vile and abominable " soever I be in God's sight, yet Jesus Christ is pre- " cious in his sight with whom I have to do."

2dly, Consider how great the acceptance with God is, that Christ doth procure to sinners whom he undertakes for. Many have found it, and such know it best: but it is but little that the best of them can tell of it: and what the gospel declares of it, believers themselves rather admire at, than fully know, or firmly believe. If you have not found it yourselves, believe others have got this acceptance.

3dly, Consider how many Christ hath made highly accepted with God, who were just such as you be; as unworthy and vile as you are, or can think yourselves to be. What were the Corinthians of whom the apostle speaks, 1 Cor. vi. 9, 10, 11.? If the Holy Ghost had not written it, we would be ashamed to read over such a bed roll of abominations: *Be not deceived: neither fornicators, nor idolaters, nor adulterers, nor effeminate, nor abusers of themselves with mankind, nor thieves, nor covetous, nor drunkards, nor revilers, nor extortioners, shall inherit the kingdom of God.* (If it be so, what then shall become of them?). And such

such were some of you: but ye are washed, but ye are sanctified, but ye are justified in the name of the Lord Jesus, and by the Spirit of our God. Every instance of Christ's grace on great sinners, (and every age is filled with many of them), should be an encouragement to every sinner to put in for a share of the same grace whereof Christ hath so great an abundance, and as great a good-will to show it.

4*thly,* Consider that Jesus Christ never refused any sinner that employed him to do this great business with God for him. It is his proper office, he hath given his word and promise for it, John vi. 37. and vii. 37. And he hath been as good as his word to all that ever trusted in him; none of them were ever put to shame, Rom. ix. 33.

Let therefore hope come in, and spring up. Say, "Though I see myself vile and lost as ever sinner "was, or can be, out of hell; though I can do no-"thing to relieve myself; yet there is help in Christ; "many have found it. I am commanded by God to "come to him, and to the Father by him; and there-"fore I will try and trust Christ in my forlorn state." Do so, and you shall prosper. Christ will undertake your cause and concern, and you shall quickly find the blessed fruits thereof. I shall conclude with an allusion to that passage in the gospel, Matth xiv. 22. 30. and Mark vi. 46----51. wherein we read, that Christ did send, yea constrained his disciples to go to sea without him. They meet with a contrary wind in this commanded voyage, and toil all night to little purpose. Our Lord knew their difficulty; and not only remembered them on the mountain at land, but made them a visit at sea, and that *walking on the sea;* and, doubtless, he that made both sea and land, could use either of them as he pleased. His *disciples saw him, and were troubled, saying, It is a spirit. They all saw him,* as in Mark vi. 50. *and were troubled;* for none of them knew him, but all mistook him, *and cried out for fear;* till he said, *Be of good cheer, it is I, be not afraid.* On this Peter, always a forward disciple, said, *Lord, if it be thou, bid me come unto thee on the water.* Christ giveth the command, *Come.* Peter obeys: but *when he seeth the wind boisterous, he is afraid; and begining to sink, he cried, saying, Lord, save me. And immediately Jesus stretched forth his hand, and caught him, and said unto him, O thou of little faith, wherefore didst thou doubt?* Christ saved him, and then rebuked him for his unbelief. Is not your condition somewhat like this? Christ cometh to you as on the waters, in the night, and in a storm; you are afraid of him: he calls you by the gospel to come to him; you essay it, but the winds and waves fright you. Cry to him, *Lord save me.* Assure yourselves, that he that calleth you, will hear your drowning, dying cry; will stretch forth his hand, catch you, and save you; and then chide you kindly for your unbelief: yea, you will then chide yourselves for it, when you find (and find you will) that Christ is more merciful than you did or could imagine. How vastly doth the first experience of Christ's grace surpass all the desires and expectations of the first adventures and adventurers, upon Christ's tender heart, and on his mighty saving arm!

SERMON

SERMON XIII.

JOHN xvii. 24.

Father, I will that they also whom thou hast given me, be with me where I am; that they may behold my glory which thou hast given me: for thou lovedst me before the foundation of the world.

YOU have heard, that this is the third thing in the matter of Christ's prayer that I have been speaking to. Wherein I proposed to speak to two things: The glory of Christ; and his people's beholding of his glory. In speaking to the first of these particulars, I did confine my discourse unto Christ's glory, as he represents God unto his people, to be savingly known by them; and as Christ represents his people unto God, to be graciously accepted by him.

It is to the latter of these I have been speaking; and have made some entrance upon the application thereof, which I would now prosecute. Last day I spoke to unbelievers; the true name of many, who will never own it, till they *get their portion with them,* Luke xii. 46.; unless the Lord open their eyes to see their disease, and stretch forth his hand, and heal it. Faith is wrought, and acteth, where unbelief is seen, and bewailed, and prayed against. Mark ix. 24. *Lord, I believe, help thou mine unbelief,* said a new-begun man in faith. I ranked unbelievers into three sorts. 1. The secure and stupid unbeliever, that never saw and felt any quarrel betwixt God and him, nor any necessity of Christ as a peace-maker. 2. The awakened and roused unbeliever, who begins to open his eyes, and to see the importance of salvation, the

danger

danger of God's wrath, and the bad state he is at present in. Such people, unless God's Spirit work true faith in them, do naturally betake themselves to themselves for relief. That great word spoke by the jailor, Acts xvi. 30. *What shall I do to be saved?* however it was meant by that distressed sinner, it hath been by many as much mistaken as the apostle's answer to it in ver. 31. The true meaning is, " I am " a lost undone creature, and have no help at home; " if there be none abroad, I am quite undone." And they take these words in vain, that use them, while they vainly and proudly think, they can do something, if they did but know it. 3. There are discouraged, despairing unbelievers, that know that they are in a bad case, and cannot believe that it can ever be altered to the better. A very great sin, and too common. Many live, and die, and perish in despair, that go not down to the pit roaring. We think their case sad, that die in expressions of despair; and their case yet worse, that destroy their own lives in despair. And indeed this last case is exceeding dreadful, if they are themselves, and are not distracted. As to the former, there may be more charity due to such as have given good proof of their faith in their lifetime, though they die in a cloud, and utter heavy unbelieving complaints. Of which sort, I have heard of a Christian near death making a heavy complaint of the Lord's withdrawing from him in that season of his greatest need; and said, he " did not think that " ever the Lord did so with any of his children." The wise and happy minister to whom he made this complaint, gave him this answer: " Know ye not that " thus it was with the Son of God, when, on the " cross, a little before his death, he cried out, *My* " *God, my God, why hast thou forsaken me?*" Which words were so blessed, that the storm ceased, and the good man died in peace. But there is a silent despair in many unbelievers, that goes along with them many days and years, and they perish in it without noise or complaint. They inwardly think, that their state is bad, and they have no hope that it will ever be better. It is like an inward wound, that a man may bleed to death of, as well as of an outward one. But can Satan and unbelief prevail to that degree in a man not in hell, as to make a perishing sinner look on Christ's saving gracious face, and say, " Either thou " canst not, or will not help me?" No; Christ is surely out of that sinner's eye in whose heart despair hath the dominion. A glance of Christ's glory as a Saviour will expel despair, and beget and nourish faith in him. Never did a sinner see Christ's face, but he looks for some good from him, and that not a little also; and that never in vain.

Exhort. 2. That which remains, is to give two exhortations to believers; though one of them will take up our time now. As I told you in the former exhortation who were unbelievers, so now I would tell you who are believers, that the exhortation may be rightly taken, and not snatched at by them to whom it doth not belong. By a believer in Christ, I mean a man that doth in heart and in experience know these two things. 1. He hath seen so much of the holiness of God, and strict purity of his law, and hath seen so much of his own vileness and impotence, that he doth despair of ever making himself accepted with God by any thing he hath or can do. And this sort of despair (if we may give so ill-sounding a name to so good a thing) is so far from being inconsistent with true faith, that no true faith in Christ can be, or be acted, without it. That sinner that hath any hopes of getting matters betwixt God and him mended without Christ, will never, and can never believe on Jesus Christ. 2. A believer is one that hath so heard and so believed God's record concerning Christ in the gospel, and his ability and good-will to save sinners, as voluntarily and deliberately to lodge all his acceptance with God for salvation on Jesus Christ alone. He seeth it to be his only shift, and a good one too.

Unto such believers I would give these two exhortations from the doctrine. 1. Study in the light of the word, and by the eye of faith, this glory of Christ in representing his people to God for acceptance. 2. Improve this truth by the activity of the same faith.

Exhort. 1. Study and behold the glory of Christ in representing his people to God. None see it once, but they will desire to see it again and again, and more and more of it. None see it rightly, but they wonder and admire at it; that not only our salvation is brought about by this representation, but that Christ's glory is great in making of it. Whenever a man seeth any thing of the glory of God, before whom the representation is made, any thing of the vileness of the persons represented, the divine dignity of Christ the representer, and the great acceptance the represented by him obtain of God; then will the man stand amazed, and cry out, " O the depths of " grace in saving lost man!" See Heb. i. 3.; where the apostle teacheth us three things concerning Christ; what he is, what he did, and what he got. He is *the brightness of his glory, and the express image of his person,* (of God the Father's glory and person), *and upholding all things by the word of his power.* The whole creation oweth its original to him, and is preserved by him, and his powerful word. Who can doubt his Godhead, that believes that these, and many such expressions, are indited by the Spirit of truth? Who would think what follows? This divine person, this equal with the Father, this creator and upholder of all things, when he comes into the world, what is his business? what doth he? *He by himself purged our sins.* His work was about sin and sinners, to purge sin, and to save sinners. Observe the phrase. It is not said, *by himself he made the world;* but only, that *God made all things by him,* ver. 2. It is not said, that he *by himself upholds all things;* but only, he doth

doth it *by the word of his power.* There is no need of the interpoſing of himſelf, or of his perſon, (if I may uſe the word); his word of command was enough to do both. But when our ſins are to be purged, a word of power was not enough: himſelf muſt come in, and be a ſacrifice; as Heb. ix. 26. *He appeared to put away ſin by the ſacrifice of himſelf.* Nothing leſs was needful, nothing leſs craved by God offended by ſin, nothing leſs offered by the Saviour of ſinners. In and by this purging our ſins, how low is this divine perſon the Son of God brought! But what became of him when he had done this work? *He ſat down on the right hand of the Majeſty on high.* He is high in his divine perſon was brought low in his work, and is exceedingly exalted when he had done it; as in Phil. ii. 6---11.

In order to the raiſing of your thoughts about this glory of Chriſt in repreſenting his people unto God, I would offer you, 1. Some generals about it; 2. Some particulars in this chapter to the ſame purpoſe.

Firſt, The generals about it ſhall only be theſe two. 1. Divine counſels about it. 2. Divine acts about it.

1. Divine counſels about this. It was the eternal purpoſe of God to have a remnant of Adam's offspring repreſented to his favour, and its fruits, by his own Son made man, and dying in their ſtead. This *eternal purpoſe was purpoſed in Chriſt Jeſus our Lord,* Eph. iii. 11. *His good pleaſure which he hath purpoſed in himſelf,* Eph. i. 9, 10. *It was in Chriſt Jeſus before the world began, but is now made manifeſt by the appearing of our Saviour Jeſus Chriſt,* 2 Tim. i. 9, 10. It is unto this higheſt ſpring your faith muſt riſe by all the lower ſteps it takes; even to the deep deſign of God in purpoſing ſalvation by Jeſus Chriſt to his choſen. And it is revealed to us in the word as purpoſed by him, to the eternal praiſe of his grace, to the exalting of his Son Jeſus, the undertaker of the

the work of saving, and to bring in a great salvation for his people.

2. What passed in time about this. In the fulness of time God sent his Son into the world. When he came, that was fulfilled, Isa. ix. 6. *Unto us a child is born, unto us a son is given.* He was born and given to us; for he came to die, and to be given for us. On this I would offer four things.

1*st*, When our Lord came, and set about his work he came for, he looked on himself, preached and declared himself, to be a representer, by his office, of his people to God; that he was the sacrifice for sin and sinners, Heb. x. 5,---10.: that his flesh and blood was the meat that came down from heaven, which he must give for eternal life to his people, and that all must feed on by faith that had any mind to live, John vi. 35,---58. Yea, when he was first made manifest to Israel, John Baptist, the first preacher of Christ as come, preacheth and points him forth to be *the Lamb of God which taketh away the sin of the world*, John i. 29. a Lamb for purity, a Lamb for sacrifice, and the Lamb of God, sent and provided by God, (as his type was, Gen. xxii 8), and acceptable unto God. But what was spoken in the ear in closets in Christ's time on earth, was proclaimed on house-tops (as he bid them, Luke xii. 3.) when Christ had done his work, and was gone to heaven. His apostles, and all his servants in all ages, have made it their business to set forth Christ as the only sacrifice for sin, and the only High Priest to introduce sinners into God's favour, in and by the virtue of his sacrifice. They have not begun to preach Christ rightly, that have not *first of all declared how that Christ died for our sins according to the scriptures*, 1 Cor. xv. 3.; and then of his resurrection, verse 4. Ministers must neither leave Christ in his grave, nor preach a glorified Jesus, without remembering his death.

2*dly*, We find that the law and justice of God dealt with our Lord, when he was come, as with a representative

sentative of sinners. There was nothing in him, that justice and law should exact on him for; he owed no debt of his own contracting; yet law and justice dealt severely with him. The Lamb of God was without spot; yet his life must go, and his blood be shed for sin. There had been no justice in the Lord's bruising of his beloved and spotless Son, if he had not been answerable at the highest bar for the sins of others, for which he was stricken, Isa. liii. 8. In that chapter, (in which it is something strange that a Jew cannot see Jesus; but far more, that any that bear the name of Christians, should make the eunuch's question, Acts viii. 34. *I pray thee, of whom speaketh the prophet this? of himself, or of some other man?* and will not take Philip's answer, ver. 35. who from *that scripture preached unto him Jesus*), in that of Isa. liii. we have the prophet preaching Christ like an apostle, concerning his work, his death, the cause and fruits of it, with New Testament brightness and glory; and this several hundreds of years before Christ came into the world. I shall touch at a few things in it that belong to my present purpose. In ver. 4. *Surely he hath borne our griefs, and carried our sorrows.* Every man is not charged with the sorrows of others, except in common sympathy, which all owe towards others in distress. Christ not only had this, but a near and close feeling of, and pressure by them, that was proper to him only; yea, he bore the sorrows of many, whose sorrows were over before he came, and of far more, whose sorrows were not begun, long after he came to bear them. Yet he did bear them to save them; for that grief and sorrow that men have, which Christ did not bear, will be everlasting sorrow. But what had Christ to do with their sorrow? In verse 5. *He was wounded for our transgressions, he was bruised for our iniquities.* His wounds and bruises were very heavy, but not without a cause; only the cause is strange: they were for *transgressions*, for *iniquities*; but these were none of his, but ours. The wounds were his;

but the sin was ours, that deserved the blows. And thus our peace, our healing cometh. But what had Christ to do with our iniquities? verse 6. *The Lord hath laid on him the iniquity of us all.* And he took the burden on him, and was only able to bear it, and did bear it away. The Lord hath resolved, that sin and sorrow shall go together. So was it with the Saviour; if sin be laid on him, sorrow shall follow it. So is it with sinners; their sin will bring dreadful sorrow, except Christ take away both. Sirs, you have formerly known, or do at present, or shall hereafter know, what a heavy burden sin is; how insupportable it is; and how surely that soul must sink into hell, that hath this burden lying on himself. And indeed, until the burden of sin be felt to be too heavy for them, and a burden that all the world cannot bear for them, men will think lightly of Christ's undertaking, and will never employ him, but in a compliment. Know this, and accordingly chuse your course: It is resolved in heaven, and declared in the gospel on earth, that every sinner's iniquity shall either be borne by the sinner himself, to his eternal damnation, or by the surety, Jesus Christ, to the believer's eternal salvation. But well did the prophet preface to this doctrine, ver. 1. *Who hath believed our report? and to whom is the arm of the Lord revealed?* This gospel-doctrine will never be welcome to an unbeliever; and none are made believers, but by the revealing of the arm, and putting forth of the power of the Lord upon their hearts. Till then, sinners will mock God, both in their contracting the debt of sin, and in their devices of paying of that debt; and both are very sinful work. God hath fixed his way of satisfying his justice, and will not alter. Men must either betake themselves to Jesus Christ by faith, or lay their account with hell. That sinner is blind, and ignorant of God's justice, and of the strictness of his law, that thinks that sin against God can be expiated by any thing, but the blood

blood of him that is God. And he that dare not trust to the sufferings and virtue of Christ's atonement made for sin, knows not God's mercy, nor *the truth as it is in Jesus*, Eph. iv. 21. Let all sinners therefore take heed, what course they take in the matter of the burden of sin. Take heed, that you mock not God in studying to pay it in false coin. All your own, all creature coin, is but reprobate metal in heaven's court and kingdom. It may pass on earth, and in a deluded conscience: but how little doth that signify? and how short while will that little last? It is but hay and stubble, which Christ hath many fires to burn it up with. But for Christians, I advise you, in reading the prophets and apostles concerning Christ and his sufferings to make use of this as a key to open up all, as a light that enlightens all, That all the sufferings of Christ were laid on him, and endured by him, and presented unto God, as he did represent his guilty people; otherwise justice could not exact on him, nor his people be saved by them. See how Christ expresseth this in the celebration and institution of his last supper. He *taketh, blesseth, breaketh*, and *giveth bread*, and calls it, *my body given for you. Likewise also the cup after supper, saying, This cup is the new testament in my blood, which is shed for you*, Luke xxii. 19, 20. I do not mind the Antichristian synagogue, (for a church it is not, but in an usurped name, or in a vain notion), who have abused and perverted these plain and easy words, more than devils or men did ever pervert any words of God or man before; and have, upon that abuse of them, set up the grossest idol that ever a Heathen worshipped; for such as worship sun, and moon, and the host of heaven, have God's glorious workmanship before their eyes; yea, the Egyptians garden and herb gods are preferable greatly to a bit of paste, knead and baked by a baker in his oven, conjured into a pitiful godhead by the mumbling of a priest, and first worshipped, and then swallowed down as other food, by the

the besotted people. Nothing less than the dreadful wrath of God can be in mens believing this lye, that the man's reason and all his senses militate against, 2 Thess. ii. 10, 11, 12. But many that are not infected with this strong delusion, understand no more by Christ's words in this sacred ordinance, than that the bread and wine, so used as Christ appointed, do signify the sufferings unto death of our Lord Jesus Christ, cruelly handled by wicked men, and severely dealt with by the justice of God; but the cause and end of his death, they mind not. This Christ puts us in mind of, in these words: " For you, and for " your sins, and for the remission of them; you, and " your sins, are the cause of my death; and my death " is the cause of your forgiveness." Christians, if you keep out that word, *for you;* if your faith do not echo to Christ's *for you,* with your *for me,* I assure you, that the bread and wine on the Lord's table, and the same creatures on your own table, will be of equal signification, as to soul-nourishment; and that is, none at all.

3*dly,* We find, that when Christ had thus been dealt with, as representing his people, there was a high acceptance of his sacrifice. The Father that put him to all this, was mightily pleased with him, and with his death. Here behold the depth and mystery of God's saving men by Jesus Christ. God's justice against sin squeezed out Christ's life, and by that squeezed out eternal salvation for them he died for. Here is wisdom, and here is love, 1 John iv. 8, 9, 10.

4*thly,* Hence it is, that all believers on Christ are graciously accepted with the Father. Whenever this blood shed for them, is sprinkled on them; whenever the virtue of this blood is applied to them by his Spirit, and applied unto by their faith, they are represented to God in it and with it, and are therefore accepted.

Secondly, Let us, in the next place, look into this chapter, John xvii. and learn something of Christ's repre-

representing his church and people unto God. It is as fit a portion of the word, as any for that end; and in it I would look to two things: 1. What is in it about Christ, the representer. 2. What of his people, whom he represents in this solemn address to his Father.

1. About Christ, the representer, we find these things.

1st, Our Lord notes the time in which he was to do his great work he came into the world for: *Father, the hour is come;* it is at hand: "the hour of "my dying for my sheep." John xii. 27. *Now is my soul troubled; and what shall I say? Father, save me from this hour: but for this cause came I unto this hour.* As if our Lord had said, "I should lose my "main end I came into the world for, if it was not "for this hour." This was that special hour, in which Christ was to make the grand representation unto God, of all his people for their redemption, and of all their sins for their expiation. This was Christ's dying-hour, and the church's redemption-hour.

2dly, Our Lord prays for the united and mutually-influencing glory of the Father and of the Son: ver. 1. *Glorify thy Son, that thy Son also may glorify thee;* as he prayed, John xii. 28. *Father, glorify thy name;* and was answered, *I have both glorified it, and will glorify it again;* and as he foretold it, John xiii. 31, 32. *Now is the Son of man glorified, and God is glorified in him. If God be glorified in him, God shall also glorify him in himself, and shall straightway glorify him.* What is this glorifying he prays for? It is of large extent. "Glorify thy Son, in making him a "sacrifice; glorify him, in accepting the sacrifice; "glorify him, in slaying him; glorify him, in raising "him from the dead; glorify him, in exalting him, "and making him head over all things to the church, "his body, his fulness," Eph. i. 20.----23.: and all this, *that thy Son also may glorify thee;* "may glorify "thy justice and thy law, in satisfying both by my "blood;

"blood; may glorify thy grace and mercy to thy
"chosen, by redeeming them unto God by my blood;
"and may glorify thy wisdom, in contriving this way
"of redemption, which is to be accomplished by my
"death, the hour of which is come."

3*dly*, This that our Lord defires of his Father, was according to the everlasting covenant: ver. 2. *As thou haſt given him power over all fleſh, that he ſhould give eternal life to as many as thou haſt given him.* "Thou haſt given him univerſal power and domini-
"on, but a particular charge of the elect; to them
"he is to give eternal life, in and by this redempti-
"on-hour now come."

4*thly*, See how our Lord nameth this eternal life which he was to give, and they that were given unto him were to receive: ver. 3. *And this is life eternal, that they might know thee the only true God, and Jeſus Chriſt whom thou haſt ſent.* A moſt ſpiritual deſcription of eternal life given by the author of it. It is begun in the ſaving knowledge of the Father and of the Son, and in the begun fruits of that knowledge. Eternal life is perfect in the perfect knowledge of the Father and Son, and in its perfect fruits: as in Eph. iv. 13. 1 John v. 20. and John xiv. 20.

5*thly*, Our Lord, in ver. 4. giveth a faithful account of his diſcharge of the work his Father had given him to do: *I have glorified thee on the earth; I have finiſhed the work thou gaveſt me to do:* all but dying: which he was now as ready and willing to do, as any thing he had done before.

6*thly*, and laſtly, Chriſt prays again (what he had prayed for in ver. 1.) in ver. 5. *And now, O Father, glorify thou me with thine own ſelf, and with the glory which I had with thee before the world was.*

2. Let us ſee what Chriſt ſaith here of his people, whom in this prayer he repreſents to his Father. It is to be undoubted by all Chriſtians, that this prayer of Chriſt doth as really concern all believers in all ages, as it did the apoſtles themſelves. And this Chriſt

Chrift tells us in ver. 20. *Neither pray I for thefe alone, but for them alfo which fhall believe on me thro' their word.* It is the prayer of our great High Prieft; and all his Ifrael were on his heart in making of it, and reap the bleffing of it.

In it, as concerning them, we find,

1ft, Our Lord names them rightly, ver. 6. They are *the men which thou gaveft me out of the world: thine they were, and thou gaveft them me; for they are thine. And all are thine, and thine are mine; and I am glorified in them,* ver. 9, 10. Well doth the good fhepherd know, and count, and tell his flock; and he feeth his Father's mark of election upon them, and his own mark of redeeming blood on them; and therefore he cares for them, and prayeth for them, and giveth them eternal life, John x. 28, 29.

2dly, Chrift tells all the good he can of them, and covers their failings: *They have kept thy word,* ver. 6. *Now have they known, that all things whatfoever thou haft given me, are of thee,* ver. 7. *For I have given unto them the words which thou gaveft me; and they have received them, and have known furely that I came out from thee, and they have believed that thou didft fend me,* ver. 8. How poorly had they received Chrift's word? how weak and ftaggering was their faith? and how oft had Chrift reproved them fharply, for their unbelief, and other faults? Yet not a word of thofe in Chrift's reprefenting them to his Father. They had fpoke one good word in John xvi. 30. *Now are we fure that thou knoweft all things, and needeft not that any man fhould ask thee: by this we believe that thou cameft forth from God.* This Chrift remembered and tells it to his Father, in ver. 8.; but not a word of what he faid to them, John xvi. 31, 32. *Do ye now believe? Behold, the hour cometh, yea, is now come, that ye fhall be fcattered every man to his own, and fhall leave me alone.* This is the conftant gracious way of our High Prieft: He makes no mention of his Ifrael's faults in heaven, but for their expiation, 1 John ii. 1, 2.; whatever reproof and correction he sends to humble his people, and to amend them, Rev. iii. 19.

3*dly,* Christ doth here represent his people to God, his Father, with their necessities and dangers, and prays for help and supply: *They are in the world,* ver. 11. *The world hateth them,* ver. 14. There is evil in the world, that they are endangered by, ver. 15.; and therefore prays for their preservation, ver. 11. 15. a. 'sanctification, ver. 17. To be kept from evil, and to increase in true holiness, are the main blessings believers need till they come to heaven. So Paul's faith acted, 2 Tim. iv. 18. *For the Lord shall deliver me from every evil work, and will preserve me unto his heavenly kingdom.* So he prays for others, 1 Thess. iii. 13. *To the end he may stablish your hearts unblameable in holiness before God even our Father, at the coming of our Lord Jesus Christ, with all his saints.*

4*thly,* Christ doth here declare to his Father, that his undertaking and sufferings were for his people's sake: ver. 19. *And for their sakes do I sanctify myself.* Christ needed no such sanctification as his people do, and as he giveth unto them, by the virtue of his death, by his Spirit. His sanctifying of himself, is his separating and devoting himself to death, as a sacrifice for his people. And in this sense a very learned foreign divine understands that dark word in Heb. x. 29. *And hath counted the blood of the covenant wherewith he was sanctified, an unholy thing,* or *common thing*: whereas commonly it is taken, as if the apostate had been ever in some sense sanctified by the blood of the covenant. This learned expositor doth natively enough from the Greek text take this *he* that was sanctified by the blood of the covenant, to be but another name of the Son of God, who is trodden under foot by such desperate apostates. So that the sense is plain and easy, and a great aggravation of their apostasy, that they not only despise the Son of God, but also his sacred blood by which himself was sanctified, and the cove-

covenant confirmed unto his people, and made to be his testament and last will. To this same purpose is that other word of the same apostle, Heb. xiii. 20. *The God of peace brought again from the dead our Lord Jesus, that great Shepherd of the sheep, through the blood of the everlasting covenant.* So that the apostle in Heb. x. 29. describes this dreadful apostasy in three things: open contempt of the person of the Son of God; contempt of his sacred redeeming blood, the only price of redemption; and despite to the Spirit of grace, that works by the gospel on mens hearts. Such must fall into the hands of the living God, who lives to revenge such bold affronts done to the most gracious and only saving appearances of God unto men; that is, in his Son, and his blood, and in his Spirit, by the gospel. All is openly and deliberately contemned and despited by such wretches; and they must perish. And though it be hard to make an application of these sad brands of ruin to any man in particular, or sort and body of men; yet this I may venture to say, that open blasphemers of the Son of God, (as all are that count him a mere man); all that count the blood of the covenant a common thing, (as they must do that count it but the blood of a mere man); and all that do despite unto the Spirit of grace; such, I say, if they have been once enlightened, as Heb. vi. 4. and have had the Spirit of grace striving with them, and if this contempt of such sacred things of God be in malice, have far more reason (though I know that such have no inclination) to fear their interest in this dreadful scripture, and in such like, than any of the poor souls, who, upon their falling from their first love, and first works, or on their falling into some gross conscience-wasting sin, have applied this awful sentence unjustly to themselves. But all such are far from it, to whom the Son of God, and his redeeming blood, and his Spirit of grace, are sacred and adorable, though they have no comfortable view of their interest therein at present: for though the case of such be sad, yet there is a door of hope for them, in renewing repentance and faith.

But, to return again unto the exhortation given to believers, to consider this glory of Christ in representing his church unto God, I would offer a few things to engage them in the studying of it.

1. Consider the necessity of this representation made by Christ, in order to the acceptance of sinners with God. Christ saw this necessity when he undertook the office. No sacrifice but that of himself was required; no high priest but himself was called, or able to offer what was effectual to satisfy the justice of God and to save sinners, Heb. x. 5,---10. A sinner must see the necessity of this representation, which Christ only can make unto God; or he will never renounce all vain shifts of his own, and betake himself only unto this. And a believer must see the necessity of this representation made by Christ, that he may admire it more, and trust to it only.

2. Consider the glorious excellency of this representation that Christ makes of his church unto God. Glorious in itself, glorious in its fruits and ends. It is the ministration of righteousness, that exceeds in glory: 2 Cor. iii. 10, 11. *For even that which was made glorious, had no glory in this respect, by reason of the glory that excelleth.* And all this glory is in the face of Jesus Christ, *who of God is made unto us wisdom, and righteousness, and sanctification, and redemption;* and that for two ends: *That no flesh should glory in his presence; and that he that glorieth, might glory in the Lord,* 1 Cor i. 29, 30, 31. If a man could have any saving wisdom but in and from Christ to know God and the way to heaven, he would glory in that; if he had any justifying righteousness to stand accepted before God in but Christ's, he would glory in that; if he had any sanctification but what is derived from Christ as its root and fountain, he would glory in that, if there was any redemption but what Christ the only Redeemer brings in, he would glory in that: yea

so

so proud, and so inclined is flesh to glory in God's presence, that sinners do vainly hunt after, and as vainly imagine they have attained some matter of glorying before God. But, saith the apostle, "Christ is so made of God unto us, as to cut off all pretensions to any glorying, but in the Lord." So that a Christian, when he finds he is made wise to salvation, must say, "This is from Christ:" when he seeth any justifying righteousness upon him, wherein he stands safe and accepted before God, he must say, "This is none of mine, but Christ's righteousness:" when he finds any sanctification in him, in his heart, and way, and worship, he must say, "This is but a few droppings from the fountain Christ; a little of the ointment that was poured in all fulness on my High Priest Jesus:" when he gets any piece of redemption, or acts his faith and hope on compleat redemption, all his acknowledgments, and all his expectations are, and must singly center in Christ the Redeemer. Yea, the Spirit of God expresseth this thing most strongly. He saith not, that Christ is made unto us the prophet and teacher, and giver of wisdom; nor the justifier, and bringer in of righteousness; nor the sanctifier, nor the redeemer; all which are true of Christ, and of God's making him to be, and oft spoken of him in the word: but he is made unto us the things themselves, *wisdom, righteousness, sanctification, redemption.* All of these are in Christ, and nothing of any of these is out of him. Wisdom out of Christ, is damning folly; righteousness out of Christ, is guilt and condemnation; sanctification out of Christ, is filth and sin; redemption out of Christ, is bondage and slavery.

3. I would recommend the considering of Christ's glory in representing his church unto God, from the profit and advantage believers do receive by this exercise. I believe most of you would answer this question, What is the best exercise, and thought of the heart? Surely it is that that hath most grace in it.

Now

Now, what are the best graces of the Spirit? Are they not repentance, faith, and love? And all those, in their lively acts and exercises, do natively flow from the right studying of Christ's representing of us to God for acceptance.

1*st*, Repentance. What do you take it to be? There is too little of it with many professors, and that because it is not well known in its true nature. Many take repentance to be that that is little better than what the devils have. We read of their faith and trembling, James ii. 19.; and this is a greater length than many are got, who are angry if they be not called good Christians. Repentance is not a bare fit of sorrow and shame for sin committed, nor fear of God's wrath for sin. This may be in ungodly men. Few malefactors go to the gallows without somewhat of this. Cain, Pharaoh, Saul, Judas, had this. But true repentance unto life, though it may begin with a discovery of some particular sin or sins that God sets in order before a man's eyes, Psal. l. 21.; yet it is not *godly sorrow that worketh repentance to salvation, not to be repented of*, 2 Cor. 7. 10. till the sinner look upon himself as lothsome and abominable in the sight of God, that it becometh one of the greatest riddles and mysteries unto him, how such a God and such a sinner should ever be made friends; how God can look upon him without abhorrence; and how such a sinner can stand before this holy God with favour and acceptance? And when the glory of Christ as the peace-maker is discovered to, and seen by him in this case, and when he is drawn to trust to it, this faith is acted in the sight and sense of his own vileness in himself. They are unhappy people, and unskilful teachers, who take up *repentance towards God, and faith towards our Lord Jesus Christ*, Acts xx. 21. and think of them, and study to act them, as if they did interfere with one another; as if repentance were the fruit of the law, and the faith and fruit of the gospel; as if
they

they could be acted separately and apart. All gross mistakes. There is no saving grace in our heart, but is Christ's work by his Spirit blessing the gospel. Repentance without faith, is the devil's repentance: and faith without repentance, is the hypocrite's faith. If they be true, they go together; if rightly acted, they act together. And as this sense of sin and self-vileness is inseparable from first believing, so it continueth in all the life of faith in all true growing believers. David dieth with the acting of repentance and faith, 2 Sam. xxiii. 5.

2dly, Faith in Jesus Christ. Bring true faith unto a narrow point, to that act in which its nature doth properly stand. For faith is a large comprehensive grace, much spoke of in the word, more talked of than acted by many; and least known, and most mistaken by them that have it not. This faith I speak of, is not a bare believing, or giving an assent unto divine truth, upon the evidence of a divine testimony; nor is it believing and expecting of good from God, upon the ground of his faithful promise; though these are acts of true faith. But faith in Jesus Christ, in its closest, nearest nature, acts thus. The self-condemned sinner, lothsome in his own sight, and persuaded that as he is in himself, he is far more lothsome in God's sight, doth, on the gospel call and promise, try and trust Jesus Christ for making him accepted with God. This is proper believing, Gal. ii. 16. And according as the measure and degree is of our knowledge of sin in us, and of the law's condemning of us for sin; and as the measure is of the light of the knowledge of the glory of God in the face of Jesus Christ; so is the measure of that faith that seeth our need of, and taketh up the glory and safety in Christ's representing us to God for acceptance, and that trusts to it.

3dly, The heavenly and everlasting grace of love, that is planted in the heart of a believer, and is nourished by the grace of the new covenant; that groweth
in

in true Christians as the new creature doth, and is the only grace that the glorified act in heaven. Other graces of the Spirit are the Christian's armour, that is laid aside when they get the perfect victory. Now, what raiseth love to Jesus Christ to the hottest flame? Is it not when Christ's loveliness in himself, and when his love to us, is best seen by us? And are not both most conspicuous in this matter of his gracious representing us to God, covering us with his own righteousness wrought out for us by his precious blood shed, counted to us freely by his grace, and intitling us to the love of God, and to all the great fruits of that love?

It follows to speak of the second exhortation to believers; but that I shall leave to the next occasion. Only, to press the first, the duty of studying in your hearts Christ's glory in representing his church unto God, I would add four things.

1. By this representation that Christ makes of you that are believers unto God, *you that were enemies are reconciled unto God*, Col. i. 20, 21. You are beloved of God. Not only there is no condemnation to you that are in Christ, Rom. viii. 1.; not only are your sins blotted out, and your natural deformity covered from the eye and hand of law and justice, by the covering of Christ's righteousness; but you are so adorned with that garment, that the Father loves you; as Christ tells believers, John xvi. 27. *For the Father himself loveth you, because ye have loved me, and have believed that I came out from God.* You are not only saved from wrath, and the curse of the law; but possessed of God's love, and have a sure right and title to glory, by this grace of Jesus Christ that is come unto you.

2. By this representation of you unto God, you are made as accepted of God as ever any believer was. This many do not rightly understand; and therefore are ready to reproach it. There are degrees of grace

on earth, and there may be degrees of glory in heaven; but neither here nor there are there any degrees of acceptance. Accepted, or not accepted, divides and diftinguifheth all mankind in both worlds. Acceptance with God relates to a man's ftate before God, and not to his frame. We fay not, that every or any believer is fo good a believer, or fo great a faint, as Paul; but yet every true believer, as to the ftate of his perfon, is as accepted as Paul was as to his perfonal ftate. The reafon is this: The acceptance of all believers with God, is only on account of this reprefentation made by Chrift for them unto God. And this is made by Chrift for all equally: all the tribes of Ifrael are equally on the heart and breaftplate of our great High Prieft Jefus Chrift. And thus we find in that triumph of faith, Rom. viii. 31,---39. all God's elect are included; and the grounds of that triumph lie equally fair for any believer: *Chrift is given, and hath died, and rifen again, fitteth at the right hand of God, and maketh interceffion for them.* Every believer may fay fo as well as Paul, though we cannot fay fo with as ftrong a faith as Paul had. The ground is the fame, and common to all believers; but they do not equally build upon this foundation. If our ftate of acceptance did ftand on any thing believers themfelves have, or do, and not fingly on what Chrift hath done, and daily doth for them; then indeed all believers, who differ fo much from others in their inherent grace, and in the improvement, exercife, and fruits thereof, could not be alike accepted.

3. You that are believers, you are, even now, as much accepted of God as ever you fhall be. I fay not, that you enjoy God as much; that you are as near, and as like to him, as ever you fhall be; but that you are as much accepted as ever you fhall be. Believers are not called to glory, nor brought unto it, for acceptance. That is paffed, and fixed for eternity,

as to all in Christ by faith, before they come there. Only their acceptance in that day is more gloriously declared and proclaimed than it was on earth, Matth. xxv. 34. And the fruits of that acceptance will be bestowed by the Lord, and enjoyed by the glorified in heaven, vastly beyond what believers can know, receive, or enjoy on earth. A state of acceptance in Christ Jesus, is the common privilege of all believers. He is all in all to all of them without difference, Col. iii. 11. And as it admits of no difference in them that are in him, and represented by him for it; so it admits of no gradations nor increase in any one believer, save as to the evidence, comfort, and fruits of an accepted state. And after building by faith on Christ the foundation, all the remaining work of a Christian stands in seeking after those blessings that flow from our state of acceptance with God by Jesus Christ.

4. I will adventure to add, in the last place, that which to some seems a hard saying; but it is not so hard in itself, when rightly understood, as some would make, or mistake it. And it is this, That a believer on Christ, and represented by Christ unto God's acceptance, is as accepted of God as Christ the representer is. The same acceptance that Christ the Mediator hath with God, the same acceptance is given to all believers. See John xvii. 23. *That the world may know that thou hast loved them, as thou hast loved me.* Verse 26. *I have declared unto them thy name, and will declare it: that the love wherewith thou hast loved me, may be in them, and I in them.* If we consider Christ and his people asunder and apart, then there is as great a difference betwixt Christ in himself, and his people in themselves, as is betwixt light and darkness, righteousness and unrighteousness, Christ and Belial. But if we consider Christ the head, and his church his body, as one, and inseparably united in this mystical representation before God; then the divine

vine acceptance on this reprefentation is one and the fame towards the reprefenter and the reprefented: as Aaron the high-prieft's was within the vail in the holy of holies, and all Ifrael's without the vail, on the day of atonement. The high-prieft was accepted as reprefenting all Ifrael, and all Ifrael accepted as reprefented by him. Indeed the difference was very great betwixt the Old Teftament type and fhadow, and the New Teftament fubftance. But all that difference is only to the greater glory of our great High Prieft, *the Son of God, who is paffed into the heavens,* Heb. iv. 14. ix. 24. and to the greater advantage of his fpiritual Ifrael without the vail, Heb. ix. 13, 14. The fame acceptance the Father giveth to his Son, Mediator, the reprefenter of his people, falls on all thofe for their happinefs that are reprefented by him. And it is to be feared, that fuch as cannot receive this truth, have a fecret refpect to fome other way and fort of acceptance with God than that that comes by Chrift's reprefenting them to God. And the danger of fuch delufions, is as great as their fouls are worth.

SERMON XIV.

John xvii. 24.

Father, I will that they also whom thou hast given me, be with me where I am; that they may behold my glory which thou hast given me: for thou lovedst me before the foundation of the world.

TWO greater, deeper, and larger themes, are not in God's word, than these; the glory of Christ, and the beholding of this glory by his people. They are such as cannot be fully known by any on earth; yet it is very useful to Christians to be exercised in the study of them while they are here.

On the first of these, the glory of Christ, I have spoken at some length, under these two heads. 1. Christ's glory, as he represents God to his church, to be savingly known by them; and, 2. His glory, as he represents his church to God, to be graciously accepted by him. The former I have finished, and would dispatch the latter at this time. After I had handled the doctrinal part, I made some application; and in that spoke to one exhortation to believers, to study, in the light of the gospel, with the eye of faith, the glory of Christ in his representing his people unto God for his gracious and eternal acceptance.

Exhort. 2. I come now to the second exhortation to believers; which is, That they should improve, by the activity of their faith, this glory of Christ. There is nothing sweeter to the eye of faith than this glory of Christ, and nothing more useful to a believer than to have his faith well exercised about it. This glory of Christ in representing, as our High Priest, his church unto God, is a matter of pure revelation. It had

had never been known, unless it had been revealed. All truths that are of pure revelation, can only be managed by faith. When a truth is discoverable by reason, it is also improvable by reason. But if the truth transcend reason, and the discovery of it is made only by divine revelation, the right improvement of that truth can only be made by faith grounded on that revelation, and that faith wrought by the Spirit of the revealer, Matth. xvi. 17. This truth about the glory of Christ, is not only of pure revelation, but it is *the great mystery of godliness,* 1 Tim. iii. 16. And *in Christ are hid all the treasures of wisdom and knowledge,* Col. ii. 3. In the improving of this truth, faith only can do any thing to purpose; and there is much work for faith in the using of it. I shall therefore on this exhortation handle these two things. 1. In what cases specially believers ought to use and improve Christ's representing them to God's acceptance. 2. In what way and manner they should improve it in all or any case.

First, In what cases specially believers ought by their faith to improve this glorious representation of them unto God. I shall name some particular cases.

1. Be careful to improve this glory of Christ, in all your daily approaches to, and appearances before God. Whenever you come to the court of heaven, and into the presence of the great King, forget not him that only must introduce you, and make your address acceptable: Heb. x. 19, 20, 21, 22. *Having therefore, brethren, boldness to enter into the holiest by the blood of Jesus.* The apostle is writing unto Christian Hebrews, who were well acquainted with the Old Testament sanctuary and worship; and he speaks to them in that dialect. They knew what the holiest was in that dispensation; and that the *high priest alone,* and *but once a-year,* and *not without blood,* might enter into it, Heb. ix. 7. And this holiest to us in the New Testament, is *heaven itself,* Heb. ix. 24.; into which our *High Priest is entered by his own blood,*

Heb.

Heb. ix. 12. and made an entrance for his people: *For the way to the holiest of all was not yet made manifest, while as the first tabernacle was yet standing,* Heb. ix. 8. Christ by his blood made an open door to heaven, and by that door we must always enter, and *climb up by no other way, lest we be as a thief and a robber,* John x. 1, 8. What is the blood of Jesus? It is the blood of the Son of God: the blood of him, as a sacrifice offered up by him as our High Priest, for the sins of his people; the blood whereby he brought in that everlasting righteousness in which all his people stand accepted before God. Now, saith the apostle, that privilege that only the high-priest under the law had, of entering into the typical holiest of all by the blood of the typical sacrifices, every believer in Jesus Christ hath now under the gospel, and hath a daily entrance into the true holiest of all by the blood of the true sacrifice, Jesus Christ. And he adds in ver. 20. *By a new and living way* (or a new slain and living way) *which he hath consecrated for us thro' the vail, that is to say, his flesh.* We need not a door of entrance into heaven only, but a way to walk in. And that way is provided by Christ, and he is it; as John xiv. 6. And Christ as slain, hath by his death consecrated it for us; like that in John xvii. 19. *For their sakes sanctify I myself.* The apostle calls Christ's flesh, *the vail,* alluding to the vail of the sanctuary, Heb. ix. 3. through which the high-priest passed into the holy of holies. There was a double use of the sanctuary-vail. It kept the holiest of all from being seen by all the people, and yet made an entrance for the high priest through it unto the holiest of all. So is the vail of Christ's flesh; it vails and hides his divine glory, as Phil. ii. 6, 7. and yet it gives a passage into the glorious presence of God unto believers. What more is needful for a believer's access and acceptance? ver. 21. *And having an high priest over the house of God.* We not only wanted a door, and a way, but an authorised introducer into heaven. And Christ is is all. He is the High Prieſt, who by his office is the introducer, the repreſenter, and preſenter, of his people unto God. Upon this comes the exhortation, ver. 22. *Let us draw near:* " Let us all go to God, " and to heaven together; you Chriſtians, and I an " apoſtle. We have the encouragements common to " us; let us jointly improve them." But, alas! moſt unbelievers think it an eaſy thing to draw near to God, though they never think of Chriſt, nor of uſing him in their approaches to God, (if they may not rather be called *departings from God*). They neither care for making them aright, nor care whether they be accepted or not; nor fear the taking God's name in vain, as all do that come not to God by Jeſus Chriſt, John xiv. 6. Chriſtleſs Chriſtians, and Chriſtleſs worſhippers of God, (if it were proper to call Chriſt-leſs men either Chriſtians, or worſhippers of God), are an abomination unto God. But that that is ſo eaſy to ſuch careleſs triflers, is far otherwiſe unto a ſerious ſoul. When ſuch a perſon ſeeth any thing of his own ſinfulneſs and meanneſs, and any thing of the holineſs and majeſty of God, it is no ſmall difficulty to reſolve this queſtion: " How is it poſſible, that " ſuch a defiled creature as I am, can make any ac- " ceptable appearance before ſo glorious a God?" The only reſolution is in this: " Chriſt our High Prieſt " repreſents me to the Father." He did all our bu-ſineſs with God as our Mediator, and that in our na-ture, and in our name and ſtead; and all that we do in worſhip to God, is to be done by us in his name; and thus acceptance comes to us. Chriſtians, when you pray, when you read and hear God's word, when you ſit down at Chriſt's table, when you perform any part or piece of worſhip to God; if you would have it acceptable to God, and profitable to you, (and theſe two are inſeparable; for no accepted ſervice is unprofitable to us: and if profitable to us, it was firſt accepted of God), let your faith be exerciſed on this: " Jeſus Chriſt makes another ſort of figure

" for

"for me in heaven, than I can make for myself on earth."

2. Improve by faith Christ's representing of you to God, in all your judgings and examinings of yourselves. Self-examination is a great duty, and a necessary one, 1 Cor. xi. 28. and 2 Cor. xiii. 5. Happy are they that mind it much, that manage it rightly, and issue it well. I believe, that of all duties required in the word of all men, it is that duty that fewest unbelievers and hypocrites are employed in. It is very doubtful, whether it be possible, that a hypocrite can be at the pains to spend some portion of time in the work of self-examination. Of all companies, an ungodly man likes least the company and conversation of his own conscience. Psal. iv. 4. *Communing with our own hearts;* dealing fairly and freely with our own consciences; and not only allowing, but charging them to reply, and do deal freely with us again, and taking well with this freedom, seems to be above the reach of a hypocrite, at least of an ordinary one. But when a Christian is setting about this work of self-examination, by and in the light of God's word, he should search his heart, his sins, his wants, his graces. But the main thing is his state in God's sight. And the designed end and issue of this trial, is, to have and pass the same judgment on himself that God doth; that he may not, as many do, commend himself, when God condemns him, or condemn himself, when God approves him. Now, we all know, that God's judgment of mens state is, as they are in Christ, or not in him. So 2 Cor. xiii. 5. Surely you must think they were bold and saucy professors, that sought a proof of Christ's speaking in and by Paul, as ver. 3. To them he saith in effect, " Instead of your trying, " whether Christ speaks by your ministers, inquire if " Christ be in yourselves or not. If Christ be not in " you, they have spoken to little good purpose to " you: and if Christ be in you, you will quickly
" know

"know who they be that speak in Christ's name "unto you, and whether Christ speaks by them to "you."

3. Improve this truth of Christ's representing his church unto God, in all the misrepresentations that are, or can be made of you to God, or men, or yourselves. They are false, if they differ from what Christ makes of his people to God. I shall name some of them.

1*st*, The devil misrepresents believers to God, and men, and themselves. *Doth Job fear God for nought?* Job i, 9. said the devil to God. "He hath been a "good servant to thee, but thou hast been a good "master to him; take from him what thou hast given "him, and he will serve thee no more, but curse thee "to thy face." Impudent slanderer, and a lying prophet! God, to try Job, and to make the devil a lyar, gives the devil a permission. He readily useth it: and Job is made a poor man in one day; but blesseth God in taking, as well as in giving, ver. 21. Yet Satan gives not over; but, in chap. ii. 5. begs one trial more of Job, on his body. It is also given, and yet not successful, ver. 9, 10. though strengthened by his wife's bad words. It is a sad, but true name of the devil, in Rev. xii. 10. *The accuser of the brethren, which accuseth them before our God day and night.* They are brethren, God is their God; but yet Satan will be the accuser of them before their God. There is little or no doubt to be made, but that the devil knows who are truly godly. Such a watchful and cunning jailor as he is, cannot be ignorant when any of his prisoners are rescued by Christ, and make their escape, 2 Tim. ii. 26.: and though he know not the hearts of men immediately and perfectly: yet having so much craft, and long experience, and intelligence, in ways unknown to us, of what is in mens hearts, how can we think that his works should be destroyed, 1 John iii. 8. and Christ's new work be begun in the heart of a man, and the devil know nothing of it? But as to Christians advancing in godliness, Satan knows and hates them, and they know him and resist him. Sirs, there is not a Christian amongst you so strong in grace and experience, but the devil can draw such a picture of you by his hellish art, from what he knoweth of God and his law, and from what he knows of your heart and ways, and can set it before your eyes, so as to confound you, if the Lord do not seasonably interpose for your relief. And it is this the devil drives at: that if he cannot hinder the believer's salvation, (as it is certain he cannot; and it is most probable he knows that he cannot), he may yet disturb his peace: for this picture and representation of a poor believer is so artfully drawn, and so cunningly exposed, that when the man seeth it, he is ready to think and say with horror, " This is the picture of a " devil, rather than of a man, or of a Christian." Take all the evil that is in the best, and expose that; and hide all the good that is in him, as if it were not, (and this is Satan's way), and you do then expose a hateful object. Now, this truth of Christ's representing his people unto God, is of great comfort to a believer; for by faith he may say, " My blessed Advo- " cate in heaven giveth another account of me, than " my malicious accuser from hell doth: and I will " trust to the one, and despise the other.

2dly, The world misrepresents believers. The world hates them, because Christ is kind to them, John xv. 19. We are forbid to marvel at it, 1 John iii. 13. And because the world hates them, *therefore they say all manner of evil falsely against the godly*, Matt. v. 10, 11, 12. And thereupon we are bid *rejoice, and be exceeding glad; for so they persecuted the prophets before us*, and the apostles, yea Christ himself. How little did Paul care for the world's opinion of him? 1 Cor. iv. 3, 4. *With me it is a very small thing that I should be judged of you, or of man's judgment; he that judgeth me, is the Lord.* " I stand at
" his

" his bar, and depend upon his sentence, and trust
" to his approbation."

3*dly*, The law makes a representation of believers, that they must not receive, but set Christ's representation against it. Whoever seeth his own face in the glass of God's holy law, seeth a hateful spotted face: *For by the law is the knowledge of sin*, Rom. iii. 20. Now, if a believer think, that just as he seeth himself in this clear glass, so doth he appear in the presence of God, that were dreadful indeed. But there is another representation that Christ makes of them unto God, that the law knows not of. The more a man knows of the law, the more he knows of his own sin and danger. And this sad condition remains, till he look beyond and above the law, unto the righteousness of Christ, who hath satisfied and fulfilled the law by himself, and makes this over to a believer, and represents him to God, as clothed with it.

4*thly*, Believers themselves are often misrepresented by believers also. Blessed be God, that his thoughts of us are not as mens are. Such men that seek after, and value themselves upon good mens thoughts and approbation, seek a thing of small worth, and what is quickly lost. Many are cast at the bar of good men, who stand accepted of God: 2 Cor. x. 18. *For not he that commendeth himself, is approved, but whom the Lord commendeth*. What better was Judas, that the eleven apostles had a better opinion of him, than of themselves, when, hearing Christ's warning of a traitor amongst them, each said, *Lord, is it I?* Believers are never the worse, if other men, worse or better than themselves, pass another judgment on them than God doth.

5*thly*, The last misrepresentation that the faith of Christ's right representing us to God should support us under, is that that our consciences make of us. This is nearer to us than all the other. The devil and the world are without, and round about us; the law is above us; believers are nearer to us: but conscience is nearest of all. Conscience never condemns a believer, but at the bar of the law, (for which, as condemning, Christ hath redeemed him), and always in and by the working of unbelief. And in a believer, his remaining unbelief acts this way: It looks on the disease, and forgets the physician; it looks on the debt, and forgets the surety, and his payment of it. Conscience saith, "Thou owest many thousand ta-"lents to the law and justice of God: is it not true, "and can it be denied?" "No, must the believer "say; the debt is not to be denied by me; nor "Christ's payment of it to be forgotten by me." The law, as a court of judgment, condemns for sin; but Christ's new court of grace acquits the believer in Christ. To this court every believer appeals, and at it he stands.

So much for the third use of this privilege of Christ's representing us to God, under all the misrepresentations that may be made of believers.

4. Improve this privilege under all dispensations of providence that you may meet with. Are you afflicted by the Lord's hand? and would ye have found consolation under it? All are sensible of afflictions, and all would fain have comfort under them. Sometimes the Lord sends an extraordinary measure of this comfort unto his people, which is above the usual activity of their faith; but though this be very pleasing and useful, it is not oft of long continuance, nor is it fit it should. But there is a *rejoicing in tribulation*, that is a duty that Christians should make conscience of; as well as there is a *joy of the Lord that is their strength*, Nehem. viii. 10. which they should seek and value. This rejoicing is only by faith; and this faith that produceth the joy, is acted on Christ, and on our interest in him. " I am heavily afflicted by the Lord's " hand, saith the believer: but I am a member of " Christ's body; my head is concerned in it, and " will support me under it. He keeps up the peace " betwixt a correcting father and a corrected child:
" And

"And as long as the peace stands, no real hurt can come to me. Are you tempted of the devil?" as indeed the most part of most Christians lives is taken up with affliction and temptation; and the whole armour of God is provided for, and to be used in and under them, Eph. vi. 10,---18. It was an odd remark of a minister of great learning and grace, "I never knew an eminent saint, but he had either singular afflictions or singular corruptions to wrestle with." The apostle tells us, 2 Cor. xii. 2. *I knew a man in Christ, caught up into the third heavens*, doubtless meaning himself. You think it is no strange thing that a man in Christ, one like Paul, should be so dealt with; especially when he saith, Eph. ii. 6. that God *hath made us sit together in heavenly places in Christ Jesus*. But this is more strange, that this man in Christ, this man new come down from heaven, should immediately after be buffeted by Satan. If you be so dealt with, how is it to be borne? The devil hath many things to say against us; some too true, that we cannot deny; and some things false, which we may justly deny, and yet do not through our weakness. But when Satan chargeth us with sin truly, which we cannot deny, I would not have believers reason and parly with him, (he is too cunning a sophister for us); but only tell him something of Christ, that we too often forget, and that the devil can neither bear nor answer. "If the devil speak against me as a sinner in myself, "I say Amen to all that is true; but if he say any "thing against Christ the Saviour, I dare say he is a "lyar." If the tempted believer can but say, "I am "in Christ, and therefore I shall prevail; Christ hath "overcome the devil, and therefore I will resist him;" the victory is near at hand.

5. Improve this privilege of Christ's representing you to God, in all the service and obedience you perform to God. All men owe all service unto God; all true Christians are in heart devoted to his service; and the best Christians mind it most, and perform it

best: but when they review their performances, they see them so faulty, and short of what they ought to be, that they see more reason to mourn over the iniquity of their holy things, than to glory in their holy things. Yet notwithstanding all the failings in the sincere obedience of a true believer, (and he alone is the man in whom sincerity is, and by whom any act of sincere obedience can be performed), yet are they *acceptable to God by Jesus Christ*, 1 Peter ii. 5. Their *fruits of righteousness* (though far from being fully ripe and perfect) *are by Jesus Christ unto the glory and praise of God*, Phil. i. 11. Far be it from me, to encourage any believer (much less an unbeliever) to put any confidence in their own works or obedience; but I am sure that it would greatly promote a believer's peace and joy, to look rightly on the fruits of his faith. And that is the right way of judging them by a believer, when he saith concerning his obedience, these four things. " 1. I, the worker, am one in Christ. " 2. The work I do, is the fruit of my faith in Christ, " and of my being in him. 3. The work is done in " Christ's name. 4. And as such is put in his hand, " to be perfumed and presented to God by him." Must not the conclusion of faith be, that Christ will procure a gracious acceptance thereof?

6. Improve this privilege of Christ's representing you unto God, as to your peace with God, and the acceptance of your persons. Build all your desires, expectations, and hopes of acceptance with God, on this alone, even on this representation that Christ makes of you to God. God's favourable acceptance of a sinner never had, nor can have any other foundation: Eph. i. 6. *We are accepted in the beloved.* Rom. v. 1. *Being justified by faith, we have peace with God through our Lord Jesus Christ.* But how comes this peace, this justification? It is by Christ, *who was delivered for our offences, and was raised again for our justification*, Rom. iv. 25. How would the peace of believers flow as a river, if their faith were active this way:
" As

"As Christ represents me to God; so do I stand accepted, surely and eternally?"

7. Lastly, Improve this privilege by faith, in all the views and prospects you have of your last appearing before God. Our appearances before God now are many and considerable. We are always in his sight; we oft draw near to him in his ordinances; he sometimes is pleased to admit us into his special gracious presence, and to manifest himself to us: but all these are small things, compared with the last, which is far greater than all that went before it. The native question that starts up in the mind of a man that thinks seriously on this appearance, is this, "How shall I be found of him in peace?" And the only gospel-answer is, "Thou must be found in Christ," Phil. iii. 9. *Abide in him; that when he shall appear we may have confidence, and not be ashamed before him at his coming,* 1 John ii. 28. None will be *found of him in peace* in that day, *without spot and blameless,* as all should labour for, 2 Peter iii. 14. but only they that are *found in him,* Phil. iii. 9. and *presented spotless by him,* Jude, verse 24. I know that the deep and serious thoughts of this awful appearance before God, are sufficient to make a sinner see the vanity of all refuges, save that of Christ's righteousness. How much more will the glory of the last day do it? Proud men, and trusters to their own righteousness, will then find too late, that that covering of their nakedness is too narrow; and that the beauty of their works, which they valued themselves upon here, will be but deformity before that tribunal. If there be but one blot, one hole in that robe that a man appears before God at last in, (and all that is a man's own, is but *rags,* and *filthy ones* too, Isa. lxiv. 6.), the sword of justice will enter in, and destroy that man. But to believers found in Christ, and covered with Christ's righteousness, there is no danger. The righteousness is perfect, and their acceptance in it perfect and eternal; and the crown of righteousness given to them, will be given by him,

and

and received by them *with exceeding joy*, Jude, ver. 24. We read that there is *joy in heaven, and in the presence of the angels of God, over one sinner that repenteth,* Luke xv. 7, 10. How much more joy will there be, when all Christ's children shall be brought home, to his Father's house? when he shall give that account of them, *Behold, I, and the children which God hath given me,* Heb. ii. 13.? Did Christ lay down the dear price with joy; and that *for the joy set before him,* Heb. xii. 2.? and will he not receive his full purchase with exceeding joy? It will be his, and his church's marriage-day, Rev. xix. 7, 8, 9. And never were there such lovers, as Christ and his bride. No such lover in heaven, as he; and no such love on earth, as that the church hath to him. And must not the joy be great, on their everlasting union and communion, at that day! So that we may say, that when a believer kneels to receive the crown of glory from his hand, who bought it for him by his blood shed in love, he cannot say with more joy, " O how " glad am I of this day of my receiving this crown!" than Christ will say, " I am more glad of the day in " which I give it:" *for in all things, he must have the " pre-eminence,* Col. i. 18. Christians, think justly, and think joyfully, of this great and notable day of the Lord, when he will make the greatest and most public representation of his church unto God, as the glorious head of his glorified body. See what food your faith can gather from that scripture, which, whatever fulfilments it hath had, or may yet have in time, is to be perfectly fulfilled (as many other scriptures) at the last day, Zeph. iii. 17. *The Lord thy God in the midst of thee is mighty; he will save, he will rejoice over thee with joy: he will rest in his love, he will joy over thee with singing.* Who of you hath faith to believe this? Where is the believer who dare apply these words with the confidence of faith to himself? Who is so bold as to say, (and yet all in Christ ought

to

to say so), "The blessed day is coming, and will surely come, when Jesus Christ will be as glad to see me in heaven, as I can be to see him, or myself there? He *will rejoice over me with joy;* that is, he will exceedingly rejoice: *he will rest in his love;* that is, he will love for ever, without wearying, or change: *he will joy over me with singing:* that is, his love and joy will break forth into a song." And indeed the joy of Christ in heaven is the best part of heaven's music. One cloud or frown in Christ's face in heaven, would put an immediate damp on all the holy and happy mirth there. But there is no danger of any interruption: for when the imputed righteousness of Christ is on the glorified in all its glory, (and that is when it appears with all the blessed ends it was wrought out for, and applied for, by Christ); when inherent holiness is perfect in them, and immediate communion with him is enjoyed in this true paradise of God; neither the tempter, nor temptation, nor sin, nor wrath, can enter. The *pillars in heaven*, as Christ promiseth to make *him that overcometh*, Rev. iii. 12. are more fixed, than those of the old heavens and earth, which he will shake and remove, Heb. xii. 26, 27, 28. Many doubting Christians get safe to heaven, that oft feared that they should never get in; but all that get entrance, are immediately assured, that they shall never be turned out again. As, on the other hand, many flatter themselves with vain hopes of heaven, who, when they find at last, to their dreadful surprise, that heaven's door shuts them out, and hell's door shuts them in, they know, that the latter door will never be opened to let them out, nor heaven's door be opened to let them in. Remember, that you will be lodged in your everlasting habitations, by the sentence of the great Judge in that day; that your sentence will be, as your interest in Christ, and his interest in you is, and appears. Do you believe a day of judgment? Then quickly run in to Christ; abide in him, as your only refuge; and let the last day find you in him; and you are safe now, and shall know and find your safety more in that day.

So much for the first thing, In what cases believers should improve this great privilege of Christ's representing them unto God. A privilege, in which, as Christ's glory appears, so the salvation and peace of believers is secured.

Secondly, A little on the second thing proposed, In what manner is this improvement of this privilege to be made?

1. It is to be improved with the deepest humility and self-abasement. We are so prone to pride, that not only are natural men proud of their rotten and filthy rags; but believers are not out of danger of being proud of borrowed raiment. The loathsome, naked infant, that had no eye to pity, no hand to help it, but the Lord's; when its beauty was made perfect through the Lord's comeliness put upon her, did yet trust in her own beauty, Ezek. xvi. 3,---15. I know, that there the Prophet, in a figure, points at Israel's low state the Lord found them in, and the high state he had advanced them to, of his mere grace and mercy; and, from both, is aggravating their sin in forgeting both, and the dreadful wickedness that people fell into from that forgetting: but, by a just parallel, it may be applied unto particular persons. If you make a question, Is it possible that a man can be proud and vain of Christ's righteousness imputed to him for his acceptance with God? I answer, 1. A man may imagine, that he is in Christ, and accepted with God on Christ's account, and may be proud and puffed up. Of this there is no doubt: for false notions in men may make them proud. If the legal Pharisees *trusted in themselves that they were righteous, and despised others,* Luke xviii. 9. when they had no ground nor reason for it; why may not a hypocrite make a groundless boast of his faith and interest in Christ, and in his righteousness, and be proud and secure upon that imagination? Much of this was in Laodicea's case, Rev. iii.

iii. 17, 18. 2. If a true believer find any vanity rising in his heart, on the account of Christ's righteousness reckoned to him; at that time that person hath the notion of this privilege in his mind and memory, rather than a right sight and sense of it on his heart by faith. For, 3. This great privilege, as it is given by God, that no flesh may glory in his presence; so where it is seen and pondered by faith, it always humbleth the happy partaker of it: for he still remembers what he was without it before he got it, and what vile nakedness in him is covered by this gifted righteousness. See the latter part of Ezek. xvi. 60, 63.; where the Lord, after all the enumeration and aggravation of Israel's sinfulness, comes in with that God-like, *Nevertheless, I will remember my covenant with thee in the days of thy youth, and I will establish unto thee an everlasting covenant.* "It would be but "a short lasting covenant, if it stood upon thy keeping, "or were dissolved by thy breaking of it." What is the end of this marvellous grace? *That thou mayest remember, and be confounded, and never open thy mouth any more, because of thy shame.* A sad-like exercise. But when is it to be done to purpose? When the Lord doth plague and rend Israel? when he sets their sins in order before them, and writes bitter things against them? No; but *when I am pacified toward thee for all that thou hast done, saith the Lord God.* Like the promise in Ezek xxxvi. 31. "When my quarrel "against thee for thy sin is laid aside by me, it shall be "taken up by thee in judging and condemning thy- "self; when thy sins are forgotten by my grace, they "shall be remembered by thee for thy self-abase- "ment." The pardoned man is only the true penitent; and that is the best repentance that is exercised in the reading of our sealed forgiveness. Therein a man seeth that dreadful roll blotted out, but only by free grace in the blood of Jesus. No sin is forgiven, but in the virtue of that blood. When therefore a believer seeth the vilest of all things, his sins, and the

most

most sacred of all things, the atoning blood of the Son of God, joined together in his charter of pardon; what thoughts the pardoned man must have of sin, of grace in forgiving, and of the way in which this forgiveness cometh, it were happier for you and me to feel, than it is easy for me to express, or for any to think, but such a happy soul that feels it. We have an instance of a great sinner greatly forgiven, in Luke vii. 39,---50. The Lord send us her blessing, and her frame. A proud pardoned sinner is a monster. Art thou a sinner, and proud of thy sin? Then art thou an open rebel against an offended God. Art thou a sinner, and proud of any thing? Thou art a fool; proud, when the most debasing thing lieth upon thee! But art thou a pardoned sinner, and not humble? What name should such a creature be called by? Canst thou be proud of thy pardon, when thy conscience tells thee truly, that thou deservest to be damned, as justly as any God ever condemned? and that only free grace made the difference betwixt you and them, in your sentence, when there was no difference betwixt their and your deserts? Canst thou be proud of pardon in Christ's blood, when both the guilt and vileness of sin is so discovered in the only way of its expiation; and when the glory of grace in contriving, using, and applying this expiation, shineth so brightly? Believers, whenever you read your charter of pardon in the new covenant, do but remember who and what is forgiven, and who he is that forgiveth, and on what account he doth forgive; and see if these will not lay thee, and keep thee low in his sight.

2. This great privilege should be improved by believers, with confidence and assurance of faith. Trembling believers may be true believers: but trembling and doubting believing is never due believing; it neither giveth the glory due to God, nor brings in that peace and fruit that is needful to the believer. Doth Christ represent you to God for acceptance, and do you

you doubt whether you shall be accepted? Is not this very sinfully to question his interest at the highest court? Say not you doubt your acceptance, because of your great unworthiness; for there is no worth but Christ's that is regarded in your acceptance. The question is not, "Am I any way worthy of God's "gracious acceptance?" But it is, "Is Christ worthy, "and able to make such an unworthy sinner as I am, "to be accepted? and is his worthiness for this, to "be fearfully or confidently trusted in by me?" See two passages about this. The one is in an exhortation to all believers; the other is in the triumph of faith of one great believer, in the name of all, and for a pattern to all. The first is in Heb. x. 19, 20, 21, 22, 23.; where we find the apostle, upon the solid and common grounds of every believer's faith, Jesus Christ, and his office, urging *drawing near* (and *to God*, as in chap. vii. 19.) *with a true heart, in full assurance of faith*. Having such a door, such a way, such a high priest, as Christ is, let us draw near, never doubting our welcome. The other place is in Rom. viii. 31,----39. *If God be for us, who can be against us?* An unanswerable question. But how do we know that God is for us? Thus, *He spared not his own Son, but delivered him up for us all*, ver. 32.; the *all* he spoke of in ver. 29, 30. But are there not many things justly chargeable on the elect believers? No, saith he, ver. 33, 34. Nothing, by any, can be laid to their charge. Why so? Are they not *by nature children of wrath, even as others*, Eph. ii. 3.? Yes: But *it is God that justifieth; who is he that condemneth?* He is a bold devil, or man, or conscience, that condemneth whom God justifieth. But how doth God justify? Is he not the Lawgiver, against whom they have sinned? Yes; but yet he justifieth and justly: *It is Christ that died*, &c. It is Christ's interest in them, his undertaking and performance for them, his representing them unto God, that is the ground of their justification before God, of their acceptance with God, and of their joy of faith; as Rom. v. 11. *We joy in God, through our Lord Jesus Christ, by whom we have now received the atonement.* Believers, look on yourselves as oft, and as narrowly as you can; judge and condemn yourselves as much as you will; but when you look for acceptance with God, mind Christ alone, and give him glory in trusting confidently for acceptance in him.

3. Improve this privilege with diligence and painfulness. It is well worthy of our diligence, and diligence is needful for us. I shall name on this but two things.

1*st*, Use diligence to keep this privilege of Christ's representing you to God for acceptance, stedfastly and constantly in the eye of your faith. The peace of Christians would not ebb and flow with every tide, as oft it doth, if this duty were more minded. This is what is called, *holding fast the confidence, and rejoicing of the hope, firm unto the end;* and, *holding the beginning of our confidence stedfast unto the end,* Heb. iii. 6, 14. This is what is required of all, in Heb. vi. 11. *And we desire, that every one of you do shew the same diligence, to the full assurance of hope unto the end.* The shield of faith, as it *quencheth all the fiery darts of the devil,* Eph. vi. 16.; so his most fiery darts are flung against it. Such as know not trials of faith, never had the truth of faith. An evil heart of unbelief (and some roots of it are in the best believers) will oft assault true faith. Great watch and ward should be kept by faith, about our precious faith; for faith doth watch itself. Faith prayed in that man, *Lord, help my unbelief,* Mark ix. 24. Hath the Lord once or oftener *caused you to hope?* as Psal. cxix. 49.; hath he taken you, and made you sit down, and rest on the precious foundation, Jesus Christ? Hold you there. *Be not moved away from the hope of the gospel,* Col. i. 23. But *as ye have received Christ Jesus the Lord, so walk ye in him; rooted and built up in him, and stablished in the faith,* Col. ii. 6. 7. If you try this work, you
will

will quickly find that diligence is needful. If you give diligence in it, you will quickly find the rich profit of it.

2dly, Use diligence in your improving of this privilege, in studying likeness and conformity to Jesus Christ. Hath he blessed you with this great grace of representing you in his righteousness for your acceptance with God? Should not you study to get Christ's image in true holiness, more and more increased in you? True gospel-holiness is only planted by gospel-grace, and nourished by gospel-arguments; and these arguments have neither light nor power on any, but such as have received the Spirit of faith; 1 John. iii. 3. *Every man that hath this hope in him,* (it should be read *on him,* that is, on Christ), *purifieth himself, even as he is pure.* He is still a-doing, a-purifying; but not perfect as yet. Thus a carnal heart is apt to say, "Since I cannot be perfectly holy in this life, and "since I hope I shall be so when Christ appeareth, I "will let the study of holiness alone till that day." No, saith the apostle; *Every man that hath this hope in Christ, of being like him, when he shall see him as he is,* ver. 2. will now study that likeness, although he cannot attain it, as he would. That man's state is naught, and his faith unsound, that finds not his hopes of his glory purifying to his heart and life. Now, set about the study, love, and practice of holiness, all you that are favoured with Christ's grace in representing you to God's gracious acceptance; and I make no doubt, but that all that have obtained this grace, and see it by faith, will be so exercised: Rom. vi. 1, 2. *Shall we continue in sin, that grace may abound?* A plausible objection, and easily drawn by a carnal heart, from what is said, Rom. v. 20. *Where sin abounded, grace did much more abound.* But if the objection be obvious, the answer is mysterious: *God forbid: How shall we that are dead to sin, live any longer therein?* It is as if he had said, "I do not wonder that they

that

"that are alive to sin, make this objection; but all that are dead to sin, see no weight in it." But how are believers dead to sin, and alive unto God? By the virtue of Christ's death and resurrection, ver. 3, 4, 5, 6. into which every believer is planted. And thence, ver. 11. he bids them, *Reckon ye also yourselves to be dead indeed unto sin, but alive unto God through Jesus Christ our Lord.* If Christians were more skilful in these reckonings of faith, they would abound more in the fruits of holiness. All true holiness is the fruit of faith; all true faith produceth this fruit; and the strongest believer brings forth most abundant fruit, John xv. 4, 5.

SERMON XV.

John xvii. 24.

Father, I will that they also whom thou hast given me, be with me where I am; that they may behold my glory which thou hast given me: for thou lovedst me before the foundation of the world.

YOU may remember, that, some weeks ago, when I first began to speak from this sweet, long, and great verse of Christ's prayer, I did take it up in two parts; the manner, and matter of it. The manner of it is in this word, *I will*; a way of praying that we do not find Christ used, but here; a way of praying that no Christian should use; for our will is so foolish and sinful a thing, that the less room it hath in our prayers, the better our prayers are: for our prayers are to be according to his will, and not ours.

Serm. XV.   *the Lord's Prayer.*   291

In the matter of Christ's prayer in this verse, I took up four things. 1. The denomination and description he gives and makes of them he prays for: *Those whom thou hast given me.* We cannot direct our prayers as Christ did; he prayed for the elect as elect, and as persons particularly and exactly known to him. 2. The blessing he prays for to those persons: *That they may also be with me where I am.* 3. The end of his praying for this blessing to them; *That they may behold my glory which thou hast given me:* Till they are where Christ is, they cannot behold it fully. 4. The argument by which Christ backs this prayer: *For thou lovedst me before the foundation of the world.*

I have spoke all I mean to say on the first two things in the matter of this prayer; and am yet upon the third part; which I would conclude at this time. In handling of which, I did propound two heads of discourse. 1. What is the glory of Christ that is to be beheld. 2. What is the beholding of it. Of the first I have spoken at length; and because the theme is very large, I comprehended all in two particulars. 1. The glory of Christ as he represents God unto his church, to be savingly known by them; and, 2. His glory as he represents his church unto God, to be graciously accepted of God. There are no saving views of God, but in Christ; and there are no gracious views God hath of men, but in Christ. If we look on God out of Christ, we are dazzled with an overwhelming, confounding majesty; if God look on us out of Christ, he seeth hateful and hated sinners. To both these I have largely spoken, both doctrinally, and with application.

II. I come now to the second thing, *What is the beholding of Christ's glory?* His glory is a divine glory; but the beholding of it is a creature's act. And because his glory is divine, and therefore infinitely great, it is a deeper theme in itself than the beholding

Vol. II.   P p   of

of it; yet some way the beholding of his glory, is darker to us than his glory. We are able to know a little more of his glory, than we can know what that beholding of it is that Christ here prays for. But, indeed, both the glory of Christ as manifested in heaven, and the glorified saints beholding of it there, are themes too deep, and too dark, for any man to conceive or express. My way therefore of speaking to this subject, of the beholding of Christ's glory in heaven, must be by way of comparison, comparing it with such beholdings of his glory as saints on earth have had, or may have. And of such we find specially these three.

1. Some beheld Christ's glory before he came into the world; before he took to him man's nature; as Abraham did, John viii. 56. *Your father Abraham rejoiced to see my day, and he saw it, and was glad.* So in John xii. 41. *These things said Esaias* (in chap. vi.), *when he saw his glory and spake of him.* This was by faith; and the light that that faith was begotten by, and acted in, was that of the divers ways and manners in which God communicated his mind to his people before the law; which doubtless carried such credentials with them, that did satisfy the faith of believers at that time, as really as God's written word now doth a new testament believer's faith. If we think that the Spirit of God, by Moses's pen in Genesis, gives but a small and short account of the patriarch's faith, and of the grounds and actings of it in them, both before and after the flood; yet he, by Paul in the new testament, giveth a fuller account of it; as in Heb. xi. of many of them; and of Abraham more largely, in Rom. iv. and in Gal. iii. 8.; where he tells us, that *the gospel was preached before unto Abraham,* in these words, *In thee shall all nations be blessed.* Ver. 16. *Now to Abraham and his seed were the promises made. He saith not, And to seeds, as of many; but as of one, And to thy seed which is Christ.* What an exact and spiritual commentator was
Paul

Paul on Abraham's gospel, *In thee and thy seed shall all nations be blessed?* repeated again to Isaac his son, Gen. xxvi. 4.; by Isaac given as his blessing to his son Jacob, Gen. xxviii. 4.; which he calls *the blessing of Abraham*, as Paul doth, in Gal. iii. 14. This blessing the Lord giveth to Jacob, Gen. xxviii. 14. How many do read these few words in Genesis, that never would have found out that deep gospel in them that Paul doth? That, 1. This promised seed, of whom Isaac was only a progenitor and a type, was Christ. 2. That this blessing to be got in him and by him, was justification. 3. That this justification implied a prior condemnation and curse that men were under, and which this blessing only could remove. 4. That all the families of the earth, to whom this blessing was designed to extend, were the *Heathen*, verse 8. *Gentiles*, verse 14. 5. That this blessing is only received by faith, ver. 7, 9. 6. That the law, which was 430 years after, could not disannul this promise and covenant of grace, ver. 17. 7. That every believer on Jesus Christ, whether Jew or Gentile, partakes of Abraham's blessing, are *Abraham's seed, and heirs according to the promise; yea, are all the children of God by faith in Christ Jesus*, ver. 26, 28, 29. How much despised by many would such a comment be, on so few, and so dark words, and words that have so fair an appearance of a less evangelic sense than the apostle puts upon them? But strangers to that Spirit that dictated the scriptures, will ever prove poor commentators upon the most spiritual part of the scriptures. By this short hint it doth appear, that the patriarchs before the law did behold the glory of Christ, though not yet come: not to speak of the prophets, *who, all of them from Samuel, and those that follow after, as many as have spoken, have likewise foretold of these days*, as Peter saith, Acts.iii. 24.

2. The next beholding of the glory of Christ was, when he came and lived on the earth, and his people lived with him; when *God was manifested in the flesh*, 1 Tim.

1 Tim. iii. 16. John i. 14. *And the Word was made flesh, and dwelt among us (and we beheld his glory, the glory as of the only begotten of the Father) full of grace and truth.* This beholding of his glory was only by faith: for many who saw with their bodily eyes this appearance of the Son of God, in man's flesh, that saw his works, *which none other man did,* John xv. 24. and heard his words, such as *never man spake,* John vii. 46.; yet saw no glory in him, nor in any thing he did, or said, or suffered; but despised and hated him; and all, because they believed not, John vi. 36. And on them was fulfilled what the Prophet foretold, Isa. liii. 1, 2, 3. Our Lord's humbled state was a great, thick, and dark vail on his glory: yet his glory shone in it, and through it; and faith beheld it, 1 John i. 1, 2. Envy not the happiness of such believers as conversed with Christ when he was on earth. though there was a great blessedness in it, Luke x. 23, 24. and Matth. xiii. 16, 17; yet Christ giveth the preference to them *that have not seen, and yet have believed,* John xx. 29. 1 Peter. i. 8 We may justly think, that never was the eye of faith more tried, than by the mean and low appearance, that so great a person, as God's only begotten Son, and coming with the high character of the Messias, and on so great an errand and work, as redeeming his church, made, when he came, and was *made manifest to Israel.* And therefore faith in him then had a special difficulty in its way, which ours hath not, when *we see Jesus crowned with glory and honour,* Heb. ii. 9. And this difficulty of believing increased, as Christ's low state did. He was at his lowest on his cross, and in his grave. Unbelief, and contempt of him, grew to a dreadful height in his enemies. Faith in him, in them that had it, and had professed it, was brought into its lowest: Luke xxiv. 21. *But we trusted. that it had been he which should have redeemed Israel.* They had once so believed. But what did they now? They were

asto-

aſtoniſhed, ver. 22.; they could not tell whether they ſhould repent of their faith, or of their unbelief. And thus they ſpoke to Chriſt himſelf, but vailed from them. But bleſſed Jeſus, though *entered into his glory*, (as verſe 26.), had the ſame pity and tenderneſs he had ſo oft before expreſſed, and gently rebukes, teacheth them, and recovers them. When he was on his croſs, his enemies ſaw no glory in him, and his friends little elſe ſave matter of ſorrow. Yet one, a thief, and a dying man too, ſeeth his glory, and ſaith, *Lord, remember me when thou comeſt into thy kingdom*. It is not, as Chriſt's enemies, and this man's companion, both in his crime and puniſhment, ſaid, *If thou be the Chriſt*. But it is as if he had ſaid, " I know " thee to be the Son of God; and though dying, yet " going to thy kingdom: give me a ſhare in that " kingdom thou art now buying by thy blood." And he was anſwered; the rareſt believer that ever was, the greateſt faith that ever was acted, and the moſt gracious anſwer that ever was given, ver. 33. Well did Jeſus, dying for ſinners, know how to receive a ſinner into heaven.

3. Chriſt's glory is beheld, when he is in heaven, and his people are on earth. And this is by faith alſo. In this caſe, though there be not a vail of infirmity on the glory of our Lord, as there was when he was on earth; yet there is a vaſt diſtance betwixt him and us; as great as betwixt heaven and earth, as betwixt the right hand of the Father, where he is in his glory, and our weak eye of faith, who are on earth. Yet this eye, in the light and glaſs of the goſpel, can, and doth *behold with open face the glory of the Lord*, 2 Cor. iii. 18. Of this beholding of Chriſt's glory, I would ſpeak in two inſtances.

1ſt, At the firſt converſion of a ſinner, when he is made a believer in Chriſt. None are truly converted to God, but ſuch as are made believers in Chriſt; and none are made believers in Chriſt, but they to whom the glory of Chriſt is diſcovered. It is by the

power

power of this discovery that faith is wrought; and in the light of it faith is acted. Some think, that a man is converted, when the secure sinner is awakened by the light and heat of God's law, when a profane person is made sober in his conversation. But if there be no more, he may be still as far, yea, farther from true conversion than before: Matth. xxi. 31. *Verily I say unto you, that the publicans and the harlots go into the kingdom of God before you.* And yet the scribes and Pharisees thought themselves in so much better case for heaven than they, that they would not entertain common converse with ordinary sinners; boasted that they were better than such; yea, turned Christ's grace to his reproach: Luke xv. 2. *They murmured, saying, This man receiveth sinners, and eateth with them.* What were they that said so? Were they not sinners? Yes; but they did not see or own themselves to be such. What should a sinner do, but go to Christ? What can come on a sinner, if Christ receive him not? Yea, what is a Saviour of sinners for, but for receiving sinners, and saving them from their sins, Matth. i. 21? And yet sinners coming to Christ, and Christ's welcome of them, makes unbelievers murmur, both against Christ and believers. So sure it is, that no man can see any glory in that grace of Christ, that he hath no sight nor sense of his own need of. But when was Paul converted, an eminent Pharisee, the best scholar in Gamaliel's school, Gal. i. 14, 15, 16.? It was when *God revealed his Son in him*. It is very likely, that Paul had heard of Jesus Christ, while a Pharisee; but it is certain, that he hated him, his very name, and all that belonged to him. But when the Lord's time was come to call this chosen vessel by his grace, when he intends to subdue and conquer Paul's rebellious spirit, a revelation of Christ is made to him; and the rebel yields, and is made a loyal subject all his days. Would you know when you were converted? If ever it was, it was when you had the first view of the glory of Christ as a Saviour. When this sight

is

is got, then the sinner employs Christ in his saving office, trusts him in it, and is saved by him.

2dly, Christ's glory is beheld by believers, when Christ is in heaven, and they on earth, in the following manifestations of Christ, and of his glory to them. Whenever Christ is seen, it is by his manifesting of himself. No torch, nor candle, nor fire, could make one see the sun, if its own shining did not. His people, to whom he hath manifested himself once, need to have it repeated again and again. And this blessing he promiseth, John xiv. 21, 23. It is very suspicious, that that man's state is bad, that never had but one discovery of Christ's glory. Those manifestations of his glory are various, both in measure, duration, and their seasons. Sometimes, upon special diligence in seeking of the Lord by faith in prayer. What Christian is there that is not able to witness to this, that the times of his special seeking have been the times of his special finding? If there was more of Moses's spirit, (though it may be there was somewhat in it that was above, both what is either allowable to ask, or attainable by ordinary believers), Exod xxxiii. 18. *I beseech thee shew me thy glory*, it would be better with us. If we were more importunate in begging new and clearer visions of the glory of Christ, and renewed visits from him for that end, he would not deny us. If we did go to himself, with that desire that some came with to one of his disciples, John xii. 21. *Sir, we would see Jesus:* can any think he would be displeased? But, alas! we receive not, because we ask not. Sometimes Christ manifests himself in a special manner to his people, in the furnace of affliction, especially if it be for his sake; yea, in the easiest of those sufferings: 1 Peter iv. 14. *If ye be reproached for the name of Christ, happy are ye; for the spirit of glory and of God resteth upon you.*

Sometimes the Lord manifests his glory to his people at their dying. And it is then very desirable. Old Simeon had a gracious promise, *that he should not*

not see death, before he had seen the Lord's Christ. He chused a sweet season of dying, when the promise was fulfilled, and when he had Christ in his arms, and faith and love in his heart bursting out into a song, Luke ii. 27,---29. The first martyr, Stephen, died happily; he died witnessing for Christ: and Christ witnessed for him, when the martyr said, *Behold, I see the heavens opened, and the Son of man standing on the right hand of God*, Acts vii. 55, 56. This was better than Moses's dying, Deut. xxxii. 49, 50. and xxxiv. 1,---5. It was a strange journey and call, *Go up and die*, and only take a view of the land that he must not enter into. He saw the land of Canaan, and that was all; but he saw by faith the true Canaan, and entered into it; and there abideth still; save one errand Moses was sent upon with Elias, to wait on their Master on the mount of transfiguration, Matth, xvii. 3.

These are a few instances of the seasons in which the Lord manifests his glory to his people, and in which they do behold it. But this text and theme I am upon, relates to somewhat far higher and greater, than all the beholdings of his glory that ever any saint on earth received. What it is, I cannot tell you, and I am sure that none can; though many may easily tell more of it than I can. There is both a danger and snare in prying within God's vail. I shall therefore content myself with comparing the beholding of Christ's glory by believers on earth, with this beholding of it that our Lord here prays for to all his people in heaven.

This only I would premise unto this discourse that such as are wholly unacquainted in their own experience, with the beholding of the glory of Christ, by the eye of faith in the gospel-glass, they will, they can, they must understand nothing that can be said of the beholding of Christ's glory in heaven.

These two beholdings of Christ's glory, the one on earth, and the other in heaven, may be compared, ed, and yet differ in several things; of which take these five.

1. They differ greatly in the measure of glory manifested by him, and seen by the beholders. Christ's glory is infinite; and no creature, in its most exalted capacity, can take a full view of it all. Therefore, though the glorified beholders of it are eternal beholders thereof, yet they never see it all fully, nor can comprehend it. The beholdings of his glory by us on earth, are according to the small measures of its discovery, and suited unto our small capacity. Our old bottles are not fit for this new wine. Believers know this well by their experience. Sometimes they have more, sometimes less of Christ's glory manifested to them; but always less than what they think they need, and would be at. This is so universal in the spiritual sense and experience of Christians, that these two seem to be established, as from the word of God, so from the common experience of believers. 1. That they whose views of Christ's glory are constantly the same, without any changes and vicissitudes of light and darkness, day and night: and, 2. That they who see as much of Christ's glory as they desire to see, such never truly saw any thing of it at all. Was ever true faith in the same activity? Do not all experienced believers witness by their spiritual sense, that sometimes in the word read or heard, there is a beam of light, and life, and power, that darts upon a word, that they often before had read and heard without any such enjoyment, and which they may remember and think again upon afterwards, without any power to recal the same mercy to their taste again? So it is in prayer, and in all ordinances wherein we seek communion with him. Some have less, some have more; and some believers, at some times of their life, have such manifestations of Christ's glory in his love, tenderness, and familiarity with them, as they can hardly contain. But the best enjoyment for kind, and largest for measure, is far short of what the smallest vessel in

Christ's upper-house is fit to receive, and doth receive. The *seeing of the Lord's power and glory in his sanctuary* on earth, is greatly and justly desired by his people, Psal. lxiii. 2. and is well made their *one thing,* Psal. xxvii. 4. and when they obtain communion with him, they all say as one did, Psal. lxxxiv. 10. *A day in thy courts is better than a thousand: I had rather be a door-keeper in the house of my God, than to dwell in the tents of wickedness.* He was a great man, and a great saint, that said it. But one hour in the court of heaven, is better than a thousand years in God's lower courts. There are *days of heaven upon the earth,* Deut xi. 21. Such are clear and bright days; but the days of heaven in heaven, are unspeakably more so. What we now receive, is, as Song ii. 9. *Behold, he standeth behind our wall, he looketh forth at the windows, shewing himself through the lattice.* But then all walls and windows, all means of communion with him, shall be removed, as useful no more: Rev. xxi. 22. *And I saw no temple therein: for the Lord God almighty, and the Lamb, are the temple of it.* Christ himself speaks of this last day, Matth. xxv. 31. *When the Son of man shall come in his glory,---then shall he sit on the throne of his glory.* Then will his glory appear, and his people shall appear with him in glory, Col. iii. 4.

2. In the next place, The way whereby we behold Christ's glory on earth, and shall behold it in heaven, differ greatly. As they differ in measures, so in the manner and ways of beholding: 1 Cor. xiii. 12. *For now we see through a glass darkly,* (or *in a riddle*), *but then face to face. Now I know in part; but then shall I know, even as I also am known.* There are three ways of knowing of things that God provides for us. Our senses, for sensible things; our understanding, for such things as fall not under our senses; and faith, for such things that are beyond the reach of both sense and reason. When Christ was first on earth, he was the object of mens senses, but few knew him; few could

could say as 1 John i. 2. And when he returns again, *every eye shall see him*, Rev. i. 7.; but all shall not have a comfortable view of him. Every one shall hear his voice, and rise when called, but to a different sentence, John v. 28, 29. *By that wisdom that God hath put in the inward parts, and by that understanding he hath given to the heart*, Job xxxviii. 36. *For he teacheth us more than the beasts of the earth, and maketh us wiser than the fowls of heaven*, Job xxxv. 11. By this noble power men know clearly and surely many things which are beyond the reach of our outward senses. But beyond both is faith, which is as the eye of the new creature, planted by the Lord: whereby the things of God, that can neither be taken up by our external senses, nor be traced by the eye of our minds, are yet, in the light of God's word revealing them, by faith seen and embraced, 1 Cor. ii. 9, 10. Heb. xi. 1. And this exercise of faith, with its fruits, is the utmost that believers reach or can attain while they are on earth. But this beholding of Christ's glory by them that shall be with him where he is, is unspeakably beyond all.

To begin with the first, our bodily senses, they will be perfect in the resurrection-state, in all *the children of the resurrection*, as our Lord calls them, Luke xx. 36. The apostle, in disputing about, and proving, and explaining of this article of the Christian faith, in 1 Cor. xv. 44. calls the body that is raised *a spiritual body: There is a natural body, and there is a spiritual body.* The raised body is a real body, and not a spirit; it is the real true body of every saint that he lived in, that he served Christ in and by; that very body that he departed from at death, and left to the corruption of the grave, that is raised again in *glory*, in *power*, in *incorruption*, as ver. 42, 43.; that same once *vile body that is then changed, that it may be fashioned like unto Christ's glorious body*, Phil. iii. 21. As the body is, so are its senses and powers. A natural body hath natural

tural powers; and as it decays, those powers decay also; elegantly described in Eccl. xii. 1,---7. But what a spiritual body is, and what its powers are, we do not, we cannot know. But this we know, that there will be a glorious appearance of Christ in that day, that will fall under, and will be taken up by those spiritual senses of the raised bodies of saints, and will be no small part of their happiness. The bodily eye of John, tho' it was used to the beholding of Christ and his glory on earth, could not bear a little beam of Christ's heavenly glory, Rev. i. 17. Strange; that John should need that Christ should tell him who he was, verse 18. But what John, while in his natural body, could not bear, every saint in his spiritual body will not only be able to bear, but will with delight behold more than what was like to have killed that beloved disciple.

Again, for the powers of the mind, they in that day will be perfect, so as that all the glory of Christ that shall be discovered, will be beheld by them perfectly, for the perfecting of their blessedness, 1 Cor. xiii. 11, 12.

But for faith, for as needful and useful as it is now, it will then be laid aside as useless. A believer now takes up a little of Christ's glory; but how? In the word, as in a glass, 2 Cor. iii. 18. No other glass but the gospel-glass discovers Christ's glory to us now; and it is not faith, but dreaming and doting, to study Christ but in that glass. But when both the glass of the gospel, and the eye of faith, shall be laid aside, (the two most useful and needful blessings to a believer while out of heaven, and useful and needful to bring him to heaven), what shall make up the want of them? Even Christ himself seen in his glory. Even as Christ come in the flesh, rendered all the types and shadows of him in the old testament no more needful: so Christ appearing in his glory, will do as to the new testament dispensation.

3. Let

Serm. XV.   *the Lord's Prayer.*   303

3. Let us consider and compare these two beholdings of Christ's glory by believers on earth, and saints in heaven, with respect to the case of the beholders thereof. How vastly do they differ? There are three things in a believer that all the glorified beholders of Christ's glory in heaven are perfectly freed from, sin, infirmity, and affliction.

1st, Sin dwelleth in us, in the best, and always while here. There are no sinless beholders of Christ's glory on earth, and there are no sinful beholders of his glory in heaven; and this makes a great difference between them. The believer, when his day is fairest, when his eye is clearest, when his faith is strongest, there is yet sin in him, a body of death hanging about him. Sin in its being in him, is like a film on the eye of faith, and mars clear seeing.

Brethren, there was never a sinless believer on earth but one, and that was Jesus Christ; and it is as far above us to know how he believed, (save that he did so perfectly), as to tell what it is to see him as he is in heaven. The first Adam while he stood, was not a sinless believer, but a sinless worker; and when he fell, he and all his posterity became sinners. When God's grace falls on any of them, they are made believers through that grace, and believers on it; yet sin remains in them still. Though its guilt is forgiven, and its filth washed away, and its power subdued; yet its being and indwelling remaineth: and this is a great impediment in the acting of faith. If any believer had that privilege, (which I think none ever had, nor none should desire), to be but a little while in the exercise of faith, without any indwelling sin in him; surely that man would believe wonderfully, and would think that he never believed before. It is true, that all true believers are sanctified, and that all true acts of faith are sanctifying; yet no believer is perfectly sanctified on earth. But it is certain also, that the first acting of faith on Christ, is in the sight and sense of our ruin by the power of sin in our nature;

ture; and the after actings of faith are from the same sense of remaining corruption in us. Proper faith is, a sinner's dealing with the Saviour of sinners for salvation from sin. Till we obtain perfect salvation from sin, we must act faith for it, and while we act that faith, sin is mixed with our very believing, so as that we must pray as he did, Mark ix. 24. *Lord, I believe, help thou mine unbelief.*

2*dly,* There are infirmities in believers, in all their beholdings of the glory of Christ, while they are on earth. There are infirmities in our bodies that all are sensible of; and such have no small influence on the actings of the soul. There are also infirmities in our souls; darkness and dulness in our intellectual powers. But above all these are the infirmities of the new creature. Although it be created in Christ Jesus, although it be supported by his power, and is maintained and fed by influences from him, as its head and root; yet is it still a weak and infirm thing, and is like a *new-born babe,* 1 Peter ii. 2. But none of these infirmities are in them that behold Christ's glory above; they have outgrown them all, and are become perfect in Christ Jesus. Whatever other times that word hath been, or shall be fulfilled in, its fulfilment will be at Christ's appearing: Isa. xxx. 26. *The light of the moon shall be as the light of the sun, and the light of the sun shall be sevenfold, as the light of seven days.* If such a dispensation in the course of nature were, that the moon shone by night as bright as the sun by day; and if the sun by day did shine sevenfold brighter than now it doth; where would there be eyes to endure it? Surely, none such as ours be. So is it as to the light of that glorious day. Our best eyes that now we have got and use, would fail us; but the Lord provides eyes suitable to the light he will make to shine.

3*dly,* Besides our infirmities we labour under, we have manifold afflictions also, which the glorified beholders of Christ's glory are free from. No affliction can

can have room in heaven, Rev. xxi. 4.: yet *through much tribulation must we enter into the kingdom of God*, Acts xiv. 22. Afflictions are trials of faith; faith is to be acted in and under them; often is faith shaken by them. Sometimes believing is strongest, when the believer is in greatest distress. But though this be a duty laid on all, it is not the attainment of all believers. But still affliction is an evil in itself, though the Lord turns it into good. Now, take all together; sin is in us, infirmities compass us about, affliction is laid on us; must not all together make a great difference betwixt us, in our beholding of Christ's glory now, from their beholding of his glory who are fully rid of all these things?

4. Consider and compare the difference betwixt our beholding of Christ's glory on earth, and theirs in heaven, as to the fruits and effects thereof. These fruits are of the same nature and kind, and so are expressed in the word. I shall name but three of them. 1. Conformity. 2. Satisfaction. 3. Expression of that satisfaction.

1st, Conformity to Christ is the native fruit of beholding of his glory. As it is beheld, this conformity is wrought in the beholder. The natural eye in seeing takes in the visible objects, species, and shape, by its faculty; the mind in knowing takes into itself the intelligible species of the things known: but above these, faith takes in Christ's glory in the gospel; and, beyond faith, the seeing eye of the glorified takes in Christ's glory as it shines in heaven, and is conformed thereunto. Compare 2 Cor. iii. 18. which relates to believers on earth, with 1 John iii. 2. which relates to the glorified in heaven. The object is the same, Christ and his glory; the effect of conformity is the same in kind, but not in degree; because the object is not seen by both in the same light, nor with the same eye. The one seeth him as he is; the other seeth him as he appears in the gospel-glass. On this I would lead you to consider.

(1.)

(1.) How any likeness and conformity to Christ begins. We all by nature *bear the image of the earthly Adam*, 1 Cor. xv. 49. And this is a vile image, of sin, and flesh, and death; nothing like, but quite unlike and contrary to Christ's image: yet, through rich and free grace, many that have borne this sad and sinful image, are blessed with the image of *the heavenly man, the Lord from heaven*. When and how is this great change made? Then only when Christ is formed in them, Gal. iv. 19. when he is revealed to them, and when they by faith see the glory of Christ as a Saviour. They begin to live, when they first look on him as lifted up as God's only ordinance for saving, John iii. 14, 15. There are two discoveries of Christ made to beginners; one is to all, the other only to some. The general to all believers is that that is both the cause and the ground of faith in him; and that it is such a discovery of Christ's ability and good-will to save, as doth engage their heart to trust him, and him alone, with this great concern of their salvation. The other is such a discovery of Christ's glory as doth produce peace in the believer: for in this he not only seeth Christ's all-sufficiency for saving, so as to trust him with it; but he seeth also, that this trustee is so good and faithful, that this concern must be safe, because it is lodged with him. This is like that faith in 2 Tim. i. 12. *I know whom I have believed, and I am persuaded that he is able to keep that which I have committed unto him, against that day.*

(2.) How this conformity to Christ is carried on and advanced. Even as it was begun, Colloss. ii. 6, 7. *Growth in grace* is by *growing in the knowledge of Christ*, 2 Pet. iii. 18. Abiding in Christ is the way to have our fruits to abound, John xv. 4, 5. Many true Christians cannot tell when they were first converted, when they first believed; but all Christians can tell when they were most holy; and that is always when Christ manifests himself most clearly to them. As to their

their first believing, they cannot determine that so well, because they cannot easily remember when Christ first revealed himself to them; he hath done it so oft, and every new manifestation of his glory to them, draws forth a new acting of their faith on him; and it may be such a distinct and strong act, as they think they never before did put forth the like. Something of this made a great believer, and an aged divine, when speaking of the time of his conversion, say, "I cannot tell it, for I have been more than an hundred times converted:" not that he was ignorant or doubtful, that a true conversion is but once, in God's working it; but that it may have many appearances in our sense and experience. David, after his sad fall, prays, Psalm li. 10. *Create in me a clean heart, O God; and renew a right spirit within me;* when before this he had God's testimony, that he was *a man according to God's own heart,* Acts xiii 22. from 1 Sam. xiii. 14. A witness not only to the truth, but to the eminency of his saintship. Christ calls that recovery unto Peter, a new sort of conversion, Luke xxii. 32. which he, in amazing grace, promiseth to him, just before his shameful fall: and yet he was a true believer before, and blessed by Christ, on his profession and acting of faith, Matth. xvi. 16, 17. Another thing may have some influence on Christians ignorance of the time of their conversion; and that is, they can better remember the alarms they had in their conscience by a law-work, than they can the still and calm voice of the gospel. The one not only makes more noise, but it is more readily felt and remembered by us, than the secret opening of the heart by Christ's love. But whatever mistakes Christians may labour under, and different thoughts and experience they may have as to the time of his love, and the day of his power; yet all true believers are of one mind as to the seasons of their greatest holiness. There are different measures of it dispensed by the Lord, and attained by his people. None of them have attained

tained as much as they would have; and they that have attained most, think least of their attainments, and press most for perfection. But all can readily and unanimously declare, when it is that their graces are most lively, their corruptions most low and least rampant, when their work is most sweet, and Christ's yoke and burden most easy and light; even when Christ is nearest to them, and they to him, and when most of his glory appears unto them: and this not from the might of their faith as it is their act, (though in such seasons it is in best case), but from the virtue and power of Christ's grace that falls on them, when he is pleased to manifest himself to them. This blessed experience of special likeness to Christ, by his special manifesting of himself to them, is not without some danger, that many saints have fallen into: for when things are so well with them, that the favour of Christ's knowledge perfumes their hearts, and that their secret corruption shrinks into a corner, (as Christ's glory and our corruptions are contraries), the believer is ready to say, as David did, Psalm xxx. 6. *I said in my prosperity, I shall never be moved;* yet quickly was he moved: and so will all be that say as he did; for the stronger that carnal and self-confidence is, the nearer is the man to a shameful fall, as Peter.

(3.) In the last place, Consider how this conformity and likeness is perfected; and that is, as it was begun and advanced, even by the discovery of Christ's glory in heaven: 1 John iii. 1, 2. *We are the sons of God; but the world knoweth us not, because it knew him not.* The world knows God's children well enough, to despise, hate, and persecute them; and so did the world know Christ: but this sort of knowledge is nothing but ignorance, both of Christ and of Christians. *And it doth not yet appear what we shall be.* But it will at length appear; when and how? *But we know, that when he shall appear, we shall be like him: for we shall see him as he is.* Yet all these things are food only

only for humble faith; every thing in it is deep and unsearchable. What is his appearing? What it is to be like him? What it is to see him, and that as he is? and, How this sight of him will make us like him! are unanswerable questions even to an apostle, and to all out of heaven. If it be a dark unintelligible riddle to every natural man, (whatever knowledge he may have of the letter of the world), how a sight of Christ by faith doth begin, and carry on a real begun likeness to Christ in believers on earth; it must much more be dark to them, yea to believers themselves, how the sight of Christ's glory in heaven doth perfect and complete this likeness! We must long for it, and believe it, and leave it to the day that will declare it.

2*dly*, On this conformity to Christ, followeth satisfaction and blessedness. Of which David speaks, Psal. xvii. 15. *But as for me, I will behold thy face in righteousness: I shall be satisfied, when I awake with thy likeness.* According to the measure of the manifestation of Christ's glory to his people, so is the degree of their likeness to him; and as this likeness to him is, so is the satisfaction and bliss of them that have it. All is begun on earth with the heirs, all is perfect in heaven in the partakers and possessors of glory. A little of both, in comparing them together. Believers on earth, that see his glory, are transformed into the same image, 2 Cor. iii. 18. This conformity always works satisfaction. David speaks of it in Psal. iv. 6, 7. *Lord, lift thou up the light of thy countenance upon us. Thou hast put gladness in my heart, more than in the time that their corn and their wine increased.* And indeed they know not the light of God's countenance, that feel not a joy in their heart that all the world can neither give nor take away. Christ promiseth us this joy, John xvi. 22. *I will see you again, and your heart shall rejoice, and your joy no man taketh from you.* Paul prays highly for this blessing, Rom. xv. 13. *Now the God of hope fill you with all joy and peace in believing,* *that ye may abound in hope, through the power of the Holy Ghost.* Peter speaks of joy, as an attainment of believers on earth: 1 Peter i. 8. *Whom having not seen, ye love; in whom, though now ye see him not, yet believing, ye rejoice with joy unspeakable, and full of glory.* The joy is unspeakable that is felt by believers, when they do (as sometimes, by his light, they do) see some begun likeness to that lovely image of Christ, that won their heart the first time they saw it, and when it darted its beams of life and love upon their dying souls, and did leave that scent of heaven in their heart, that they cannot rest, till they *apprehend that for which they were apprehended of Christ Jesus,* Phil. iii. 12. In the day that Christ apprehended them, and said to them in love, "Stop, sinners, "in your race to hell: follow me, and I will give you "eternal life;" then do they in faith answer, "Behold, we come unto thee, and cannot leave thee; "for thou hast the words of eternal life." And thus is fulfilled that blessed saying of our Lord, John iv. 14. *Whosoever drinketh of the water that I shall give him, shall never thirst: but the water that I shall give him, shall be in him a well of water, springing up into everlasting life.* The original spring is heaven and eternal life; and this given well will spring up as high as its original. Can there be any satisfaction comparable to this, to behold by faith, eternal life, descending from heaven unto us, in Christ's love and grace; and to find at the same time this same faith climbing up to the possession of this life? This happiness is great enough to disgrace and disparage the poor portion of the worldling, that not only perisheth with the using: but he that hath it, must perish, because he hath no better things, nor things that accompany salvation. But yet, though the believer, in and by his fellowship with the Father and the Son, by the Spirit, hath a joy that the stranger cannot intermeddle with; yet his joy, when most full, is greatly short of theirs in heaven. Only where perfect seeing is, perfect likeness

is;

is; and where perfect likeness is, there perfect satisfaction is.

3*dly*, This satisfaction and blessedness is expressed by the enjoyer, in love and praise. Groaning under misery, is not more natural to the afflicted, than exultation is to the happy. As believers feel their present, or see their future greater happiness, so is their praise and their love. But how feeble are all their expressions of it? Our best praises on earth are little better than sweet and delightful groanings under the heavy, yet dear load of loving-kindness. David, the best artist at praise of any saint, how doth he praise? 2 Sam. vii. 18, 19, 20. *Who am I? and what is my house, that thou hast brought me hitherto? And is this the manner of man, O Lord? And what can David say more unto thee?* He asks questions he cannot answer; he is silenced as soon as he begins to praise, and thus he praiseth rightly. Whoever thinks he hath balances to weigh mercy in, never felt the load of mercy; and that man is farthest from right praising, that thinks he can praise, and is best pleased with his praising. But perfect praising is reserved for heaven; and none can learn that song, but they that are with the Lamb in that mount of Sion, Rev. xiv. 1,---4. Perfect seeing of Christ's glory, perfect likeness to him by that sight, perfect happiness by that likeness, and perfect expression of that happiness, are all within the vail; and all we have and know on earth, are but faint and dark shadows thereof.

5. and *lastly*, Consider and compare the beholding of the glory of Christ in earth and in heaven, in the duration of them. In this they differ as much as in any of the former. The one is a time-enjoyment, and for a little time too; the other is eternal. If a believer get a view of the glory of Christ by faith now, it is but a transient glance, very sweet, but very short. In our sweetest enjoyments of Christ's company on earth, he may please to awake, and leave us without it, Cant. ii. 7.; and not only reserveth he a sovereign

latitude in giving or with-holding his sensible presence, but, in love and wisdom for our good, he draws near, or withdraws; and his people are made to feel their profit in these changes. But no such changes in heaven. Changes are only for time, not in eternity. I believe, that as soon as any man passeth out of time into eternity, he knows immediately and certainly, that he is now come into an eternal and unalterable state. The light of eternity demonstrates it. So that the saint entering into heaven knows, that the everlasting doors that were opened to let him in, are shut on him to keep him in that state to eternity; and this is a great part of his blessedness. And the damned that go down into the pit, do know, that the bars of hell are locked upon them, that they can never get out; and this adds to their begun, but never-ending misery. It is indeed an amazing both fruit and proof of the power of unbelief in men, that though they pretend they know this, yet most men do not in earnest think where, and in what place and condition, they shall be for eternity; and yet bestow many careful thoughts about the condition wherein they may spend their short time on earth.

So much for the doctrinal part about the beholding of Christ's glory in heaven.

APPLICATION. 1. Learn from this to behold and understand Christ's last design on his people. It is to have them to behold his glory. Christ will never leave any whom the Father hath given him, till he hath brought them to this. Let believers learn to give Christ his will and his way; give him trust, and give him time, and wait patiently. Art thou given to him? art thou a believer on him? Behold with faith what his design upon thee is. It is to bring thee into that place where he is, that thou mayest behold his glory. Many strange and deep ways and methods doth he use to carry it on. Submit to these, and believe the end of the Lord.

2. Is this Christ's design, to have his people with him where he is, that they may behold his glory? Then see that it be your design too. Many desire to be in heaven, that have nothing of this end in their desires. If your end in desiring to be in heaven, be not the same with Christ's end in desiring it for you, how can you think that your desire is right, or will be accomplished? Some men desire to be in heaven for ever, because they cannot stay always on earth: but if they might live in health and ease, if it were a thousand years on earth, they would never make a hearty prayer for heaven. But these are earth-worms, and God will destroy them. Others desire to be in heaven, only because they think hell is bad quarters, and that they would be kept from. In effect, all carnal mens desires for heaven amount to no more but this, " Lord, save me from hell." They think, that heaven is better than hell, but not so good as the earth, if they might stay comfortably in it. They know, that they must be eternally in heaven or hell; and that the states are so different, that it is easy to chuse which is best for them. But how can a natural, unrenewed man desire heaven? A heaven of his own imagination he may desire; but true heaven, heaven described in the gospel, a state of bliss in the beholding of the glory of Christ, this no unbeliever can have any relish of, or desire after. He can never say a hearty Amen to Christ's prayer in my text; they know not Christ's presence; they never saw any thing of his glory, as it surpasseth all glory. Never will a man desire to make a voyage through death, to see that in heaven that he never had any relish of, nor favour of, on earth; yea, it is impossible he should.

3. *Lastly*, Let us from hence learn to praise *the dead that die in the Lord*, Rev. xiv. 13. I allude to the word in Eccl. iv. 2. *Wherefore I praised the dead which are already dead, more than the living which are yet alive*. Christ will have them where he is, that they may behold his glory; and when he calls and takes

takes them, they do behold it. This is their happiness; and we should bless them, and rejoice in their bliss. We have an affecting passage in Acts xx. 37, 38. after a farewel-sermon and prayer of Paul's: (Here we have an apostolic pattern for farewel sermons and prayers; but no where have we any for funeral ones): *They all wept sore, and fell on Paul's neck and kissed him, sorrowing most of all for the words which he spake, that they should see his face no more*, verse 25. You may justly think, that as the elders, and others of the church of Ephesus, were excellent persons, and were full of love and value for such an eminent apostle as Paul was; so their grief was great at this sad parting. You in this city have frequently the cause of the like sorrow, if ye had the same spirit as they had. Not that I mean to compare any ministers you have, or have lost, with this apostle: for as I am persuaded we have none like him; so am I, that if there was any liker him than any of us are, considering the spirit of the day we live in, that minister would be the most despised and reproached of any; though, I hope, some would be found to discern his true worth. If, upon such occasions of the loss of faithful ministers, or useful Christians, you are sorrowing, and saying, " I shall " see his face no more, and hear his voice no more, " and see his tender walking no more;" call this also to mind, " If I shall see his face no more, he seeth " Christ's face for ever; which is better for him, " than the other would be to me." There is not a believer in heaven, but he knows this text better than all divines on earth can. Whenever a believer is entered within the gates of the heavenly Jerusalem, this blessed beholding of Christ's glory is better known to him, than angels or men can teach him now. This is indeed *the white stone, and in it the new name written, which no man knoweth, saving he that receiveth it*, Rev. ii. 17. I would only add, that it would be sweet speaking, and sweet hearing of heaven, if we at the same

same time felt something of it: and though we cannot yet get up into it; yet if, through his grace, something of heaven did come down to us; if the joy of our Lord did enter into our hearts, as an earnest of our entering into it, Matth. xxv. 21, 23.; for in that day it will be too big to enter into them. All our work now is to be well acquaint with Christ as the way. Christ is both the way and the home. We must walk in him, and be travelling towards him; and he is our guide and leader in the way. The work and life of grace is in living on him by faith, and the happiness of heaven is in living with him for ever. O come and see, go and see. He will call you up in due time. Blessed is that believer who is as willing to be in heaven, as Christ is to have him there.

SERMON XVI.

JOHN xvii. 24.

Father, I will that they also whom thou hast given me, be with me where I am; that they may behold my glory which thou hast given me: for thou lovedst me before the foundation of the world.

THE last clause of this verse only now remains to be spoken to. And it is, as you have heard, the *fourth* and *last* thing I took up in the matter of Christ's prayer here. The argument which Christ useth to back his desire of having his people with him: it is in these words, *For thou lovedst me before the foundation of the world.* This I would briefly speak to, and at this time conclude this text. And this argument of Christ I would speak unto two ways. 1. Unto the words in themselves; and, 2. As they are used by our Lord, relating to his prayer.

I. *As these words are in themselves.* They contain Christ's asserting of the eternal love of the Father unto the Son. For this word, *before the foundation of the world*, and another, *before the world was*, and *before the world began*, are all to the same purpose, and are the Holy Ghost's expressing of eternity prior to time: for before the world began, there was nothing but eternity; and God *inhabiting* it, as the prophet speaks, Isa. lvii. 15. Of this eternal love of the Father to the Son, I would speak briefly.

1. Consider this eternal love in the Father to the person of his Son. This I own is too deep for us to fathom; but it is a blessed deep to swim in. The manner of the everlasting begetting of the person of the Son by the Father, is unsearchable by all creatures, and, it may be, will be so eternally. The state of glory was not designed for satisfying curiosity, and instructing men in points of mere speculation, or in things beyond all created reach. So it passeth our understanding to know how the Father loveth his only begotten Son. How one divine person loveth another divine person, who but a divine person can understand? There are some sorts of love that I would name, all which this love greatly transcendeth.

1*st*, The love of one creature to another. This is sometimes very strong, and is in some cases allowed to be very great. 2*dly*, The love wherewith a believer loveth Christ, is yet greater. For though the lover be but a creature, yet the beloved is more than a creature, and deserves more love than we can pay. Christ cannot be over-loved; but any creature may. 3*dly*, There is the love of God towards his chosen. This is greater than the former. It is this love that God is called, *love*, from 1 John iv. 8.---16. 4*thly*, There is the love Christ bears to his church, that is
exceeding

exceeding great, and much spoke of in the word, Eph. iii. 18, 19. and v. 25, 26. In the first love, one creature loveth another, and with a love that hath bounds and limits set to it by God's will, lest it exceed. In the second, a creature loves God. In the third, God loves a creature, In the last, Christ loveth his own body, and every member of it. So that in all of them, either the lover or the beloved is a creature. But where God the Father is the lover, and God the Son is the beloved, who can tell what that love is! But I pass it, as too deep for us. Here faith must believe and adore, and cry out, *O the depths!*

2. Christ is eternally beloved of his Father in his office of Mediator betwixt God and man. Unto this office he was from eternity designed; and as soon as sin entered, and the breach between God and man was made, he entered upon this office. In it he is *God's servant whom he upholds, his elect in whom his soul delighteth,* Isa. xlii. 1. Under the name of *Wisdom,* he speaks in Prov. viii. 22,---31. *The Lord possessed me in the beginning of his way, before his works of old. I was set up from everlasting, from the beginning, or ever the earth was.* And after an elegant account of the work of creation, he adds, that before any thing was made, and when all things were a-making, *then I was by him, as one brought up with him; and I was daily his delight, rejoicing always before him; rejoicing in the habitable part of his earth, and my delights were with the sons of men.* Here are adorable delights and rejoicings; the Father delighting in his Son, the Son delighting in the Father; yea, the Son rejoicing in his people, and in that earth they were to live on, though neither they nor it were as yet created. And why may not our faith take in the comfort of this thought, that these uttermost parts of the earth where we live, and where the greatest harvest hath been in these latter days, were in Christ's heart and eye with delight from eternity! Christ the Redeemer *was verily fore-ordained before the foundation of the world,*

world, but was manifest in these last times for you, 1 Peter i. 20. Yea, he is called in Rev. xiii. 8, *the Lamb slain from the foundation of the world.* This high office of Mediator, the Father, in love to, and for glorifying of his Son, put him in, Heb. v. 4, 5. In this office he did always please his Father, and his Father witnessed to it often and many ways. It should be a great encouragement unto all that have business with Christ as Mediator, to consider how the Father delights in him in his office. Salvation is given to a believer in Christ, with as good will, by the Father, as the price of salvation was laid down by the Son. No man can please the Father better, nor so much, as by believing on the Son, and by giving him employment in his office and calling of saving.

3. Jesus Christ, the Son of God, is eternally beloved of the Father, as he is the head of his body the church; as he is the second Adam, the representative of all his people. Of which already at some length.

4. Christ was beloved of the Father in his lowest estate, and when dying. This is what is in the text. Christ was now near his lowest when he asserts this love. He was going to the garden, and to his agony in it; he was there betrayed, and apprehended, carried to judgment, condemned, and put to death next day, and buried next evening. This was the depth of the eclipse of the Sun of Righteousness. Yet in all this the eternal love of the Father to him did not cease. When Christ came into the world first, we find what great joy there was on that account. An angel first published the good news to the shepherds, and then a multitude of the heavenly host sung a song of praise for it, Luke ii. 9,---14. The Father proclaims him on his coming as the object of heavenly worship: Heb. i. 6. *When he bringeth in the first begotten into the world, he saith, And let all the angels of God worship him.* There is no angel so high, nor so great in power

power and might, 2 Peter ii. 11. but muſt ſerve and worſhip the Son of God in his loweſt and meaneſt appearance on earth. He was *ſeen of angels*, 1 Tim. iii. 16.; and it was their duty, their glory, and their bliſs, to worſhip and ſerve him. When Chriſt comes into the world, Heb. x. 5, 6, 7. he ſaith, as rejoicing, *A body thou haſt prepared me; Lo, I come to do thy will, O God*. And that will was to make a ſacrifice of that body; and he did offer it with delight. When he is baptized, Matth. iii. 17. the Father, by *a voice from the excellent glory*, 2 Peter i. 17. witneſſed his love to his Son: *This is my beloved Son, in whom I am well pleaſed, hear ye him*, Matth. xvii. 5. In Luke ix. 30, 31. we have a ſpecial hint of the ſubject of the diſcourſe that Moſes and Elias had with our Lord on the mount of transfiguration, *who appeared in glory, and ſpake of his deceaſe which he ſhould accompliſh at Jeruſalem*. We would be ready to think, if it was not for this hint, that glorified ſaints come from heaven, and waiting on their Lord in his begun glory, ſhould rather have ſpoke of his approaching perfect glory, than of his deceaſe. But as that deceaſe was the appointed way to his glory, as Luke xxiv. 26.; ſo this tells us, that Chriſt's death is a theme fit for the moſt heavenly perſons in their moſt exalted heavenly ſtate. The ſong of the redeemed is principally on his death, and its fruits, Rev. v. 9, 10, 12. As it is the root of all our ſalvation, ſo it ſhould be the ground of all our ſongs of ſalvation.

But here an obvious objection riſeth. It is ſaid, That Chriſt was beloved of his Father in his loweſt ſtate. But what brought him into this low ſtate, but his Father's anger? Did it not *pleaſe Jehovah to bruiſe him, and to put him to grief*, Iſa. liii. 10.? How could this eternal love, and his ſore ſufferings, conſiſt? I would premiſe ſome things more generally for removing this difficulty, and then come cloſer to the matter.

1. There is ſomething amongſt men required of God, and practiſed by them; and that is, in parents

correcting their children in love. It should always be so, but is not, Heb. xii. 10. He tells us what is too common, that earthly parents *chasten their children after their own pleasure*, or to vent their displeasure. Parents cannot distinguish betwixt the child and the fault, as they ought.

2. We have a greater instance in Abraham's dealing with Isaac at God's command, Gen. xxii. Isaac was innocent, Abraham loved him; yet the Lord commands him to offer him for a burnt-offering. Now the Lord did not command, nor allow Abraham to abate ought of that love to his son, that both nature and grace had planted in his heart towards Isaac; and no doubt but love continued in Abraham's heart in all his journey to the appointed place, and in all the preparation he made for the offering the commanded sacrifice: only Abraham was a strong believer, and therefore was all obedience. His love to Isaac did not turn to hatred, when he *stretched forth his hand, and took the knife to slay his son*, ver. 10. But only his love to Isaac shrunk up as it were to nothing, through the strength of his faith, and his readiness to obey the will of his God. Isaac's question to his father was an addition to Abraham's trial, ver. 7. And Abraham's answer to it was a great act of his faith in his trial, ver. 8. Isaac said, *Behold the fire and the wood; but where is the lamb for a burnt-offering?* The instruments for the burnt-offering were ready and seen: the wood was on Isaac's back, and the fire and the knife were in Abraham's hand, ver. 6. but no sacrifice was visible. Abraham answers, *My son, God will provide himself a lamb for a burnt-offering*, ver. 8. Little did Isaac think that himself was the commanded sacrifice, and to be sacrificed by his own father's own hands; though, without doubt, Abraham did afterwards tell Isaac the command of God, when he *built an altar on the place God had told him of, and laid the wood in order, and bound Isaac his son, and laid him on the altar upon the wood*, ver. 9. And as little did

Abraham think of any other sacrifice but that of his son Isaac. But by Heb. xi. 17, 18, 19. Abraham's faith did act on divine power, that could raise Isaac to life again, when Abraham had shed his blood, and the wood and fire had burnt his body; being persuaded, that as no command of God was to be disputed, so no promise of God would fail of its accomplishment. And the issue of this trial was in the Lord's gracious acceptance of his obedience, in stopping the execution of Isaac, and substituting a ram in his stead, and in adding of a divine oath unto that promise of God, that Abraham's faith was so strongly fixed upon. Compare Gen. xxii. 11,----19. with Heb. vi. 13,----20. where we find the grounds of Abraham's faith are common to all believers under the new testament, whatever trembling and sinful shortcomings are with us in the acts and exercise of our faith.

3. So our Lord requires of his people in the case of suffering for him: Luke xiv. 26. *If any man come to me, and hate not his father, and mother, and wife, and children, and brethren, and sisters, yea, and his own life also, he cannot be my disciple.* A positive hating of our relations is forbid to all, by the law of nature, and by the word of God. To be *without natural affection*,' is a great sin, Rom. i. 31. But when the glory of Christ and his truth is so concerned, (as oft it is, that a man must either deny Christ, or forego all for his sake; then is he called to testify by his choice, like Moses's, Heb. xi. 24, 25, 26. that Christ is dearer to him than all. Thus the martyr said, when some spoke to him of the desolate state he was to leave his wife and children in, " God is my witness, that " if I had all the riches of the world, I would chear-" fully give it all to live with my wife and children ; " but now when my testimony to Christ and his gos-" pel, by my death, is called for, I as chearfully leave " all."

4. The Lord's dealing in love, and yet in apparent anger with his people : Rev. iii. 19. *As many as I love,*

I rebuke and chasten. Heb. xii. 6. *For whom the Lord loveth, he chasteneth, and scourgeth every son whom he receiveth.* It is a common, but a sinful way of arguing with many Christians, that they are not God's children, because they are so much corrected by him. To question our state because of affliction, or to conclude our state to be good because of prosperity and ease, are equally false and foolish, though not equally dangerous; for it is far more so, falsely to conclude a good state when it is not, than unbelievingly to disturb a good state where it is. It is certain, that the Lord loveth his people with *an everlasting love,* Jer. xxxi. 3.; that *his mercy is from everlasting to everlasting to them,* Psalm ciii. 17.: and that this love and mercy runs through, and is mixed with all his dealings with them. Yet how hardly is this owned by them? Let us begin with the Lord's beginning to deal with them, to draw them to himself, to bring them into Christ's chariot of salvation, *the midst whereof is paved with love,* Cant. iii. 10. Doth not the Lord appear at first to them as an enemy, not only declaring war against them, but using his irresistible arms against them, and his arrows pierce their hearts, as Psal. xlv. 5.? Little did Paul think of Christ's love to him, when he *fell on the earth, trembling and astonished,* Acts ix. 3, 4, 5. Yet afterwards he well knew it, and did count it as long as he lived, the best day he ever saw. Then when the Lord hath subdued their hearts, and *given them rest in their souls,* his yoke and his burden is laid on them, Matt. xi. 28, 29. Whatsoever *is common to man,* 1 Cor. x. 13. or to a believer, that they should lay their account with. The cross of suffering any thing for Christ's sake, is oft laid on them, and always in love; yet it is judgment, 1 Peter iv. 17. and a fiery trial, ver. 12. Manifold outward afflictions are laid on them. And let all Christians in this furnace say, if they find it easy to believe his love to them, when his hand presseth them sore.

fore. Beyond thefe is Satan's fieve of temptation, Luke xxii. 21. Can there be love in the Lord's letting the devil loofe upon one of his own children? Yes, fo did the Lord with Job; Paul, 2 Cor. xii. 7.; yea, with Chrift himfelf, Matth. iv. 3. But above all, is the Lord's hiding his face, and dealing as an enemy, and that for fin; when *his wrath is kindled but a little,* as Pfalm ii 12. and in the light and heat of that fire, *the fiery law* (as it is called in Deut. xxxii. 2.) is read in the confcience, who can believe love in this, that looks fo like hell? Yet David did fo, Pfal. cxvi. 3.; and Jonah did fo, chap. ii. 2, 3, 4.: and after a life of *fightings without,* and *fears within,* (as 2 Cor. vii. 5.), when the Lord is to finifh his work and defign of love on his people, then the laft enemy is to be fought with, 1 Cor. xv. 26. Death, that to nature looks like the wages of fin, is made the door to glory. But how hard is it to believe it? He muft have a ftrong faith, that can call his own dying a *fleeping in Jefus,* as 1 Theff. iv. 14.; that can make ufe of Jacob's words concerning his fleeping place, Gen. xxviii. 16, 17. *This is the gate of heaven.* It is the great work and difficulty, and yet duty in Chriftianity, to believe unfeen and unfelt love, in and under well-feen and well-felt diftrefs. Sometimes the Lord joins them, as in 2 Theff. i. 6. and 1 Peter iv. 14. and then it is eafy. But oft the wrath is felt, and the love is hid in the promife, and there only active faith can find it.

But all thefe inftances are fo far fhort of this we are fpeaking of, that they afford very little light about this. Therefore I would come nearer, and offer a few things that may help to direct your thoughts unto a due reconciling of this eternal love the Father had to the Son, with the hard fervice he put him to as Mediator.

1. It was the anger of an offended judge and law-giver, and not the anger of an offended father, that fmote Jefus Chrift. Chrift fuffered, he was flain, and died;

died; and the bitterness of that low condition was from the justice and wrath of God, which he felt in his soul: which was well expressed by a godly minister, "Christ's soul-sufferings were the soul of his "sufferings:" that is, the main and most bitter part of them. Yet in the depth of all these Christ was pleasing to his Father, and highly so: John x. 17. *Therefore doth my Father love me, because I lay down my life, that I might take it again.* Who took Christ's life away but his Father? The wicked instruments used in this work, were of no consideration in the matter. To the chief of them, Pilate, the cowardly self-condemned judge, he said, John xix. 11. *Thou couldest have no power at all against me, except it were given thee from above.* It was this interest his Father had in his sufferings, that made him say as in John xviii. 11. *The cup which my Father hath given me, shall I not drink it?* Our Lord on his cross, our Lord when dying, when dead, was as lovely in his Father's eyes, as ever before or since. But the justice and law of an offended judge exacted thus upon him.

2. This stroke of justice fell only on the man Christ, on his human nature. His divine person was untouched and untouchable by his sufferings. Christ's body was the sacrifice; it was his soul and body that the sword of divine justice did pierce. So that this stroke was some way but like a blow on a man's garment. The divine person of the Son of God dwelling in flesh, was neither reached, nor reachable by the sword of divine justice; though the dignity of his divine person did infinitely inhance the merit of the suffering of the man Christ.

3. This stroke of divine justice on the man Christ, was not for any fault of his own, (for he had none), but for the sins of his people, Isa. liii. 5, 6. Christ's sinlessness in himself, and his dying for the sins of his people, are the fundamentals in Christian religion. If he had had any sin of his own, he could not have been a fit sacrifice for the sins of others. If he had not died

for

for our sins, all sinners must have died in, and for their own sins. Now, proper insupportable divine displeasure is for a person's own sins. This is *the cup full of mixture*, Psalm lxxv. 8.; and this is of wrath with wrath; and *without mixture*, Rev. xiv. 10. without any mixture of mercy with it: nothing but mere wrath in it. This cup all that die in their sins, must drink of: but he that died for the sins of others, did not drink of it. It is true, that all the wrath that their sins deserved, he did drink of; but the sin deserving it, was none of his own. If hard usage from men be lightened from this, as David found it, Psalm lix. 3. *Not for my transgression, nor for my sin, O Lord;* if a good conscience be a continual feast, surely Christ had this in perfection in all his sufferings. He had a troubled soul, but a most quiet conscience in all. The soul may be troubled by the imputed sin of others; but conscience is never disquieted, but for one's own sin. That Italian martyr understood this well, and used it nobly; who being asked by one, " Why he " was so merry at his approaching death, when Christ " himself was in an agony before his death?" answered, " That Christ sustained in his body all the " sorrows and conflicts with death and hell due to us; " by whose suffering we are delivered from sorrow, " and fear of them all."

4. The Father knew the perfect sufficiency of his Son, to bear all that was laid on him. If it be an act of his grace on his people, *not to suffer them to be tempted above what they are able,* 1 Cor. x. 13.; much more was it so in his dealing with Christ, Psal. lxxx, 17. and lxxxix. 19. He knew (what we cannot conceive) what a vast load of wrath this strong one could bear. None but Christ could stand before an angry God, could bear his wrath, and satisfy justice. If I may use such a similitude, when the sword of justice was drawn against Christ, and pierced through his soul and body, the Father knew well that his Son was so armed, that he could not be hurt thereby. His

divine nature, and his Father's presence with him, John xvi. 32. and the ineffable union betwixt the Father and the Son, were as armour of proof about the man Christ; that though justice slew him, it did him neither any wrong, nor real hurt, whatever smart was in the stroke.

5. The Father knew the glorious victory that his Son would obtain in, and by, and over all his sufferings; that *for the suffering of death, he should be crowned with glory and honour*, Heb. ii. 9.; that he should *be highly exalted*, Phil. ii. 9. So that what Christ was put to, was but like a father's sending his son to a stormy sea, and a dangerous voyage, from which he knew he should return safe and rich; or like a king's sending his son to war, wherein he was sure he should conquer, and return in triumph. Divine prescience is another thing in God's eye, than angel or man can possibly think. And this was eminently in Christ's sufferings, Acts ii. 23. and iv. 28.

6. There were great and glorious ends God had before him, in all the sufferings that Christ was put to endure; great glory to his grace, great glory to his Son, and a great salvation to his people: of which the word is full. And all that read, or hear, or think of Christ's death and sufferings, without regard to the ends thereof, they mind only a bare history and matter of fact, without any fruit thereby.

7. *Lastly*, The Father loved the Son in dying and for dying, as in John x. 17, 18. For Christ in dying offered up the highest and most acceptable worship and service to God that ever was offered; Eph. v. 2. *Christ loved us, and hath given himself for us, an offering and a sacrifice to God for a sweet-smelling savour.* And it is the sweet smell of this sacrifice that drowns, as it were, the stink of all the sins and sinners it was offered for. His death could not be a propitiation, if it were not so. The two greatest sins that ever were, were the first Adam's first sinning. All mens sins since,

and

and Adam's own sinning after, (as doubtless he did for nine hundred and thirty years), were all the sinning of sinners: but his first sin was a sinless man's sinning; besides, it was the most damning sin that ever was, or can be. The other great sin, was the crucifying the second Adam, the Prince of life, and the Lord of glory. It is not only charitably believed by the church of God in all ages, that Adam obtained mercy; but hath been proved by some hints in the word, that both Adam and Eve were believers. But for the other great sin, the murdering of the Son of God, it is past doubt, that many guilty of his blood were forgiven in the virtue of it. A singular case were they in. The cry of Christ's blood defiled and disturbed their consciences, (and most justly); and the voice of this blood sprinkling their consciences, purged and pacified them. Now, if to these great sins you add all the sins of all the sinners that were ever forgiven, (and no man can count them, or weigh them), conclude, that there was somewhat offered to God, more pleasing to him than all sin was displeasing; and this was only the sacrifice of Jesus Christ. Abraham's offering up of his Son at God's command, was highly pleasing to God; but it was but a type and shadow of *Christ's offering up of himself without spot unto God*, Heb. ix. 14. Abraham in that action on the mount was to be a priest, and his son the sacrifice; but he only did offer to be so, and the Lord did accept the will for the deed. But when Christ came to offer himself, for all the perfect will he had to do it, the sacrifice must be offered, and was; and therein was performed the greatest, highest, and most acceptable worship to God. None was ever like it before; and none comparable to it, will, or can ever be. The praises of the glorified in heaven will be high and acceptable worship; but no way to be compared with that worship Christ paid, and God accepted in Christ's death.

And

And thus much to these words in themselves, as they assert the eternal love of the Father to the Son.

II. I would now speak to them, *with respect to Christ's scope in using them;* and therein would observe three things.

1. Our Lord Jesus Christ was now near to his lowest; and he comforts himself with the faith of his Father's eternal love. So must Christians do. Whatever the Lord brings you to, if it were to the brink of death, you must study to imitate Jesus Christ, and take in the comfort of his everlasting love. For tho' the love the Father hath to the Son, and that love he hath to believers, do differ vastly; yet they agree in this, that they are both eternal; and in this also, that the faith of this love is supporting to his people, as it was to Christ himself. It is no wonder that believers have so little comfort; even because they do not by faith seek out and dig up the right springs and wells of consolation, and are so little exercised in drawing and drinking out of them. I say not, that this spring of consolation, eternal love, is the first, and plainest, and easiest to come at; but only that it is the strongest, when a believer can find it out, and use it.

2. Consider this word of Christ, as it is an argument backing his prayer, and every petition in it. He calls God *Father;* and rightly, *because thou lovedst me before the foundation of the world.* " Glorify thy Son, " for thou lovedst me. I pray for thine and mine, *for* " *thou lovedst me.*" How boldly may a believer pray, when he hath this argument in the hand of his faith to pray upon: " Lord, hear me; for thou hast " loved me in thy Son before the foundation of the " world."

3. The main thing in the scope of these words of Christ is this, that the Father's love to Christ is the fountain of all good to his people. Christ is praying in this verse for the greatest good to his people, even

for

for heaven; and this suit he urgeth on this argument, *For thou lovedst me before the foundation of the world.* You would think, that the argument would have run more plainly, (but it would not have run so sweetly, and so strongly), if it had been thus: " I will that " they may be with me where I am; that they may " behold my glory: for thou hast loved them, and " I have loved them before the foundation of the " world." But it is best as Christ useth it, *For thou hast loved me.*

On this truth, That the Father's love to Christ is the fountain of all good to his people, I would give a few instances of it, and conclude this text with a few words of application.

Instances are, 1. Election, that sovereign *purpose and grace* of God, *is given us in Christ Jesus, before the world began,* 2 Tim. i. 9. *We are chosen in Christ before the foundation of the world,* Eph. i. 4. Christ did not purchase the grace of election for us; yet there is no election but in Christ, and unto *the sprinkling of his blood,* 1 Peter i. 2. The end, salvation; the way and means reaching to this end, faith and sanctification, are joined in this purpose, 2 Thess. ii. 13. and Christ's interest in it, 1 Thess. v. 9. *For God hath not appointed us to wrath, but to obtain salvation by our Lord Jesus Christ:* and this salvation in Jesus Christ, with eternal glory, is obtained by the elect, 2 Tim. ii. 10.

2. The grace of redemption comes to us from the Father's love to his Son. This love sent him to be Redeemer, and accepted the price of his life for his flock. Abstracting from his eternal counsel and covenant, God was at liberty to have left man in the pit he had thrown himself in, and to appoint no Redeemer. But, not to trouble our heads with such unprofitable speculations, it is plain, that the whole business of redemption by Christ was transacted before time, promised in time, and dispatched in the fulness

of

time, in love to Chrift the Redeemer, as well as in love to the redeemed.

3. Chrift's interceffion in heaven. Whence is it fo prevalent, but from that great favour Chrift ftands in heaven in? It is from the love the Father hath to the Son, that Chrift's defires for his people are fo fuccefsful. It is upon this love that Chrift prays for heaven to his people in this text. And this whole prayer in this chapter, was a mediatory prayer of Chrift when on earth, and the beft copy we have of his interceffion in heaven.

More particularly, 1. The quickening of a finner dead in fins and trefpaffes, is from the Father's love to his Son. All the difpenfations of converting grace on finners, are acts and fruits of the Father's love to Chrift: John vi. 44, 45. *No man can come to me, except the Father which hath fent me, draw him.* " And " when he is drawn, and cometh, I will welcome him, " and give a good account of him one day." And *I will raife him up at the laft day.* But how doth the Father draw men to Chrift? By his way of teaching: *It is written in the prophets, And they fhall be all taught of God. Every man therefore that hath heard and learned of the Father, cometh unto me.* Till Chrift's Father, by his Spirit, teach a finner, and tell him good news of Chrift the Saviour, he will not, he cannot come to Chrift by faith; for divine teaching doth at the fame time reveal Chrift as the object of faith, and work the grace of faith, and draw forth the act of faith. We are oft complaining, (and not without caufe, if we had a right frame of heart in it), that many finners continue dead under the report of Chrift in the gofpel; and that converfion and quickening of the dead is rarely heard of, and feen. What is the caufe of this rarenefs? Is it not that finners are without man's teaching, but becaufe Chrift's Father doth not teach them; and till he do, they will never mifs, nor value, nor feek divine teaching. They feek but the fhell of the gofpel, they feek but the field where
the

the treasure is hid, Matth. xiii. 44.; and that they think any minister can show them. But the finding the hid treasure in it, no apostle was ever able to teach a man to do. All they can say is, that this enriching treasure is in the field of the gospel, and no where else; but it is hid in it; and till there come light from heaven, you will never find it, but die as poor as your father Adam left you, and in worse case than if you had never heard of this field. But what should we do in this sad condition? Wait on the Lord, who hath the times and seasons in his own hand; and while you wait, pray and cry for his teaching, and make use of this argument of the Father's eternal love to the Son. Say, " As thou lovest thy Son, teach " me, and many perishing sinners like me, to know " thy Son."

2. The justification and acceptance of a sinner with God, comes only from the Father's love to his Son. *We are accepted in that beloved,* Eph. i. 6. and *are translated into the kingdom of the Son of his love,* Col. i. 13. All the love believers partake of from God, is but a drop, a sprinkling of that love he hath to Jesus Christ. Therefore saith our Lord in this prayer, ver. 23. *I in them, and thou in me, that they may be made perfect in one, and that the world may know that thou hast sent me, and hast loved them, as thou hast loved me.;* and ver. 26. *And I have declared unto them thy name, and will declare it: that the love wherewith thou hast loved me, may be in them, and I in them.* No love, no grace, no favour comes from the Father immediately, but all in and by Jesus Christ the Mediator. Without a Mediator the Father dealeth not with us when he doth us good; and without a Mediator we must not deal with God, if we would please him.

3. Believers are preserved in Jesus Christ in this accepted state, Jude, ver. 1. Every one that is raised up by Christ is preserved as safely in a state of grace, as Christ is in the state of glory. *Because I live*

live, ye shall live also, John xiv. 19. and x. 27, 28, 29. The weakest lamb in Christ's flock, that hath heard the great and the good Shepherd's voice, and follows him, though feebly, and with many fears, shall have eternal life; and he shall be kept by the power of God through faith, till he possess it, 1 Pet. i. 5. Christ's arm, and his Father's arm, are more than we can conceive; and yet no less than is needful, to secure the weakest, against the greatest dangers.

4. *Lastly,* The bliss of glory in heaven is the joy of our Lord, Matth. xxv. 21, 23. All the eternal embracements of divine love they get there, are on the account of the Father's love to the Son. It will mainly be fulfilled then, what Christ promised, John xiv. 20. *At that day, ye shall know that I am in my Father, and you in me, and I in you.*

APPLICATION. 1. How should this endear Christ to us, the Father's love to us in him, and all the fruits of this marvellous love? How precious to us should all be? Should not all say, as one did, Psal. xxvi. 7. *How excellent is thy loving kindness, O God!* Did ever a man see it by faith, did ever one taste that the Lord is gracious, did ever any hope for it, that did not count it *marvellous loving kindness,* as it is called, Psalm xvii. 7. and xxxi. 21.? The love of such a God as he is, unto such vile creatures as we be; and this love flowing to us in such a channel as this, God's love to his own Son, and streaming forth in all the blessings of grace and glory, is a love that all that know it wonder at, and that all that taste of it know best, and wonder most at. Enjoyments of this love, and admiring at it, are inseparable, both in earth, in believers; and in heaven, in beholders. You have not come under the warm beams of this love, that do not stand astonished at its nature and greatness, and who do not find something both of the depth and blessedness of that word, 1 John iv. 16. *We have known and believed the love that God hath to us. God is love;*

and he that dwelleth in love, dwelleth in God, and God in him. Try to say this particularly of yourselves, and you will find its difficulty. If you attain to it by the Spirit of faith, you will find its blessedness. Yea, what are all the blessed beholders and enjoyers of this love in heaven, but a blessed company of wonderers at this love? They are in the midst of the ocean of this love, (whereof a few drops tasted by them on earth, made a begun heaven to them), blessedly swiming, diving, drinking, and admiring. But it is but very little of what they get there, and of what they do there, that we do or can know while we are here. Yet, believers, do you receive any spiritual blessing? Is it not a lovely spring it flows from, the Father's love to his Son, Eph. i. 3.? Is it not a sweet name that thou shouldst by faith give to thy pardon, to thy sanctification, to the Spirit of prayer, and to any fellowship with God: " This, and that, and all " and every good I obtain, is all from the love of " God in Jesus Christ my Lord, Rom. viii. 39.? This way of conveyance proclaims, that all is of free grace; and this way makes the blessings sure and sweet. Thankfulness for his unspeakable gift would rise higher, and be purer, and more constant, if we could read the name of the Father's love to his Son written (as surely it always is, though not always read) on all our mercies. This would make a crumb from the Master's table be earnestly begged, when we are hungry; and would make us, when we get it, prize it more than the greatest revenues of the wicked. This love of God in Christ is an ingredient in mercy, that makes the mercy swell up to heaven. It is an ingredient in the bitterest cup of affliction, that not only prevents any poison apprehended to be in it (and what is more usual to our unbelief than to call God's physic poison?), and promotes our health thereby; but it doth also cool the fiery furnace, and sweeten it, and make it the place of love and praise; as it was to the three children, in Dan. iii. 25.

2. Learn

2. Learn, Christians, to use this argument in Christ's prayer, in your prayers also. You see our Lord prays for his people on this argument, *For thou lovedst me before the foundation of the world.* Let your faith chime to this prayer, and say, " Father, I would be " with Christ where he is, that I may behold his glo- " ry which thou hast given him; for thou lovedst him " before the foundation of the world." You daily hear, that you should pray to the Father in Christ's name. Now, what is it, but to raise our faith, and to embolden our confidence with God, merely on the account of that high love the Father bears to the Son? Blessed is the believer that can plead with God on the argument of the Father's love to his Son, That tho' we have nothing in us that is lovely in God's sight; though we can do nothing to make ourselves accepta- ble, or our desires successful; yea, though there be a cloud upon God's love to us, yet we build all our hopes of acceptance and success, and all these hopes strong and high, on this lovely and beloved one Jesus Christ, and on the Father's love to him. Whatever you want of God, you may ask, and ask it on the same grounds Christ prays for you upon. You will say, May every one ask on this argument? I answer, E- very believer may, and ought; and if he be wise, he will; and if he doth plead thus, he will prevail. But how may I know that I am a believer on Jesus Christ? The Spirit of Christ sometimes suddenly satisfies the doubting soul; and that is a great mercy. He shines on the promise, and makes it bright; shines on faith, and makes it strong and active; and manifests Christ's glory to as that the heart cannot forbear to believe, and love, and know that it doth so. But the common way, and the way of our duty, is, to satisfy our hearts as to our being true believers on Christ, by repeating the acting of faith on him. I say not, Believe that you do believe; but I say, Believe on Jesus Christ, and you shall know that you are believers on him; as in 1 John v. 13. *These things have I written to you*
that

that believe on the Son of God; that ye may know that ye have eternal life, and that ye may believe on the name of the Son of God. Faith is *the evidence of things not seen,* Heb. xi. 1.; and the Spirit of faith in believers giveth evidence to faith itself. By this Spirit we *know the things that are freely given us of God,* 1 Cor. ii. 12. and faith is a special gift of God. The word in 1 John v. 10. is of great extent, *He that believeth on the Son of God, hath the witness in himself.* I dare be bold to say, that there are few true believers, who are in the lively exercise of faith in Christ, and while in that exercise, but they are some way persuaded, that they are believers: in so far, that if Satan should say to the contrary, yea, or if the Lord himself should seem to say to the contrary; yet they cannot deny that they are believers on Christ. How can this be? say you. I answer, It is from the sense and inward feeling of the workings of their hearts, in dependence and trust on Jesus Christ for salvation. Is it not thus with you, Christians, whenever you are thoughtful about salvation; whenever you are terrified by the law; whenever Satan assaults you by the remembrance of your sins and ill-deservings: yea, whenever *God writes bitter things against you, and maketh you to possess the iniquities of your youth,* or riper age, Job xiii. 26.? What do ye do? Whither do ye go? Is it not always to Jesus Christ by faith? Every true believer can readily answer these three questions, which no unbeliever can, Isa. x. 3. *What will ye do in the day of visitation, and in the desolation which shall come from far? to whom will we flee for help? and where will ye leave your glory?* Every believer can answer, " Come what " desolation will, I know what to do, I know whi- " ther to go for help, and where to leave my glory; " even on Jesus Christ by faith." You have no other answer to give to the law of God condemning you, to the devil accusing you, nor to your own conscience challenging you, but only this: " Jesus Christ came " into the world to save sinners; his Father, in love

"to him and sinners, sent him; he came and died in
"love to sinners: and I, on the good report of him
"in the gospel, do daily come to him to be saved by
"him, and do look for salvation in him, and by
"him, and from him; and all my sins, and unwor-
"thiness, and fears, and the sad grounds of these
"fears, are all but so many cords to draw me more
"and more to Christ by faith, and to bind me faster
"to him. And if I am a believer on him, I am one
"of those he prayed for in this chapter, and in this
"verse, *Father, I will that they also whom thou hast
"given me, be with me where I am; that they may be-
"hold the glory which thou hast given me; for thou
"lovedst me before the foundation of the world.* If
"Christ prayed so for me, I may surely pray so for
"myself; for a better copy I cannot follow. If Christ
"prayed so for me, he was surely answered, and the
"blessing will be given; and I may firmly believe,
"and patiently wait for the salvation of God. And
"I may also use the same argument for strengthening
"of my faith, that Christ used to enforce his suit;
"even the eternal love of the Father to his Son."

This is indeed a great and marvellous salvation which God hath provided for his people. Marvellous in the way, Jesus Christ; and that the gospel doth now declare. Marvellous in the beginning and progress of this salvation. A sinner must feel grace before he *knew the grace of God in truth*, Col. i. 6. He must have faith wrought in him, and acted by him, before he know what *believing to the saving of the soul* is, Heb. x. 39. He must be in heaven, before he know well what heaven is: yea, which is
strange, the believer must be in heaven, before
know perfectly the way to heaven. We know that Christ is the way; that we must enter into him by faith, as he is the way; that we must walk in him, and abide in him, and live on him, till we come home to his Father's house. But how Christ became the way to heaven; how he is the new and living way:

how

how he confecrated himself as the way ; how he was beloved of the Father, and bruifed with divine wrath at the fame time ; how Chrift the living head draws dead lumps of hell, and makes them lively members of his own body ; how he knits and nourifheth them by fpiritual joints and bands, Col. ii. 19. till he perfect them in himfelf, Eph. iv. 19. and Col. i. 28. ; how he gives the laft pull and drawing at death, and receiveth them unto himfelf, John xiv. 2, 3. ; what Chrift is now doing in preparing a place for them ; and what he will at laft do, in receiving them, and prefenting them to his Father ; thefe, and many fuch things, are matter for our daily exercife, in faith, and hope, and wonder. Our main work while we are here, and without the vail, is, to be ftriving to get more and more into Chrift by faith ; and not only to get within the gates and walls of this city of refuge, (and *the walls are falvation, and the gates praife,* Ifa. lx. 18.), but alfo to get into his palaces, where he giveth his loves. *His love is better than wine,* Song i. 2. The tafte of this love would quickly make all the wells of this world's confolation to be as taftelefs and empty to us as they are in themfelves. Unfpeakably both ftrong and fweet is that mortification and deadnefs to the world, that is wrought in the believer, by *the fhedding abroad of the love of God in his heart by the Holy Ghoft,* Rom. v. 5. You live in an evil world. It will mock you, and hate you : but do you pity it. A believer is a pitiful creature in the eyes of the ungodly ; *looking at things that are not feen, and not looking at things that are feen,* 2 Cor. iv. 18. ; defpifing this world and all things in it as a portion, and feeking an unfeen and future glory in an unknown world to come. To build all our hopes of partaking and poffeffing of it on an unfeen Chrift ; to bottom our faith on him, upon a word from him ; to live and die upon his promife, and to do both chearfully, are the glory of a Chriftian. But this glory is turned into fhame by the thoughts and reproaches of

all

all unbelievers. *But let the righteous hold on his way; and he that hath clean hands, shall wax stronger and stronger,* John xvii. 9. *Your path is as the shining light, that shineth more and more unto the perfect day,* Prov. iv. 18. Pass through this world, believers in Jesus, liking nothing in it, caring for nothing in it, content and satisfied with nothing it can give, moved with nothing in it; neither much taken up with the much evil, or the little good of it; neither cast down with the frowns, nor lifted up with the smiles of this vain deceitful world. Pass on, and *press forward for the prize of the high calling of God in Christ Jesus,* Philip. iii. 14. You have greater things to look to, greater things to fix your hearts and hopes upon, than all this world: even to that blessed state, when we shall be with Christ where he is, and shall behold his glory which his Father hath given him: for the Father loved his Son and our Saviour before the foundation of the world.

The END *of the* SECOND VOLUME.

www.ingramcontent.com/pod-product-compliance
Lightning Source LLC
Chambersburg PA
CBHW031849220426
43663CB00006B/545